Lost Relations

'*Lost Relations* is a quiet masterpiece. In a meditation on his family, his country and his craft, Graeme Davison shows us why he is Australia's most creative and original historian. It will delight and instruct family historians and general historians alike as he seeks his lost relations, all the while conducting a conversation with his readers about historical imagination and truth.'

—*Professor Janet McCalman, University of Melbourne*

'Graeme Davison's latest publication departs from his usual historical output in being a study of his own family history, but it is written with the same depth of research and breadth of historical understanding as his more academic oeuvre, and with his usual grace and wry intelligence. It will appeal especially to family historians, but also the wider audience who enjoy Australian social history.'

—*Professor Marian Quartly, Monash University*

Other books by the author

The Rise and Fall of Marvellous Melbourne (MUP 1978 and 2004)
The Unforgiving Minute: How Australia learned to tell the time (OUP 1994)
The Use and Abuse of Australian History (A&U 2000)
Car Wars: How the car won our hearts and conquered our cities (A&U 2004)
University Unlimited: The Monash story (with Kate Murphy) (A&U 2012)

Lost Relations

Fortunes of my family
in Australia's Golden Age

GRAEME DAVISON

ALLEN&UNWIN
SYDNEY·MELBOURNE·AUCKLAND·LONDON

First published in 2015

This project has been assisted by the Australian
Government through the Australia Council,
its arts funding and advisory board.

Allen & Unwin
83 Alexander Street
Crows Nest NSW 2065
Australia
Phone: (61 2) 8425 0100
Email: info@allenandunwin.com
Web: www.allenandunwin.com

Cataloguing-in-Publication details are available
from the National Library of Australia
www.trove.nla.gov.au

ISBN 978 1 74331 946 8

Internal design by Kirby Armstrong
Set in 11.5/15 pt Janson Text by Bookhouse, Sydney
Printed and bound in Australia by Griffin Press

10 9 8 7 6 5 4 3 2 1

For Helen
and in memory of our mother
May (Hewett) Davison
1909–2004

Contents

SIX GENERATIONS OF HEWETTS

John Hewett m. **Jane Parsons**
1796–1839   1791–1875

Henry
1822–1855

John
1823–1888

Lucy
1824–1912
(Maxfield)

Frances
1826–1826

Mary Ann
1827–1892

Robert
1828–1894
m. **Elizabeth Fenwick**
1824–1879

Richard
1830–1882

Jane
1832–1928

Susan
1834–1893
(Maxfield)

Annie Mary
1852–1924
(Swalling)

Clara Jane
1853–1942

Elizabeth Jane
1855–1945

Robert Henry
1859–1933
m. **Susan Stephens**
1856–1918

Edward John
1862–1862

Francis D.
1863–1954

Victor Stephens
1882–1957
m. **Emma Seller**
1874–1968

Reuben Francis (Robert)
1883–1960

Frank Lloyd
1890–1946

Robert John (John)
1894–1984

(Emma) May
1909–2004
m. George Davison
1911–1998

Gwendolyn Ruth
1911–1979
(McConnell)

Joyce Stephens
1913–2013
(Bowater)

Marjorie Evelyn
b. 1915
(Jackson)

Florence Susan
b. 1919
(Lear)

Graeme John
b. 1940

Helen Margaret
b. 1943
(Hobbs)

Janet Barbara
1946–2000
(Tranter)

INTRODUCTION
The great-aunt's story

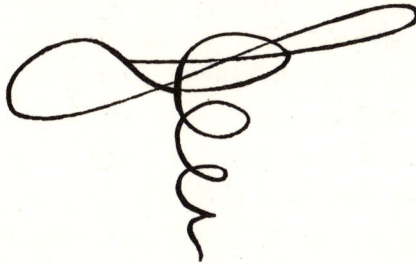

We Australians are a nation steeped in stories of our immigrant forebears. In every migrant's story there is a moment of arrival, when the newcomer steps ashore, the emigrant becomes an immigrant, and memories of the old country give way to prospects of the new.

This is the arrival story my mother told me:

In July 1850, 'before the gold rush', Jane Hewett, a widow, and her eight children entered Port Phillip Bay after a four-month journey from England. They climbed down the ship's ladder and landed at Sandridge, or Port Melbourne as it became known, then walked three miles across the swamp to Prince's Bridge, the only Yarra crossing, and stayed their first night at the Globe Inn in Swanston Street.

Jane Hewett was my great-great-great-grandmother, and my mother learned her story from my grandfather, Vic Hewett. He heard it from the lips of Jane's daughter, another Jane, the second youngest of the family and the last survivor. Vic visited her, still single and a resident of the Old Colonists' Homes in North Fitzroy, sometime before her death in 1928 at the age of 96. He took her photograph—a stooped, wizened old lady in a long black dress—and recorded the outlines of her story together with a sketchy genealogy in a notebook he later passed on to my mother.

When I eventually read Vic's notebook, written in his characteristic clear printer's hand, I noticed details omitted from my mother's condensed version, as well as some curious gaps in Jane's. Nowhere, for example, does Jane mention the name of the ship, or explain why the passengers were obliged to climb down a ship's ladder, tumble into boats and walk overland to their destination rather than being transferred by tender as most passengers were. But she adds other intriguing details, such as the fact that five of her siblings, including my great-great-grandfather Robert Hewett, married young people they met on the voyage. The emigrant ship was evidently a nineteenth-century love boat!

A nuclear family when they embarked, the Hewetts had already begun to pair off by the time they arrived in Port Phillip. The new couples dispersed to points west, north and east, leaving the mother and two daughters, 23-year-old Mary Ann and eighteen-year-old Jane, to form a household of their own. Read in the light of this abrupt change, the details Jane does recall—the frightening climb down the ship's ladder; the walk across the swamp; the first night at the Globe Inn, one of Melbourne's rowdiest—hint at a landfall that was as chaotic as it was momentous. Those four months at sea and that tumultuous arrival would shape the family's fortunes for the next half-century.

It is odd that Jane did not mention the name of the ship, for the voyage of the *Culloden* was one of the most famous, or notorious, of its time. Prominent politicians, including Sidney Herbert, the later champion of Florence Nightingale, were there on the dock at Gravesend to farewell it. The novelist William Thackeray, author of *Vanity Fair* (1848), also witnessed its departure. Future prime minister William Gladstone had been briefed on arrangements for the voyage. An artist from the *Illustrated London News* sketched the scene, and reports appeared in all the major newspapers, from *The Times* and the *Morning Chronicle* to *Punch* and the Chartist newspaper *The Northern Star*.

The voyage that began with such fanfare, however, would end in scandal and confusion, with its passengers abandoned, its crew in rebellion, its captain and surgeon in disgrace, and its organisers embroiled in notoriety and recrimination. The *Culloden*, the bearer of many hopes, would become a symbol of shame and disappointment. I wonder if that was why Jane made no mention of its name.

Simply because it was so fragmentary, Jane's account of her arrival inspired questions and conjectures. Why did the Hewetts embark on the great adventure, abandoning the Hampshire village where their forebears had farmed for generations? Who were their fellow passengers, and why did the voyage that began with such hopes end so badly? Who was the woman that Robert met on the ship and where did she come from? What became of Jane's other brothers and sisters and the partners they had met on the voyage? And what befell their widowed mother and Jane herself?

Unknowingly, the voyagers had arrived in the colony at a threshold in Australia's history. Within months, the Port Phillip District would separate from New South Wales and become the new colony of Victoria. A catastrophic bushfire would sweep through the countryside, the new colony's first environmental disaster. (One of the Hewetts' fellow passengers, a painter named William Strutt, would immortalise it in an epic painting.) And soon a lone shepherd tending his sheep in a paddock near Clunes would pick up a nugget of gold, precipitating a mineral rush that would utterly transform the colony, creating a vortex of economic opportunity that would draw the

Hewetts into paths, both pleasant and unpleasant, they could never have imagined when they embarked.

This book tells the story behind Jane's story, the one she must have known but did not tell, or perhaps did not even think worth the telling. Little remains in writing of the Hewetts' own words. So I have had to reconstruct their story through the words of others, listen for clues to their thoughts in the voices of people like them, and try to put myself in the situations they faced. This is a risky business. Some would say it is too risky: if the evidence allows little to be said beyond the bare bones of genealogy, then silence, they say, is the only alternative. Others, like some recent Australian novelists, take an even braver course, stretching conjecture into invention, filling the gaps in the evidence with fictions, the silence with imaginary conversations. Rather than silence or invention, I invite the reader to accompany me on my journey, sharing my discoveries, disappointments and surprises.

I did not get far along the road before realising that family history is a very different pursuit from academic history, my day job. It is not a search for general historical truth but a quest for personal identity. Identity, says the philosopher Charles Taylor, is a 'dialogical concept': 'We define our identity always in dialogue with, sometimes in struggle against, the things our significant others want to see in us.' In pursuing the Hewetts' history, I am continuing a conversation with my significant others, not just my parents and sisters but also the long-forgotten relations who preceded them. Much of the satisfaction of doing it lies in the search rather than the discovery, the journey rather than the arrival. By making the resources of the world's archives and libraries searchable and accessible from one's own desktop, the digital revolution has democratised family history and multiplied the possibilities of tracing families across countries and generations. Yet the excitement of connecting with kin, living and dead, in cyberspace cannot entirely substitute for the experience of revisiting the real places they inhabited or finding their traces in the paper, ink and stone of past eras. When we pause by the grave of a forebear, or recover a fragment of their everyday lives, we are engaged in something akin to what Aboriginals do when they go 'Back to Country'.

For most of my life I have avoided family history. The crowds of chattering genealogists in public libraries and archives are one of the daily hazards of the academic researcher. I have written critically about the perils of 'speed-relating', the craze for online genealogy, and the business activities of Ancestry.com and the other commercial genealogical websites. As a young man, eager to be 'captain of my soul and architect of my fate', I probably minimised the influence of inheritance and kin on my own life. My parents, my father especially, tended to discourage interest in the family's past. Australia, not England, the future, not the past, was what he cared about—or so he said. Only as I grew older and my parents passed on did I begin to recognise how much of my life had been shaped by family tradition and expectation, not to mention genetics; although even now, when temptations to reminiscence and nostalgia grow stronger, I resist them, conscious of their distortions. In the end, however, encouraged by my family, I succumbed to the appeal of family history, not only because I wanted to better understand who I am, but also in order to think more concretely about the relationship between the familial and the communal pasts. And 'doing' my own family's history, or a part of it at any rate, seemed the best way to tackle it.

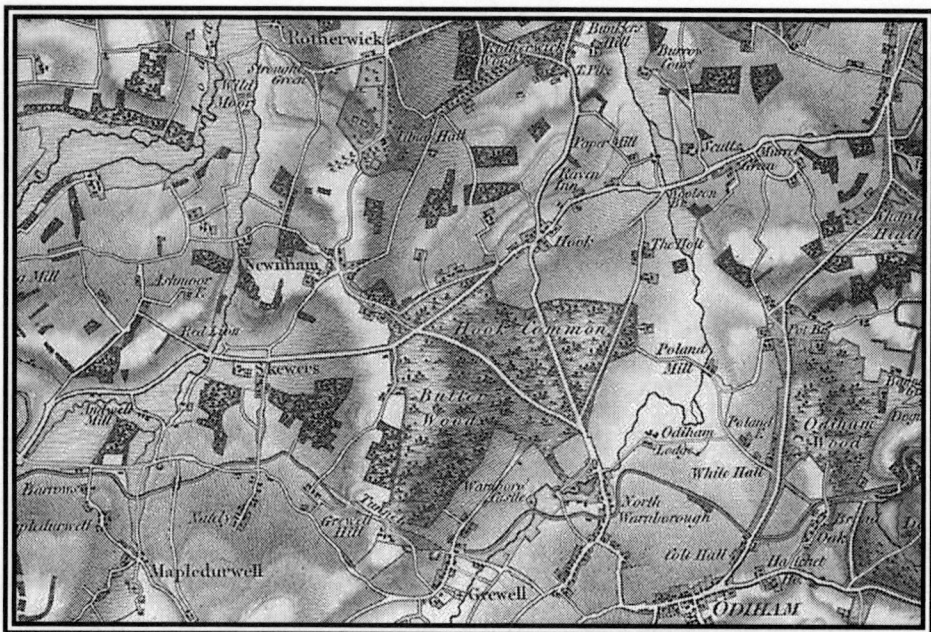

Northeast Hampshire in the early nineteenth century. The hamlet of Hook (centre) is strategically located at the crossroads between the London road, bisecting the map diagonally from northeast to southwest, and the subsidiary north-south connections to Reading in the north and the nearest market town, Odiham, in the south. The village of Newnham, with its manor and parish church, lies immediately to the west. Hook Farm is indicated by the patchwork of open fields and woodland to the northwest of the junction. With the growing traffic along the road, Hook will wax and Newnham will wane. (Ordnance Survey First Series, 1817, Sheet 12 (detail), British Library)

CHAPTER ONE
Hook Farm

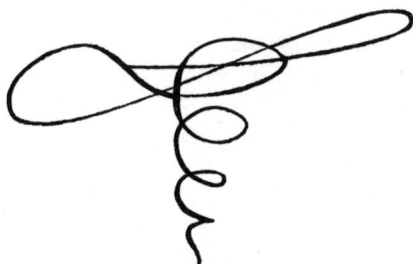

One Sunday afternoon almost twenty years ago I visited my sister Helen, who lives in a village about eighty kilometres from London, close to the border between Surrey and Hampshire. Like many young Australian women of her generation, Helen had embarked on the Grand Tour to England in the late 1960s. There she fell in love with an Englishman before marrying and staying on. After lunch she suggested we drive to another village, Newnham, just twenty minutes away on the other side of the M3. The rough genealogy in my grandfather's notebook, based on his conversation with Great-Aunt Jane, associated the Hewett family's origins with 'Redding' in Hampshire, a name we simply couldn't find on the map. Someone else had suggested that they came from Farnham in Surrey, birthplace of the writer and political radical William Cobbett. But Helen had just received a letter, together with a large genealogical chart, from a distant cousin, John Boothroyd,

THE HEWETTS OF HOOK FARM

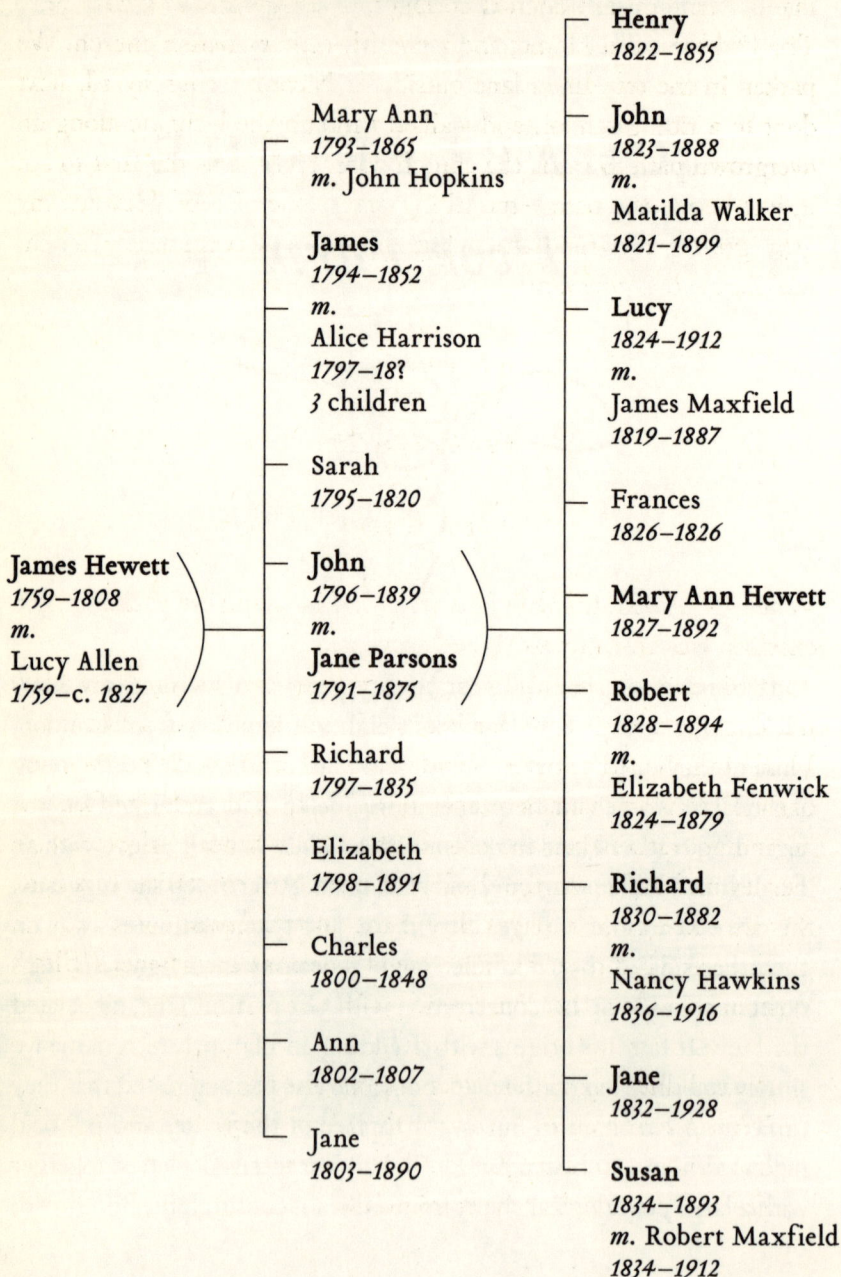

James Hewett
1759–1808
m.
Lucy Allen
1759–c. 1827

Mary Ann
1793–1865
m. John Hopkins

James
1794–1852
m.
Alice Harrison
1797–18?
3 children

Sarah
1795–1820

John
1796–1839
m.
Jane Parsons
1791–1875

Richard
1797–1835

Elizabeth
1798–1891

Charles
1800–1848

Ann
1802–1807

Jane
1803–1890

Henry
1822–1855

John
1823–1888
m.
Matilda Walker
1821–1899

Lucy
1824–1912
m.
James Maxfield
1819–1887

Frances
1826–1826

Mary Ann Hewett
1827–1892

Robert
1828–1894
m.
Elizabeth Fenwick
1824–1879

Richard
1830–1882
m.
Nancy Hawkins
1836–1916

Jane
1832–1928

Susan
1834–1893
m. Robert Maxfield
1834–1912

who had traced the family back to Newnham in Hampshire. So with his letter in our hands we set off to visit our ancestral home.

Newnham is a picture-postcard village with a sixteenth-century manor farmhouse; thatched cottages; a village green; a cosy pub, The Old House at Home; and a twelfth-century parish church. We parked in the tree-lined lane outside St Nicholas' churchyard, next door to a riding school, and walked through the lychgate along an overgrown path towards the church door. Helen was the first to see it, just beside the path—the tilting gravestone of John Hewett, my great-great-great-grandfather. The epitaph, now obscured by lichen, was simple but poignant:

> *In memory of*
> *John Hewett*
> *who died Jan 10th*
> *1839*
> *Aged 42 years*

When John died, his wife Jane was 47. The youngest of their eight children was five, the eldest only seventeen.

It was a strange feeling to stand beside the grave, trying to imagine the circumstances of my forebear's life and death. As a historian, I had often visited cemeteries and graveyards and pondered the lives of the famous and humble people buried there. The tomb is often the beginning, rather than the end, of the family history pilgrimage, a journey undertaken in the shadow of one's own mortality. It is here that we come closest, physically, to the ancestral past.

The scene before us reminded me of Thomas Gray's famous 'Elegy Written in a Country Churchyard' (1751).

> *Beneath those rugged elms, that yew-tree's shade,*
> *Where heaves the turf in many a mouldering heap,*
> *Each in his narrow cell for ever laid,*
> *The rude forefathers of the hamlet sleep.*

. . .

For them no more the blazing hearth shall burn,
Or busy housewife ply her evening care;
No children run to lisp their sire's return,
Or climb his knees the envied kiss to share.

. . .

Let not Ambition mock their useful toil,
Their homely joys and destiny obscure;
Nor Grandeur hear, with a disdainful smile,
The short and simple annals of the poor.

The life of John Hewett had been like that of many other villagers, simple and short. The grief of his family was like that of many others in an age when birth and death were frequent callers. But for us, his descendants, the discovery of his grave stirred something more than the pity we felt for other villagers cut off in their prime. John Hewett was *my* great-great-great-grandfather. His life and death had significance, not because he was famous or did anything remarkable, but because he was, in some obscure way, connected to *my* life and identity.

The link between us was not just biological—the fact that the DNA in my body was encoded in similar ways to the DNA in whatever remained of John Hewett in that grave. I am not much attracted to biological or mystical notions of blood and inheritance. My natural inclination is to question the links that aunts and grandmothers are always finding between granddad's fiery temper and grandson's misbe-haviour on the football field. In the perennial debate between nature and nurture, I lean to the environmental side. I abhor the pernicious use of genealogy and genetics to attribute inborn characteristics to families and ethnic groups and to discriminate accordingly. I care little for notions of family pride or ancestral distinction, perhaps because there is little in my pedigree to boast about. Yet I could not deny that the person buried in that grave—that farmer whose useful toil had been so prematurely cut off, whose destiny was indeed so

4

obscure—meant more to me than the many others who shared his fate but were unconnected to me by the accident of kinship. I began to wonder why.

Our discovery prompted further questions. Where did John Hewett live? What kind of life did he lead? And what prompted his widow and her eight children to quit this beautiful village and set off, almost a decade later, across the seas to distant Port Phillip? We knocked on the door of the churchwarden, Mr Nigel Bell, who, it turned out, was also the local historian. He showed us the parish registers in which the baptisms of John's children were recorded. And he pointed us towards a plot of land, now covered with houses, in the nearby village of Hook that John Hewett had once tilled as a yeoman farmer. Nearby, just across the London Road, was the coaching inn, the White Hart, once run by his brother James. Little by little we began to fill in the picture, a process that accelerated as online genealogical sites brought the world's archives onto our computer desktops. But the question 'Why did they leave?' remained unanswered.

THE YEOMAN

The Hewetts had been Hampshire folk for at least two centuries. The name, a diminutive form of Hugh, is said to originate in Dorset, although by the time of the 1841 census, when we can plot its distribution on the map, its bearers appear to cluster in Hampshire, to the south around Portsea Island and in the north around the market towns of Basingstoke and Odiham. In a society still only half-literate, there was uncertainty about the spelling of the name, with the same family, including ours, using the spellings 'Hewett' and 'Hewitt' almost interchangeably.

John's father, James Hewett (1759–1808), a yeoman farmer and also a native of the village, had married John's mother, Lucy Allen (1759–*c.* 1827), in 1792. John was the second son and fourth child in a family of nine. After Mary Ann (born 1793–1865), whose birth was recorded in Odiham, St Nicholas' parish registers record the names of James (1 May 1794–1852), Sarah (15 February 1795–1820), John (1 May 1796–1839), Richard (5 June 1797–1835), Elizabeth (5 August 1798–December 1891), Charles (7 December 1800–20 July 1848), Ann (10 January 1802–1807) and Jane (19 June 1803–December 1890). Even in an age before artificial birth control, Lucy's fertility was remarkable. Women are less likely to become pregnant while breastfeeding, so the short spaces between Lucy's babies—from nine to fourteen months—suggest that she was either weaning them early or employing a wet nurse. One of the nine children, Ann, died in childhood and another, Sarah, in her mid-twenties.

On James's death in 1808, at the relatively early age of 49, his estate passed to his wife Lucy, then on her death to James, the eldest son. Sometime in the interim, James had become publican of the Raven Inn, leaving John, the second son, to take over the farm. Of the Hewett sons, only the eldest, James and John, my forebear, appear to have married and formed families of their own. In a rural society where wealth came from the soil, the marriage prospects of landless or unskilled younger sons and daughters were often slim. The two younger sons, who worked as agricultural labourers, died young. Two single daughters, Elizabeth and Jane, lived longest, supported by modest annuities and lodging together in Odiham, Weymouth and Dover. They died a year apart in the early 1890s and lie together next to their brother John in the Newnham churchyard.

James Hewett senior called himself a 'yeoman'. For centuries, 'the yeomen of England' had been venerated as the sturdy, independent heart of the nation. By the early nineteenth century, however, the word and the class itself were in flux. From the late eighteenth century, new forms of commerce, linked to new agricultural practices, had begun to break down the traditional structures of English rural society. Open fields were enclosed, and scattered holdings consolidated, crops were rotated, stock breeds improved, and new technologies—ranging from seed drills and harrows to deep-furrowing ploughs and threshing machines—adopted. In the 1820s, William Cobbett observed that: 'Those only who *rent* . . . are, properly speaking, *farmers*. Those who till their *own land* are *yeomen*; and, when I was a boy, it was the common practice to call the former *farmers* and the latter *yeomen-farmers*.' Many of the biggest and most successful farmers were now tenants, rather than freeholders, yet they called themselves 'yeomen', as did James Hewett. 'The English "yeoman", the proud, independent owner-cultivator, was more a figure of fiction than reality,' writes the historian G.E. Mingay. James's son John would continue to call himself 'yeoman', for example in his 1835 will. James's daughter-in-law Jane and his other descendants, however, would call themselves 'farmers'.

Bordering Berkshire to the north, Surrey and Sussex to the east, Dorset to the west and the Solent to the south, Hampshire was the heart of the old kingdom of Wessex, centred on the cathedral town of Winchester. Its rolling downs and green pastures live in the popular imagination as quintessential English countryside, evoked, in different ways, by the novels of Jane Austen, a resident of Winchester's satellite village Chawton; the Reverend Gilbert White's classic *The Natural History and Antiquities of Selborne* (1789); and Richard Adams' popular animal adventure tale, *Watership Down* (1972). The heart of Hampshire, the undulating chalklands known as the Downs, was largely pastoral and, in the 1830s, still thinly populated. Here life still moved slowly, and the pace of agricultural innovation was moderated by deep attachment to traditional ways of life. Along its edges, however, the tempo of life was increasing. The ocean ports and shipyards of Portsmouth and Southampton were capturing more of the nation's maritime commerce, while to the north, where the county touched the edges of the Thames basin, it came within range of what Cobbett called 'the Mighty Wen'—the magnetic, corrupting metropolis of London.

The parish of Newnham, which includes the neighbouring village of Hook, is almost a hundred kilometres southwest of London, close to the main transport corridor now defined by the M3 motorway and the London and South Western Railway. It lies along a ridge in the northeast corner of Hampshire, close to the Surrey border, and between the valleys of the Whitewater and Lyde rivers. Between 1801 and 1831, it grew from around 250 to 350 people (about the same as today). The ancient, and once rich, market town of Odiham (population 3000 in the 1840s) was about five kilometres away, within easy riding and regular walking distance. The surrounding countryside was generally lower, flatter and less fertile than the light soils of the South Downs. Charles Vancouver, an agricultural expert who surveyed the area in 1810, noted its 'strong, brown and grey loam, upon a tough, blue, and yellow clay', and warned that the 'raw damps' it exhaled were 'supposed to produce rheumatisms and to be otherwise unfriendly to the inhabitants'. The main form of local agriculture was mixed farming, with about half the land under crop, mainly wheat, and the rest devoted to pasture and woodland.

Hook Farm comprised about 250 acres of mixed arable land, pasture and woodland. The largest portion, 125 acres, was located in the parish of Newnham and included about thirty allotments, ranging in size from a few perches to seventeen acres, clustered on the north side of the London Road and along the road to Reading. (When I read the name 'Reading' it rang a bell. It seemed my grandfather did *not* mishear—though he misspelt and misunderstood—his great-aunt Jane when he wrote in his notebook that her birthplace was 'Redding'.) A second parcel, of 87 acres in fifteen small allotments, lay to the north in the parish of Rotherwick; a third, of 25 acres in seven allotments, in the parish of Nately Scures to the south; and the smallest, of seven acres in two allotments, in the parish of Odiham. From the higher ground near the London Road, the farm descended towards the valley of the Whitewater River, where several mills turned the farmers' wheat to flour. To an Australian eye, this patchwork of irregular fields, strips, woods and commons, crossing parish boundaries, is more like a map of feudal principalities, each with its own name and distinctive character, than an ordinary farm. Indeed, its origins go back at least to Elizabethan times, when the farm was part of the estates of the bishop of Winchester. Behind each name—Wood Plain, Long Slip, Washbrooks, Little Mead, Carter's Close, Ash Coppice, Wild Herons, Ash Wells, Gutter Close—lay a history, natural or human. Together they attest to the long-evolving intimacy between the farmer, his work and the natural world.

The nucleus of the farm, sometimes described as the 'homestead', was a 'substantial' building with a scattering of outhouses, their outlines clearly visible on the 1840 tithe assessment map. It stood at the junction between the London, Reading and Portsmouth roads, directly opposite the White Hart. John's brother James was previously landlord of the Raven Inn, a mile or so up the London Road, but after John's death he took over the White Hart, perhaps because of its commercial appeal, but maybe also to be closer to his brother's bereaved family. One imagines a constant flow of people, produce, hospitality and gossip between the households. The Hook farmhouse has long since disappeared, but the White Hart still stands at the intersection, the eighteenth-century coaching inn now joined to a modern roadhouse hotel.

In his survey of the county, Vancouver divided the farmers of north Hampshire into two categories. The larger proprietors—'a sober, industrious sort of men, seldom leaving home but when their business calls them to fairs or markets'—were the main agents of agricultural improvement. Gradually increasing their holdings and introducing the new techniques of marling (adding lime to break up the clay), harrowing and crop rotation, they were slowly squeezing out the smallholders. John's namesake George Hewett, a large tenant farmer at nearby Elvetham (famous in Tudor times as the seat of the Seymours), was typical of the new breed of modern farmers, enjoying 'most of the comforts and conveniences of life' and 'getting on in the world'. The smaller tenants, with a hundred or so acres, had barely sufficient land to be viable, and survived by carting wood, repairing public roads or providing winter pasture for the sheep of their southern neighbours. By such means, Vancouver believed, 'they contrive to rub on tolerably well; and if lucky with their little stock and horses, by frugality and good management, do rather more at the end of the year than make ends meet'. At 250 acres, Hook Farm was a viable holding, at least for a small family. But what could support a man, his wife and a few young children might not suffice for an ageing widow and eight adult children.

THE FARMER TAKES A WIFE

John Hewett was 25 years old and Jane Parsons almost five years older when they married on 12 September 1821 in the Newnham parish church. Jane had grown up just a few miles up the London Road at Murrell Green, where her father was the publican. In an era when social status was more sharply defined than it is today, and travel more restricted, people tended to marry partners from their own level of society and often from their own locality. John and Jane were folk of the 'middling sort'—the class of small farmers, publicans, builders, shopkeepers and skilled tradesmen who comprised about a quarter of the men in the village. They were a step above the rural proletariat of agricultural labourers—more than half the male workforce—but well below the 10 per cent or so of gentry, clergy, lawyers and large farmers who comprised the local elite. Jane Austen spoke for the gentry when she made her heroine Emma say: 'The yeomanry are precisely the order of people with whom I feel I can have nothing to do.'

Austen's novels describe a marriage market for the gentry centred on London and the spa and coastal resort towns such as Bath and Lyme Regis. By the 1820s, the 'middling sort' had also begun to look beyond their immediate locality for marriage partners. While John Hewett married a local girl, his elder sister, Mary Ann, married a Wiltshire farmer, John Hopkins, and James, the eldest brother, married Alice Harrison, born over two hundred kilometres away in Shropshire, although she was living locally by the time she married. An increasing number of locals sought their fortunes, and spouses, in a wider world (about 12 per cent of Newnham natives were living outside Hampshire in 1851, many in London), but no more than a dozen or so villagers came, like Alice, from outside the county.

The first duty of a farmer's wife was to produce a good crop of children. Tending chickens, milking cows, and lending a hand at harvest time, they were an integral part of the rural workforce. Over the following twelve years, Jane bore nine children, of whom eight survived to adulthood: Henry (born 1822), John (1823), Lucy (1824), Frances (1826), who died a month later, Mary Ann (1827), Robert (1828), Richard (1830), Jane (1832) and Susan (1834). Like her mother-in-law, she was blessed, or cursed, with high fertility, producing babies at almost yearly intervals until the arrival of the youngest, when she was 43. Her family was large, but only a little larger than average among farming communities. Her sister-in-law Alice, the publican's wife, by contrast, had fewer babies and at longer intervals: Mary, the eldest, was born two years after the marriage, followed by a long gap to James, born in 1834, who died six months after birth, and the son and heir George, born in 1837, when she was 41.

By the mid-nineteenth century, Hampshire was at the forefront of large-scale capitalist farming in England. The average farm now approached two hundred acres in size, and 90 per cent of farmers employed at least two men aside from family members. The days of the traditional family farm, supporting a family on two hundred acres or less, were numbered. Those who survived now derived the bulk of their income from outside work as tradesmen or labourers on public works or larger farms. In 1835, a parliamentary inquiry into the state of agriculture interviewed a large Hampshire farmer, Robert Stares. 'We have an increased population, yet we are selling our produce at less than our forefathers did when the population was not half of what it is now,' he estimated. Unless the farmer had enough capital to acquire more land and carry out improvements, 'the farms become deteriorated and the farmer is ruined'. As for the tenant farmer: 'He has gone, he cannot go on.' Perhaps he spoke too soon, but not by much.

Mechanisation had begun to threaten the livelihood of agricultural labourers and the survival of smallholders. The first horse-powered threshing machines were small, no bigger than a piano, but by the 1830s larger steam-powered machines began to appear. In the summer of 1830, discontented labourers, under the banner of their mythical leader 'Captain Swing', rampaged across the southeastern counties, rioting, burning haystacks and breaking threshing machines in an epidemic of small rebellions. Hampshire, one of the three counties where mechanisation and the concentration of landholding proceeded fastest, was an epicentre of revolt. After a meeting in Odiham, three hundred special constables were sworn in to repel the insurrection, and the cavalry at nearby Dogmersfield was readied for action. Rioting seems to have been more prevalent in the south, close to the Sussex border, in the west near Andover, and further north towards Berkshire than around Hook Farm, but it contributed to the mood of simmering discontent in the countryside.

LAST WILL AND TESTAMENT

In October 1835, 'John Hewett, Yeoman' drew up a fresh will. He must have ridden or walked into Odiham to arrange it, for the document was witnessed by 74-year-old Eli Lee and 69-year-old William Trickett, who both lived near the vicarage, the residence of Reverend William Harriott, curate of All Saints, who would later witness its execution. What prompted John to take this step? Could his health have already begun to fail, or had the arrival of his ninth (and last) child, or perhaps the two combined, focused his concern? Whatever occasioned its writing, the document offers an interesting insight into his hopes and fears.

It presents the picture of a modestly comfortable household, able to afford at least some of the good things of life. He left the perishable contents of the house—'all my stock of wine, beer, fuel and provisions'—and 'also my own wearing apparel for her own use, benefit and disposal . . . to my dear wife Jane'. The rest—'all . . . my household goods, in particular plate, linen and china and all my own live and dead farming stock and crops, implements and utensils in husbandry, debts, chattels, moneys and securities for money and all . . . other personal estate and effects'—was left in trust to his brother James Hewett, the publican, and his friend Edward Hellis, a builder in Odiham. When the will was eventually proved, the estate amounted to 'not more than £1000', no small sum if that figure was a conservative estimate of John's worth.

Under the trust, Jane was 'to carry on and manage my [her husband's] trade and business as a Farmer for the maintenance and support of herself and all and every my children'. Only when the youngest child turned 21 would the estate be divided between Jane, who would receive half, to be invested in 'government or real securities for her sole use', and the children, who would receive equal shares. John evidently had confidence in his wife's ability to 'carry on and manage' the family business for the foreseeable future but anticipated her need of advice in financial matters from his brother and friend. While contemporaries usually expected farmers' widows to continue on the land, they did not always make it easy for them. The hard-dealing that farmers needed to survive in a competitive business was sometimes seen as incompatible with proper feminine behaviour. Landlords were also often mistrustful of widows' ability to manage their farms along modern lines. In one of her short stories, the novelist George Eliot, herself the daughter of an estate steward, recounts an imaginary conversation between a landlord and a widow endeavouring to fulfil her husband's dying wish that she would stay on the farm. 'You are about as able to carry on a farm as your best milch cow,' he declares.

Significantly, John's will made no distinction between older and younger children, or between males and females, in distributing his estate. Farming families traditionally tended to pass their estate to the eldest son, with smaller bequests to siblings if their wealth permitted. This practice, known as primogeniture, was designed to transmit the family's property undivided into succeeding generations. It was especially prevalent among landed families, but as the historian Barry Stapleton has shown, it was the commonest single pattern of inheritance among all classes in Odiham, not just the landed. Of a sample of 104 wills gathered over two and a half centuries, just under half gave the bulk of the estate to the eldest son. Most of the rest favoured another son or sons together, and only eighteen of the 104 divided the estate equally between the children. Living in an age of greater gender equality, we are inclined to applaud John and Jane for not favouring a single male child over the others. But in this decision they may have jeopardised the survival of the family business. As Stapleton shows, the prospects of a family conserving their fortune over successive generations were lessened when—as with the Hewetts—the family was large, child mortality low, and one of the parents died prematurely. Dividing the estate between the children could further reduce their chances of survival—although defying primogeniture, he argues, was not as disadvantageous as other factors. John's clear message was that the family came before the interests of its individual members, and that their future was best secured by sticking together and staying on the farm.

While putting family first, however, John could not disregard the circumstances threatening the viability of their family business. He recognised that not all of his children would necessarily become farmers, by providing that, with the agreement of his wife, his trustees might advance from their presumptive inheritance sums of up to £60 'for the purpose of putting or placing out him or her to go in any trade business or profession or employment or otherwise for his or her benefit or advancement in the world'. Over the next few years, all of his sons, with the exception of the eldest, Henry, who also became a farmer, would be apprenticed to trades: John as a butcher, Robert as a carpenter and Richard as a miller. Their earnings would help to offset the family's static or declining returns from crops and livestock.

John also realised that Jane might eventually find the challenge of running the farm beyond her. 'In case my wife should not elect to carry on my said farming business . . . [or it] cannot be longer continued with advantage to my family', he directed that his personal property, together with the stock and effects of the farm, should be sold and the proceeds distributed just as if it had continued until the youngest child became an adult. In the meantime, however, the trustees should invest the shares of any children still under the age of 21 until they reached their majority. Over the decade following John's death, as she entered her fifties and the difficulties of running the farm increased, these clauses of her husband's will must have been a subject of anxious discussion between Jane and her brother-in-law James.

A DISTURBANCE IN THE VILLAGE

As they listened to the gossip in the bar of the Raven Inn and watched the flow of traffic along the London Road, the Hewetts could recognise the signs of the times. Hook was no longer a rural backwater but a lay-by on an increasingly crowded highway. After the end of the Napoleonic Wars in 1815, the growth of maritime trade, propelled by the introduction of larger, faster sailing vessels, increased the importance of the transport corridor between London and the southern ports. In the 1790s, the Basingstoke Canal, a mile or so to the south, was completed, enabling the cheaper carriage of agricultural produce to London, and the supply of coal from the industrial north. The turnpike linking London to Land's End used to run close by St Nicholas' Church and Newnham. But the new coaching road (the precursor to the A30) bypassed the village and proceeded through Hook, where it forked, one branch heading south towards Portsmouth and the other west towards Southampton and

Plymouth. By the 1830s more than thirty coaches passed or stopped at the inn each day. When James later left the Raven and became publican of the White Hart, he cannily sought to capture some of that growing passenger trade.

Just a few months before John's death came the biggest shock. From the east, cutting a swathe through fields and woodland, the London and Southampton Railway irrupted into the village. Its arrival had been anticipated for almost a decade. 'A new era is dawning on Southampton,' the local newspaper announced soon after the formation of the railway company in 1830. Surveying and construction began in the mid-1830s, but only in early 1838 did work begin on the 40-kilometre section between Woking and Basingstoke. An army of navvies, mostly moonlighting local farm labourers, camped along the line, filling the air with curses and the clang of hammers, eating at mobile kitchens and carousing in local inns. In less than a year, with the aid of only picks, shovels and horse drays, they transformed the local landscape, excavating an 80-metre tunnel under Scures Hill and raising a mile-long embankment between Hook and Newnham. From his farmhouse, John could see the new line, barely three hundred metres away, as it passed through the village, almost touching the southern edge of his farm. In September, the first train from London, carrying a party of politicians and railway officials, arrived in Winchfield, about a mile up the line, where 'a large assemblage of gentry and rustics' awaited them. After congratulatory speeches, the gentry, including the local parson, Reverend Mr William Harriott, adjourned to the Wellesley Inn at nearby Murrell Green for a celebratory dinner.

I wonder what the Hewetts thought about the arrival of the railway. As an academic historian I would not even attempt to answer the question: it is too conjectural. I would be better off examining the opinions of people who actually wrote them down. But the people who wrote things down are not the people whose feelings I want to know. Ancestry inspires the assumption that our forebears, being our own flesh and blood, are somehow more accessible, as

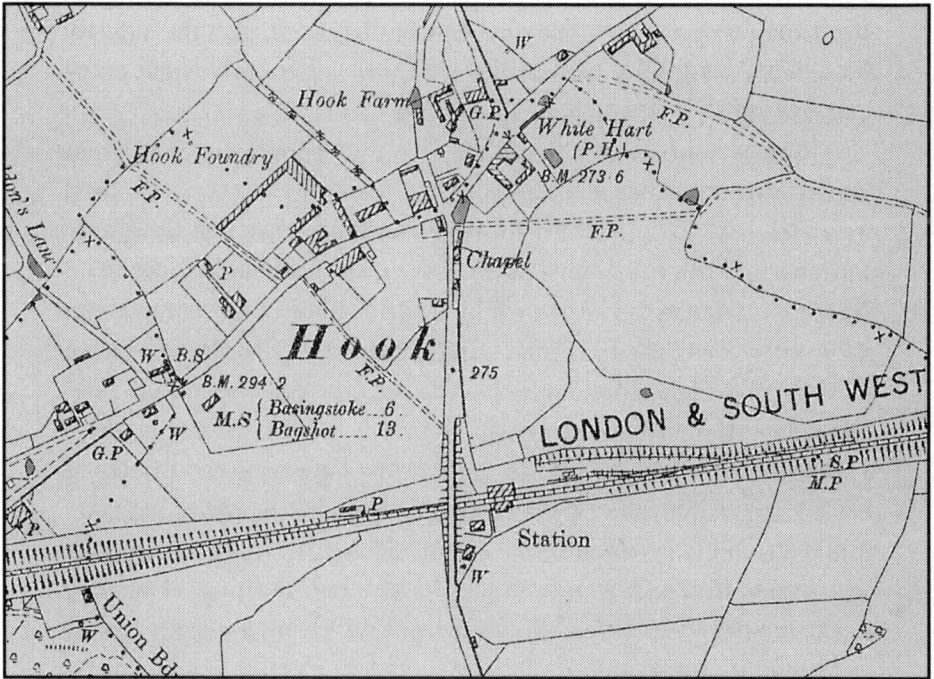

The coming of the London and Southampton Railway in 1839 transformed the village of Hook. In 1897, when this map was made, the outbuildings of Hook Farm were joined by a small foundry, and shops had begun to appear along the main street. The White Hart Inn and the Independent Chapel, the pivots of the local community, are clearly visible. (Ordnance Survey Six Inch Series, Hampshire and Isle of Wight, XIX NE, 1897, National Library of Scotland)

well as more important, to us than other dead people. At the end of our pilgrimage we imagine ourselves sitting in a room with our ancestor, as we would with a lost relation, joined by an unspoken bond of understanding. When I ask, 'What did John Hewett feel about the coming of the railway?', I am hoping that blood relationship will do what evidence and scholarly understanding alone cannot. As 'patriality' once entitled the children of British emigrants to enter the United Kingdom, so kinship, we think, offers privileged entry into the family past.

However, our distant forebears were not people just like us in period costume. They were inhabitants of another country, the past, where they did things differently. If I were able to have that imaginary conversation with John Hewett, the gulf between us might prove to be almost unbridgeable. The French historian Fernand Braudel imagined a conversation with the great philosopher Voltaire. If they were talking philosophy, Braudel believed, the conversation would flow easily, since the men of the eighteenth century are our contemporaries at the level of ideas. 'But if we spent a few days with the master of Ferney, all the details of material life, even his personal hygiene, would shock us,' he contended. 'Tremendous differences would open up between him and us: lighting in the evenings, heating, transport, food, illness and its cures.' My visit to Hook Farm, I suspect, could be even more surprising. I might be as shocked by John's ideas as by his teeth and body odour, by his prejudices and insularity as much as his domestic arrangements.

The idea that we can actually put ourselves in the shoes of our forebears is a harmless enough delusion, but a delusion nonetheless. The philosopher R.G. Collingwood said that the historian aims to rethink the thoughts of people in the past. Historical events are not 'spectacles to be watched but experiences to be lived through in his own mind'. Even Collingwood, though, did not suppose that the historian could directly experience past feelings. Yet even if we cannot feel the emotions of people in the past, something may be gained in the attempt. By reconstructing the situations they faced, taking account of the beliefs and attitudes of the time, comparing their situation with that of others, we can begin to understand their actions, even if we cannot enter their minds or hearts. This is what historians call the discipline of historical context. It begins by treating our own forebears not as special but as ordinary people of their time, and it ends—I would argue—not by enhancing family pride but by expanding our common humanity.

When I ask the question 'What did the Hewetts feel about the coming of the railway?', I peer through a glass darkly. The glass has been darkened by the many contemporary observers, from Dickens and Tolstoy to J.M.W. Turner and Karl Marx, who depicted the remorseless advance of the locomotive as a sinister portent of the industrial age. In the year that the railway arrived in Hook, Dickens watched the London and Birmingham Railway arriving in the outskirts of London 'with a shriek and a roar and a rattle, and no trace to leave behind but dust and vapour: like as in the track of the remorseless monster, Death!' Sympathy for my ancestor, so soon to die, and knowledge of what was to become of his family—not to mention literary effect—might tempt me to lend a similar colour to the arrival of the railway in Hook.

Yet the sceptical historian urges caution. Perhaps John Hewett was actually among the 'gentry and rustics' who welcomed the railway. Perhaps he was excited by the prospect of reaching London in less than a third of the time it had taken by coach, and 'with an ease and smoothness that seemed the very perfection of locomotion', although I wonder if he could have afforded the seven-shilling second-class fare. I hear him saying gruffly, 'And pray, sir, why would I want to go to London?' While passengers on the new line gained 'a series of delightful prospects' of 'a most fertile tract of country which everywhere exhibits unequivocal proof of the rich luxuriance of the country', the Hewetts may have been more troubled by the disruption the construction of the line caused to the operations of their farm. None of them, at any rate, could have known how the railway age, and what Dickens called 'railway dreaming', would shape their lives for both good and ill on the other side of the world.

~

John Hewett died in the interval between the arrival of the first locomotive in September 1838 and the completion of the line the following June. Since 1837, when the new system of compulsory state registration of births, marriages and deaths came into force, local registrars were obliged to record the cause of death as well as the deceased's age and occupation. Actuaries, doctors and experts in public health wanted this information in order to generate more reliable statistics of mortality. John's brother James, who is named on the death register as the informant, gave his date of death as 8 January, two days before the date recorded on his tombstone, and its cause as 'appoplexy' (*sic*). Church officials may well have followed the custom of recording the date of burial, 10 January, rather than that of the death two days earlier. The given cause of death may also have been approximate. The term 'apoplexy' was often used loosely to cover what we call a stroke, as well as other sudden attacks such as heart failure. Little was then known about the physiology of hypertension or cholesterol. People believed that people with thick, short necks and ruddy complexions were especially prone to apoplexy, and that an attack was often brought on by excessive exertion, or indeed excitement of any kind. 'Where a predisposition to apoplexy is suspected,' one authority advised, 'the individual should avoid strong bodily exertion; venereal [sexual] excitement; the excitement of drunkenness; violent mental emotion; straining at stool; long stooping; tight neckcloths; too much indulgence in sleep; and warm baths.' A man who followed this advice to the letter might just as well be dead, you might think. It is unlikely that John Hewett, a 42-year-old with a 250-acre farm and a large family, even tried to do so. Yet coming after his own father's early demise, John's sudden death may have left his widow and children wondering whether a hereditary disposition to apoplexy could blight their lives as well.

The death of the last Hewett 'yeoman' and the coming of the first railway signalled a mighty transition, although what that transition signified was less clear. By the early 1840s—'the hungry forties' as they were sometimes called—English agriculture was heading into more troubled times. Historians have often viewed the era through the eyes of its most radical thinker, the Communist Karl Marx, and his vision of the imminent overthrow of capitalism. Contemporaries, however, took more notice of the prophecies of a rural clergyman, Thomas Malthus, who feared that population was increasing faster than the means of subsistence. His ideas shaped angry debates about the provision of relief under the New Poor Law of 1834, pleas for agricultural protection and the necessity for emigration. Living close to the soil, and struggling to support a large family of hungry adult children, Jane Hewett was better able than most to appreciate the force of his dismal logic.

LIFE ON HOOK FARM

For a time, little seemed to change at Hook Farm. When the census taker called on 6 June 1841, Jane and her eldest son, nineteen-year-old Henry, were both described as 'farmers'. Missing from the household on census night was eighteen-year-old John, an apprentice butcher, probably living with his master. Thirteen-year-old Robert was still living at home, although probably already apprenticed to a local builder or carpenter. The household also included a 60-year-old lodger, Mary Webb; a twenty-year-old domestic servant, Henrietta Stanley; and three agricultural labourers, twenty-year-old Daniel Lavington, and George Drewett and Henry Petter, both fifteen. Female domestic servants, like Henrietta, the daughter of agricultural labourer William Stanley and his wife Ann, were usually locals, but agricultural labourers, like Daniel Lavington from Stratfield Saye, about eight miles away, often travelled further in search of work, especially during the harvest season.

By employing so many young people, Jane was probably economising. A boy of fifteen might earn about half to two-thirds of a man's wage, or about six shillings a week plus board. At harvest time, when labour was short and the work more arduous, labourers were usually paid piece rates. Family, servants and farm labourers traditionally lived together, eating at the same table, although by the 1830s the tradition was dying, according to Cobbett, who lamented its decline. A household like Jane's, with eleven people under twenty, was voracious, consuming a good proportion of what it produced. 'The ordinary breakfast of farm-servants is bread and skimmed milk, with the remainder of what bacon was left the day before; their lunch or noonchine [snack], consists of bread and cheese, with the small beer they take in their kegs to the field,' Vancouver observed. 'Their dinner is usually prepared between three and four o'clock, and consists of pickled pork or bacon, with potatoes, cabbages, turnips, greens and broths, seasoned to the palate with a variety of garden stuff and pot herbs, thickened with wheat flour.' There was little on this menu that could not be produced on a Hampshire farm, at least in the warmer months, and what could not be eaten fresh could be pickled or preserved.

Among the old stuff left in my great-great-grandparents' house in Castlemaine was a battered volume with the handwritten title 'A Collection of Valuable Recipes by Mrs Hewett'. The recipes have been written into a small cashbook with an 1858 calendar or almanac in the flyleaf. The word 'Melbourne' has been written three times, in different hands on the title page. It is not certain whether the Mrs Hewett of the title was the farmer's widow, Jane Hewett, or her daughter-in-law Elizabeth, but it is probable that, like many such collections, it is a compilation from several sources, including Jane. As we read the recipes for parsnip wine, ginger beer, 'common buns' and apple cakes, it is easy to imagine ourselves standing beside her in the kitchen of Hook Farm, watching as she beats and stirs, boils and bakes to turn the seasonal produce of the farm into food and drink for her large family. We would only have to make up the recipes ourselves to experience the tastes and aromas she created. The instructions for preserving damson plums, pickling hams and making sour wine sweet take us back to an age before cans and refrigerators, when summer bounty had to be eked out to ward against winter famine. The remedies for chapped hands ('it protects the hands against the action of the severe frosts') and damp walls evoke the physical hardships of rural life, while her 'cure for cancer' ('this preparation converts the tumour into perfect carbon and it crumbles away in a few hours') reminds us how close Jane lived to the era of the quack and witch doctor and how far from the victory of scientific medicine.

THE LANDLORD

While local conditions worsened, the Hewetts' future was also being shaped by a family crisis on the other side of the country. Like all tenant farmers, they were dependent on the continuing goodwill of their landlord. They may never have met Samuel Tyssen, or certainly not for some time. He was a large landed proprietor with estates near the family's ancestral house, Narborough Hall in Norfolk, as well as houses in Hackney, and scattered holdings, including Hook Farm, in Hampshire. The Tyssens had come to England from Flanders in the seventeenth century and later made a fortune in slave plantations in Antigua. By the early nineteenth century, they were country gentlemen, with a grand Georgian mansion, Felix Hall, in Essex. Their children followed the traditional careers of the landed gentry, the elder sons buying commissions in the army and two of their four daughters marrying clergymen.

After the death of their mother in 1828, however, the family's fortunes took a turn for the worse. In 1835, Samuel suffered a serious illness, probably a stroke. During the next ten years—'a living death', according to his sister—he was unable to attend to the affairs of the estate. Unwilling or unable to arrest the drift, his sons pursued their

Parsnip wine

To 12 pound of parsnips, cut in slices, add
4 gallons of water; boil them till they
become quite soft. Squeeze the liquor well
out of them, run it through a sive, and add
to every gallon 3 pounds of loaf sugar. Boil
the whole three quarters of an hour, and
when it is nearly cold, add a little yeast.
Let it stand for ten days in a tub, stirring it
every day from the bottom, then put it into
a cask for twelve months: as it works over,
fill it up every day.

own careers, sometimes to the ends of the earth. In 1842, when Henry, the youngest son, died in Geelong in faraway Port Phillip, his elder brother William, a captain in the 80th Regiment of Foot, was supervising convicts at the Towrang Stockade in New South Wales. Only when the father was on his deathbed in 1845 did his heir, Charles, a captain in the 70th Regiment, hasten home.

Samuel's death brought an overdue reckoning with his legacy. For ten years, decisions had been deferred and debts had accumulated. Thousands of pounds had been borrowed against the Hampshire estates to buy commissions for his sons and marriage settlements for his daughters, so that by 1846, Hook Farm was mortgaged to more than half its value. Samuel's will, dated 1833, written in an archaic but now almost unreadable lawyer's script, recognised the reluctance of most of his children to live on the land. Charles, the eldest son, would inherit most of the estate, but the lands in Norfolk and Hampshire were to be sold, his debts and mortgages discharged, and £10,000 distributed equally among his younger children. In 1843, he added a codicil making further provision for his second son, William, who had retired from the army to a farm in South Africa. Perhaps he feared that Charles, still unmarried at 35, would not produce an heir. If so, his intentions were nullified by William's death only two years after his own. When Charles inherited, he sold the ancestral homes in Norfolk and Essex and bought a more modest house, Clanville, deep in the Hampshire Downs, where he lived, still unmarried and alone save for three servants, until his death in 1863.

The sale of the Hewett farm, together with the White Hart, James Hewett's inn, took place by auction on Friday, 8 May 1846. A handbill advertising the sale, with a map and inventory of the various fields, is the fullest contemporary description of the farm we have.

The Hewetts had rented Hook Farm from the Tyssens for almost fifty years. At the beginning of the century, the usual lease on Hampshire farms was for 21 years, but by the 1840s many farmers were 'tenants at will', leasing their land year by year by mutual agreement. This insecurity of tenure had become a sore point in the

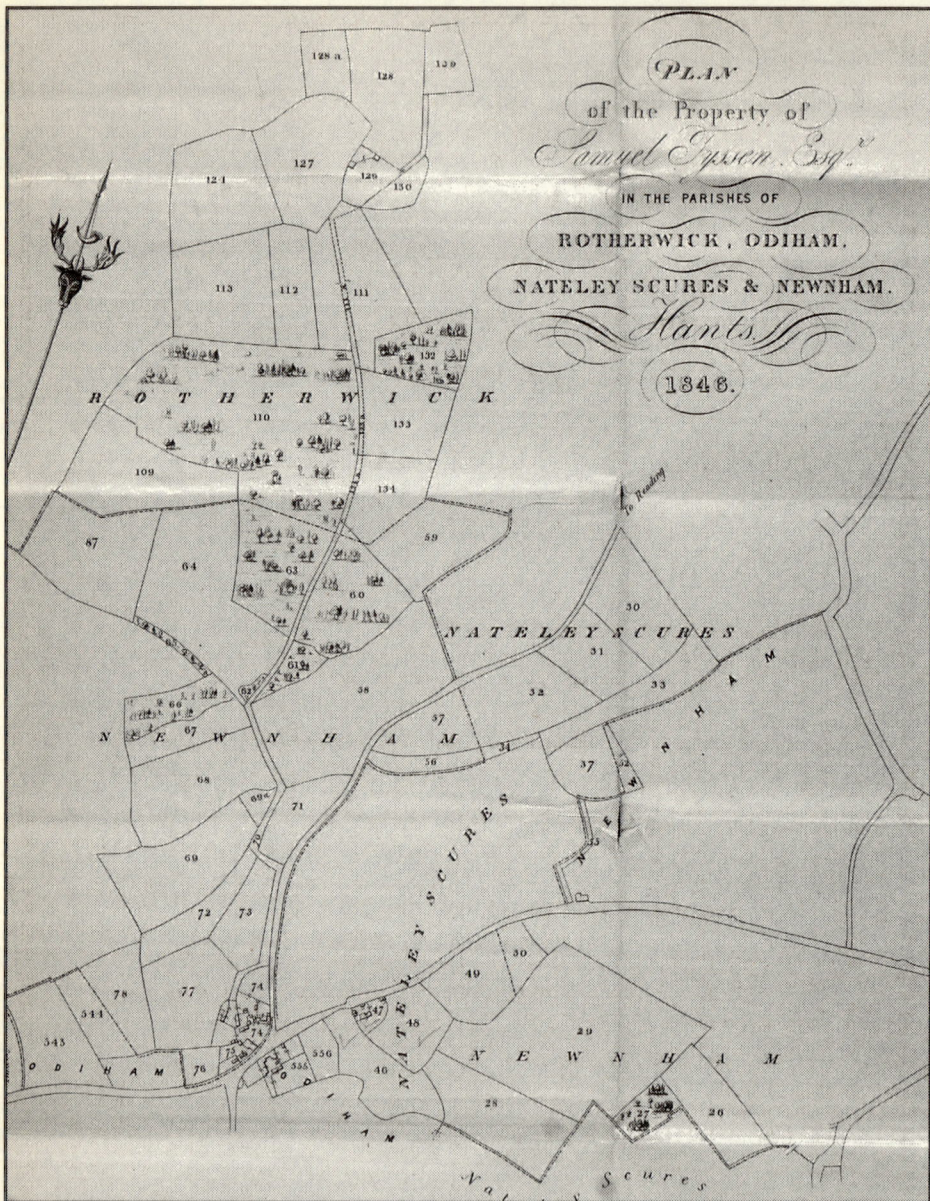

Plan of the property of Samuel Tyssen prepared for the sale of Hook Farm in 1846. The Hewetts' 'homestead' and associated farm buildings appear on the north side of the road junction in the lower left-hand corner opposite James Hewett's coaching inn, The White Hart. (Hampshire Record Office 10M57/SP527)

PARTICULARS AND CONDITIONS OF SALE
OF

FREEHOLD ESTATES,

IN HANTS

WITHIN THREE MILES OF THE SOUTH WESTERN RAILWAY STATION AT WINCHFIELD

Very Eligible for Investment or Occupation

CONSISTING OF AN
EXCELLENT FARM
OF NEARLY
TWO HUNDRED AND FIFTY ACRES
OF
Arable, Meadow, and Woodland,

MOST ADMIRABLY ADAPTED FOR THE PRESERVATION OF GAME
AND GROWTH OF TIMBER

Known as "HOOK & NIGHTINGALE" FARM

ALSO A
CAPITAL INN

AT THE JUNCTION OF THE READING AND PORTSMOUTH, WITH
THE LONDON AND SOUTHAMPTON ROADS, KNOWN AS THE
"WHITE HART" AT HOOK

With about 14 Acres of very superior Meadow Land attached.

TWO FREEHOLD HOUSES
ELIGIBLY SITUATED FOR BUSINESS

AND SEVERAL DETACHED PIECES OF MEADOW LAND

THE WHOLE LYING IN THE SEVERAL PARISHES OF

ODIHAM, ROTHERWICK, NATELY SCURES
And NEWNHAM, HANTS.

relationship between farmers and landlords, especially as economic conditions worsened.

While a change of ownership did not necessarily bring a change of tenant, it often did. When the Tyssen estates were put up for auction in 1846, they were advertised as 'very *eligible* for investment or occupation'. The cultivated lands, the advertisement continued, 'are let on Lease to an *eligible* Tenant with Lots 3 & 6, for a term of 14 years from September 29th, 1840, determinable by the Landlord at the expiration of the first 5, 7 or 10 years, on giving two years notice, at the annual Rent of £205' (my emphases). The use of the word 'eligible' in the two passages is interesting: in the first it appears to mean 'deserving' or 'suitable', but in the second it may mean no more than 'available'. Since the prospective purchaser was invited to consider occupying the farm himself, the question must have arisen: how soon could the sitting tenant be required to quit? The seventh year of the Hewetts' lease would expire in September 1847, leaving insufficient time, however, for the new owner to give the required two years' notice. The next opportunity would not arise until September 1850, though, of course, once the owner's intentions were clear, an earlier exit could always be negotiated or forced.

The successful bidder, Thomas Chalcraft, a grocer from Headley, offered £4810 for the farmland and a total of £5847 for the entire estate, including woodland. He may have been bidding for his son, also Thomas, who later settled in Odiham, but by the early 1850s the sale seems not to have gone through and the property reverted to Charles Tyssen. In the meantime, however, perhaps as a casualty of the incomplete transaction, the Hewetts had quit the farm and set off for Australia.

HARD TIMES

Quite apart from these uncertainties, the sale of Hook Farm could hardly have come at a worse time. In 1846, the government of Sir

Robert Peel repealed the Corn Laws. These laws had previously forbidden the importation of foreign grains until the price of locally grown corn reached a high set price of 80 shillings a quarter (in today's money about $1600 a ton). The advocates of repeal, the Anti-Corn Law League, inspired by the free-trade doctrines of Adam Smith, argued that this tariff increased the cost of living to English workers, drove up wages, and blocked innovation in agriculture. But their promise of cheaper bread for workers and lower costs to manufacturers sowed panic among tenant farmers, who predicted that imports of cheap foreign grain would drive them to the wall. 'Gentlemen—You are really to be pitied,' a sympathiser wrote to *The Times*. 'With the exception of the men who work for you at 7s a week wages, you are of all classes of society, at this moment, the most unfortunate.'

While the price of his produce fell, the tenant farmer could not control his most significant cost, his rent. Every year, before she began to pay wages and other costs, Jane had to pay her landlord £205 rent. 'Surely, if ever we required help from our landlords, it is at the present time when every article of farm produce is at a full 25 per cent lower than it ought to be to meet the rents and taxes, and this, too, with failing crops,' a Gloucestershire farmer pleaded. Meetings of desperate farmers across the agricultural counties petitioned landlords to reduce their rents in line with the anticipated fall in agricultural prices. The market reformers replied then, as they do still, that inefficient farmers should increase their productivity by modernising their methods. To many small farmers, with limited capital and expertise, their advice seemed both impractical and insulting. As a sympathiser observed:

Every agricultural meeting presents the sad spectacle of the naughty tenantry being scolded for their misdoings; their stubbles are shamefully high, their hedges disgracefully untidy, their drains ignorantly placed; they use four horses where two would do the work, their farmyards waste rather than provide manure; they sow too thick, they plough too shallow . . . Now, Sir, what is this but a delicate intimation to the farmer that unless they can produce more corn

than they do now from the same area of soil, they must give up all
legal protection of the price of what they do grow?

Even before the repeal of the Corn Laws, the price of corn had been falling steadily. Between 1839 and 1849, the annual average price of wheat sold in the Winchester market fell from 66.3 to 44 shillings a quarter. 'The crops are ripening and the markets are falling,' *The Morning Post* reported in September 1849. Just when the farmers at last had a bumper harvest, the fall in prices wiped out their profit. Many were simply selling off their possessions, often at a quarter of what they had paid for them, and walking off the land. 'I have tried in vain to let the farm,' one lamented, 'but no one will pay the old rent, and my landlord refuses to take it off my hands except under the sacrifice of my £5000 invested in his land.' More than three hundred distressed farmers in Surrey signed a petition calling for the reintroduction of protection. The proud yeomen of England had been reduced to beggars.

If tenant farmers left or were forced off the land, where were they to go? All their choices were bad. If they became landless labourers, they found themselves competing on a depressed market with their old employees. They fell from the 'middling' to the lower ranks in a village society where such falls were conspicuous and pitiable. If they went elsewhere in England, their options were little better. Most of their skills were rural, and while some, like the Hewett boys, could find jobs elsewhere as carpenters, millers or butchers, what was to become of their mothers and sisters? Whatever opportunities England offered seemed to entail the splitting up of the family.

We do not know whether Jane and her family were actually forced off Hook Farm or whether they departed with whatever dignity remained before they were evicted. Either way, by 1851, when the census taker called again, the farm was being tended by a bailiff, Joseph Mott. But their circumstances suggest that by the late 1840s the aperture of opportunity in England was closing and their accumulating difficulties were pushing them to seek another life elsewhere.

SLIPPING THE MOORINGS

As economic hardship loosened the Hewetts' hold on their farm, their relationship with the local community was also changing. The growing traffic along the transport corridor from London had cut Hook adrift from its once-dominant neighbouring villages. The old patterns of authority, based on the rule of squire and parson, were fading. The local magnate, Lord Dorchester, and the Hewett's landlord, Samuel Tyssen, both absentees, took little part in local affairs. Hook had no parson of its own; the nearest churches, St Nicholas in Newnham and St Swithin's in Nately Scures, were more than a mile away. Its only religious building, just across the London road and a few doors from the White Hart, was a tiny Independent Chapel established in 1816.

The Independents, or Congregationalists, were the spiritual descendants of the Puritans. In 1643, when Cromwell's soldiers reputedly gathered at the old White Hart Inn, Hook stood close to the battlefront of the English Civil War. Two hundred years later, the Independents, who claimed about one-fifth of Hampshire's church-going population, mostly tradesmen and shopkeepers, were still fighting religious oppression. They led the popular movement to abolish the tithes or compulsory church rates levied on local landowners, a cause that hard-up farmers like the Hewetts often supported. Like his father, John Hewett had been a churchman, but the interests of his widow and sons, now working as independent tradesmen, were less clear-cut. Proximity as well as fellow feeling may have drawn them towards the Independents. Significantly, soon after their arrival in Melbourne, John, Robert and Lucy Hewett were married in the residence of the Independent Minister Alexander Morison, each 'solemnly declaring' that 'I do hold communion with the Independent or Congregational denomination of Christians'. A yearning for independence, religious as well as economic, may have helped to broaden their horizons.

A WAY OUT?

The English had long regarded emigration as a form of exile, a fate scarcely better than death. It was tainted by memories of its association with slavery, convict transportation and poverty—'shovelling out paupers' was the unflattering description given by one contemporary politician. Only in the late 1840s did public opinion begin to turn strongly in its favour. Like a safety valve (an image with obvious appeal to an industrial society), emigration simultaneously relieved the pressure of surplus population in Britain and supplied the human energy needed to develop its colonies. Ambitions frustrated in the homeland could be realised in another England overseas. People began to speak of emigrants as 'settlers' or 'colonists', words that made them heroes in a great national enterprise, the British Empire.

English statesmen and colonial officials preached the new gospel of salvation by steerage. Agents employed by the colonial governments toured the country, handing out pamphlets on the benefits of emigration. Articles appeared in the national and provincial press describing the successes of settlers in Canada, New South Wales and Port Phillip. A Colonial Land and Emigration Commission offered assisted passages paid for out of the revenue generated from the sale of colonial land to suitable settlers, especially young men with agricultural skills. It is easy to imagine how news of these developments might have penetrated the countryside of north Hampshire, lying athwart the swelling traffic between London and the southern ports. Perhaps the Hewett boys overheard conversations in the White Hart about old friends or neighbours now doing well on the colonial frontier. Or perhaps someone drew their attention to this letter from Geelong in the 7 July 1849 issue of the *Hampshire Advertiser*.

EMIGRATION TO AUSTRALIA

Dear Father, Mother, Sisters and Brothers,
and all inquiring friends,

I hope these few lines will find you quite well, as it leaves me, thank God. After a most beautiful voyage of four months all but one day we dropped anchor on the 7th of December . . . There were masters enough to employ three times the number, if they had been here, they were offering from £20 to £25 a year, and 12 lb of meat, 10 lb of flour, 2 lb of sugar, and quarter of a pound of tea weekly, for single men and from £10 to £20 a year for single women . . . I am living in the largest butcher's shop I ever saw; they kill 6 bullocks every day and 100 sheep every week; the prime joints 2d a pound, and the others 1d . . . It is a very fine country . . . Who would stop in old England and starve, when they can make their fortunes in ten years if they keep from drinking? Do not hesitate one day, but go and get your papers, and come out here to the Land of Paradise.

The wages offered to the newcomers may seem modest enough to us, but we may gain a better sense of how this letter might have been read in the England of 1849 when we compare the situation of the young immigrant with a contemporary reporter's description of the lot of an agricultural labourer in Berkshire with a wife and eight children. While the former earned £20 to £25 a year, the latter earned barely £18. And while the colonist gained in addition a plentiful supply of good food, the second subsisted largely on bread and tea with skerricks of cabbage and bacon.

Emigration often followed a chain pattern, with new departures following the path blazed by relatives, friends or neighbours. Hampshire had not been one of the prime recruiting grounds for government-assisted migrants to the Australian colonies in the 1830s and early 1840s; those lay mainly to the southwest in Wiltshire, Dorset, Somerset and Devon, or to the east in Kent and Sussex. But the late 1840s brought a shift away from the recruitment of male agricultural labourers towards a more balanced migrant intake. As 'emigration' was redefined as 'colonisation', British politicians and Australian emigration advocates began to think beyond the economic to the moral and social attributes of the new colonists.

A central figure in these debates was Caroline Chisholm, a formidable 42-year-old Englishwoman who had recently returned from New South Wales. Her influence would become another strand in the web of circumstance drawing the Hewetts to Australia.

Caroline married her husband, Captain Archibald Chisholm, a retired officer in the East India Company, when she was 22, and converted to Roman Catholicism. In 1838, they settled in New South Wales, where she took up the cause of friendless immigrant women, finding them homes and employment, and attempting to shelter them from the moral perils of colonial life. By the late 1840s, when she arrived back in England, the focus of her efforts had changed. Rather than rescuing vulnerable girls in New South Wales, the secret of successful emigration policy, she decided, was to send out emigrants in family groups, relying on the parents to exercise a wholesome influence over their children. She toured the provinces, speaking tirelessly in favour of emigration. Back in London, in their rented house in Islington, the gallant Captain Chisholm maintained the command centre of the campaign, answering letters from the thousands of prospective emigrants seeking Mrs Chisholm's advice.

Early in 1849, she set out her ideas about emigration in a series of long articles in London's *Morning Chronicle*. Alongside journalist Henry Mayhew's sensational revelations of poverty and distress in the metropolis and provinces, readers were offered Mrs Chisholm's antidote, 'family colonisation'. The trouble with government schemes of emigration, she contended, was that they divided families instead of strengthening them. In her pamphlet *The ABC of Colonization*, published in January 1850, she painted a heartrending picture of the scenes on the wharf as parents said farewell to children they would never see again and unprotected young women fell among strangers. 'But what scenes take place before they have got this far; what conflicts of nature are endured before they ever leave their homes,' she exclaimed. 'What wailings in the cottage! What sad farewells outside the village!' Only if families could emigrate together, taking their ageing parents with them, keeping their daughters under the protection of parents and older siblings, could they enjoy the benefits of emigration without its moral hazards. Mrs Chisholm's Family Colonization Loan Society, a scheme to advance passage money to respectable people migrating to Australia in family groups, was launched to great acclaim in the early months of 1850. 'By means of its family groups, emigration at once ceases to be exile, no longer implies banishment from kindred and friends, but becomes simply a change, an advantageous change moreover, of locality,' she explained. It was an idea with wide appeal in a society where Home and Family stood next to Queen and Country in popular esteem. Several of the great and good, including the politician Sidney Herbert, the factory reformer Lord Ashley (the Earl of Shaftesbury) and the novelist Charles Dickens, rallied to her cause.

When the Hewetts boarded the *Culloden* at Gravesend in February 1850, Caroline Chisholm's family colonisation scheme had been launched, but the first group of passengers under the scheme did not embark at Southampton until April. Considering their circumstances, with a widowed mother, four strapping boys and four, mainly younger, daughters, the Hewett family look like model applicants, yet the timing suggests they came some other way. We know from their arrival papers that they did not come as assisted immigrants under the Colonial Land and Emigration Commission, but the cost of bringing nine adults as private passengers may have been beyond the Hewetts' means. ('Intermediate' berths on the *Culloden* were advertised for £20, or about £200 for the whole family.) Some English parishes, including Odiham, were assisting hard-up families to emigrate by paying at least some of their passage money, but the Hewetts, who had until recently been substantial farmers, were unlikely to have been eligible, and there is no record of their being helped in this way. Could the Hewetts' old friends and neighbours have taken pity on their plight and interceded with the parish overseers to help them onto the boat? We do not know for certain, but there was another possible explanation, one that becomes more credible when we examine more closely the background of their shipmates aboard the *Culloden*, as we will do in the next chapter.

WHY DID THEY LEAVE?

Historians have long debated the motives for migration. Were the voyagers to the New World pushed or pulled? Was their decision forced upon them by adversity at home—poverty, political or religious oppression, family or ethnic conflict? Or were they inspired by the promise of a better life in the new land, a promise held out by emigration agents or fellow countrymen who had gone before them? Was the decision a coolly rational one, based on plenty of information and a careful calculation of the opportunities and risks? Or was it impulsive, based upon emotion and sentiment more than reason?

The answer, of course, is that it could have been all of these, or rather combinations of them, according to each individual's circumstances. In most cases, while migration may have been the decision of a moment, the circumstances that led to it had been developing for some time. When John Hewett died, it is unlikely that the thought of emigration had entered his widow's mind. Yet, in retrospect, his premature death was the first in a series of small disruptions—the coming of the railway, the death of their landlord and the sale of the Tyssen estate, the repeal of the Corn Laws and the collapse of agricultural prices—that together drove the family to the point of crisis. One could even argue that their misfortunes began a generation earlier, with the untimely death of John's own father in 1808.

But while these forces, acting cumulatively, gradually prised the Hewetts away from their inherited way of life, they did not necessarily point to migration as the inevitable result. Thousands of other rural émigrés settled elsewhere in the United Kingdom. Many of those who did finally emigrate had first moved from the village to a small town, from a small town to a larger one or to the fringes of the metropolis, and only then overseas. The Hewetts were unusual in moving directly from the village to the migrant ship. Many more emigrants chose the United States or Canada before Australia. Port Phillip, so far away and so expensive to reach, would have seemed an unlikely destination but for the success of figures like Caroline Chisholm in making 'family colonisation' a popular cause. There do not appear to have been any Hewett relatives or friends already in Australia encouraging them to come. But the 'emigration mania' of the late 1840s was enough to break down any remaining reservations. To the extent that we can read their motives from their actions, it was the opportunity to transplant their entire family, and reconstitute their old life in a new environment, that inspired them. It was a touching testament to the strength of their family bond and their determination to maintain it. Once they left Hook Farm and set sail into the great unknown it would be tested as never before.

The West End. In 1841, John Fenwick and his family were living in Dacre Street, a narrow street off Broadway, only a block from Westminster Abbey and the Houses of Parliament. In the mid-1840s the construction of a new main road, Victoria Street, forced many poor families, including the Fenwicks, to move on. By 1851, they had moved across St James Park to 97 Regent Street, a few blocks from St George's Hanover Square, the church where they had married in 1825. (Payne's Illustrated Plan of London, 1846 (detail), National Library of Australia)

CHAPTER TWO
London

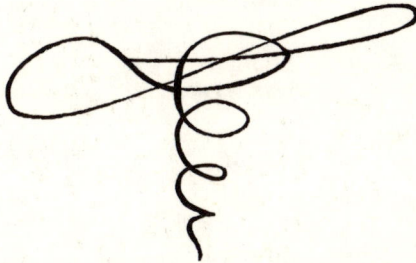

Family history is a search for roots. Nowhere are the roots buried deeper than in the soil of an ancestral homeland. By beginning my family story with the death of an English yeoman and his burial in a country churchyard, I yielded to a romantic English vision of the past, one with a strong appeal to many Australians. When the historian Keith Hancock defined the identity of an earlier generation of Anglo-Australians, he wrote of being 'in love with two soils'. More recent generations of Australians return in spirit to country graveyards in Italy, Greece, Turkey or China. Others, seeking a spiritual homeland on Australian soil, identify vicariously with the long ancestral past of the Aboriginal people at Dreaming sites in Kakadu or Uluru. As Australia becomes more post-industrial, urban and multicultural, the urge to 'return' to such places, far from the

THE FENWICKS OF WESTMINSTER

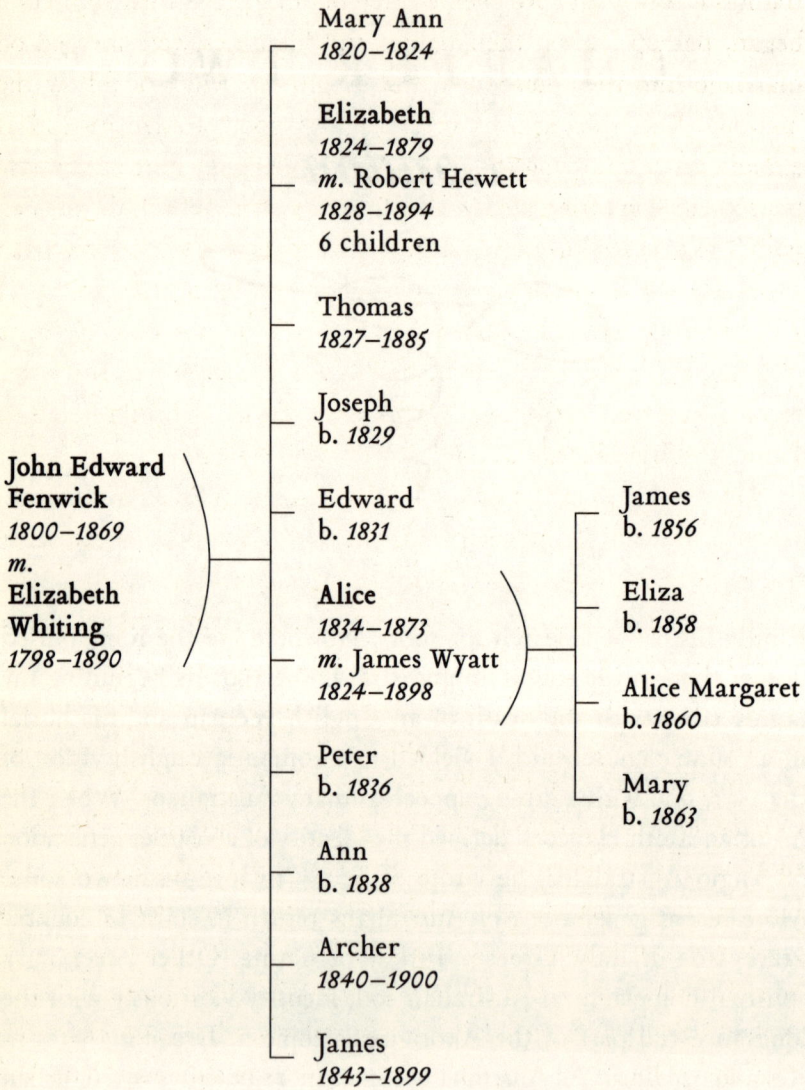

John Edward Fenwick
1800–1869
m.
Elizabeth Whiting
1798–1890

Mary Ann
1820–1824

Elizabeth
1824–1879
m. Robert Hewett
1828–1894
6 children

Thomas
1827–1885

Joseph
b. *1829*

Edward
b. *1831*

Alice
1834–1873
m. James Wyatt
1824–1898

Peter
b. *1836*

Ann
b. *1838*

Archer
1840–1900

James
1843–1899

James
b. *1856*

Eliza
b. *1858*

Alice Margaret
b. *1860*

Mary
b. *1863*

madding crowd, where we join the spirit of the ancestors seems to grow stronger.

In beginning my story with a man, John Hewett, I was following another tradition: the male or patrilineal path into my family's past. Most family historians are women, and they sometimes question this tradition. If women have been written out of history, their subjection began, perhaps, when their names and identities were merged on marriage into their husbands'. So, in protest, why not follow the maternal line, tracing a proud lineage of good women instead of automatically following the male line? Some rebels start out bravely but soon give up, frustrated by the difficulty of recovering the maiden names of great-great-grandmothers in records that seldom recorded them. Recently, feminist genealogy got a boost from the advent of DNA testing. Mitochondrial DNA passes from mother to child, so enabling researchers to trace female lineages invisible in the paper record. But even with biology apparently on her side, the feminist family historian battles strong patriarchal headwinds.

My mother was the eldest of five daughters in a family with no sons. But in tracing their family history they followed the male line back to John Hewett. His third son, Robert, became my great-great-grandfather, marrying Elizabeth Fenwick, one of his shipmates on the voyage to Australia, in 1851, nine months or so after their arrival in Melbourne. Of Elizabeth, however, we knew almost nothing, save for a brief note in my grandfather's notebook that she was 'born on the Old Kent Road, London'. Was she a victim of genealogical discrimination? Or was the silence about Elizabeth more ominous—born, perhaps, of a suspicion that enquiries into her past might lead to somewhere less picturesque than a country churchyard in Hampshire? The Old Kent Road was at the other end of the Monopoly board from Mayfair and Park Lane. Its name evoked a South London of dockyards, tanneries and gasworks, cloth caps and jellied eels, and the cheeky old music hall song 'Knocked 'Em in the Old Kent Road'.

Elizabeth was indeed a Londoner, through and through. Her mother, Elizabeth Mary Ann Whiting, was born in the parish of St George's Hanover Square, and baptised in Lambeth, south of the Thames, in 1798, while her father, John Edward Fenwick, was born in St Margaret's Westminster, close by the Abbey, in 1800. They married in 1820 at St George's Hanover Square in fashionable Mayfair, where a galaxy of notables also wed, including Byron, Disraeli, George Eliot and the famous dancer Lola Montez—the last bigamously. When Elizabeth, the Fenwicks' eldest surviving child, and Thomas, their eldest son, were born, in 1824 and 1827 respectively, they were living on or near the Old Kent Road in Southwark. By the mid-1830s, however, they had moved back across the river to John's old stamping ground, St Margaret's Westminster. Over the next thirty years they moved several times, but always within the City of Westminster.

By 1840, London was the world's metropolis, the capital of the British Empire. Westminster was the historic heart of London. All the sacred sites of English power were concentrated within a one-mile radius of the Fenwicks' home: Buckingham Palace, home of Queen Victoria; the Palace of Westminster, home of the 'Mother of Parliaments'; and Westminster Abbey, the home of the English Church. Together they formed the hub of the West End, the playground of the English aristocrats, who arrived each spring as regularly as the cuckoo for a season of debutante balls, receptions, royal levees and sporting events known as 'the Season'. Around the great squares of Mayfair and Park Lane, in the handsome terraces of Kensington and Bayswater, the noblest, richest and most famous in the land gathered, to see and be seen, dance and play, and, above all, to splurge their wealth.

Arab sheiks and American billionaires still come to Savile Row and Burlington Arcade to buy bespoke suits, designer gowns and handmade shoes, craftsman-made furniture, gold watches and diamond bracelets. In the 1840s, London's consumer economy fluctuated with the ebb and flow of social activity in the West End, especially the London Season. The livelihood of tens of thousands of

London tailors, shoemakers, jewellers, furniture makers, watchmakers, furriers and carriage builders hung on the whims of 'the upper ten thousand' of the country's richest families. When we think of the Industrial Revolution our first thought is of cities like Manchester and Leeds, with their barracks-like mills topped by giant smokestacks and each employing thousands of spinners and weavers. London was an industrial city too, but its workforce was diffused among thousands of small workshops. Rather than dominating the horizon, London's factories were hidden along narrow lanes and courtyards, and in lofts and cellars almost invisible to those who drove along its fashionable streets only metres away.

John Fenwick occupied one of the last carriages in this national gravy train. He was a coach trimmer, an upholsterer who made the seats and padded interiors of coaches and carriages. Private carriages were a luxury, and the average Londoner, according to a contemporary observer of the trade, was 'but little aware of the delicacy, the elegance, and the attention to comfort, displayed in the interior fittings of a pleasure carriage'. The centre of the London coach-building trade was Long Acre Street near Covent Garden. In the 1840s, more than fifty of the 140 houses in the street were devoted to the coach-making business. Within each house, the various specialised trades—wheelwrights, body builders, carriage-makers, painters and trimmers—had their own departments, separated vertically on different floors. Each trade occupied a distinct slot on the hierarchy of skill, status and pay. Body builders were at the apex, but trimmers, who selected and worked the silk, leather, lace, horsehair and other expensive fabrics used to fit out the carriage's interior, stood well above ordinary tailors and shoemakers, for example, earning two or three pounds a week.

Like other luxury trades, however, coach manufacturing was a precarious business. Around April, the order books of the carriage builders began to fill up. If it was a good year, the workshops would be busy throughout the summer, but by November, as the landed families headed back to their estates, trade subsided, and workmen could be left to fend for themselves through the winter months. The good earnings of a workman in high season were offset by the high cost of housing in inner London and the dearth of work in the off-season. In 1843, the London Statistical Society published a study of the condition of poor families living in St George's Hanover Square. 'There was a general complaint made of the difficulty of obtaining employment during the past season,' the investigator reported. 'In winter many families stated that they were in the habit of pawning part of their furniture and releasing it in summer, as they can only obtain employment during the "season".'

In 1841, John Fenwick and his family were living in Dacre Street, Westminster, a short walk from St James's Park and Buckingham Palace. When you come out of the St James's Park Underground station it is just across the road. The famous rotating illuminated sign of New Scotland Yard stands on the corner, but only three or four brick shops and warehouses remain of what was once a busy Victorian street. Entering their forties, the Fenwicks had eight surviving children, five boys and three girls, ranging from seventeen-year-old Elizabeth down to eight-month-old Archer. (Another child, James, would be born in 1843). Housing in inner London was expensive, and becoming more so as houses were demolished to make way for roads, railways and commercial buildings. Many poor families were forced to live in crowded courts and tenements, often sharing a single room and sleeping three or four abed. Some paid out more than half their earnings for a single crowded room. John Fenwick may not have been among the lowest-paid Londoners, but the cost of feeding and housing his large brood pushed the family to the brink of poverty.

Dacre Street bordered a notorious slum, 'the Devil's Acre'. By 1841, it had been selected by the government for a program of 'metropolitan improvement'. A new thoroughfare, Victoria Street, named after the newly crowned monarch, would open up its festering courts and rookeries to the cleansing glare of scrutiny. 'Immediately a street is widened . . . a more respectable class of occupants is induced to come and live in the houses,' one of the improvers promised. What he didn't say was that the new residents would be fewer as well as richer, and that many poor people would be forced out to make way for them. By the end of the decade, about two hundred houses were destroyed in the Victoria Street neighbourhood, displacing some 2500 people, including the Fenwicks. Like many others, they migrated northwards towards the parishes of St John's and St George's Hanover Square, Elizabeth's old parish. 'I've always been a-moving and a-moving on, ever since I was born,' remarks Jo, a young crossing sweeper in Dickens' novel *Bleak House* (1853). 'Moving on' was a fact of life for poor families like the Fenwicks well before Elizabeth and her younger sister Alice set sail for Australia.

When the census taker next found them, in 1851, John and Elizabeth were living at 97 Regent Street in Mayfair. Between 1817 and 1823, the famous architect John Nash, creator of Regent's Park, superimposed a broad elegant thoroughfare upon the axis of the old Swallow Street, bending its southern section, where Regent Street joins Piccadilly Circus, into a handsome arc of shops and dwellings known as the Quadrant. Number 97 is at the opening of the Quadrant, just where an arched entryway connects Regent Street with a truncated remnant of Swallow Street. Today it is one of the most expensive tracts of real estate in London, a showcase for fashionable brands like Burberry and Austin Reed. In the late 1840s, however, the colonnade and adjoining lanes of the Quadrant were a notorious centre of prostitution and gambling, which had spread northwards from their traditional haunts around the Haymarket and Piccadilly Circus. 'If Piccadilly may be termed an artery of the metropolis,' a contemporary observed, 'that strip of pavement between the top of the Haymarket and Regent Circus is one of its ulcers.' On a walk along Regent Street from Haymarket to Portland Place, William Acton, author of the classic study *Prostitution* (1857), claimed to have counted no fewer than 185 prostitutes. In 1847, lessees of the surrounding properties had appealed for the demolition of the colonnade on the ground that it had become 'so notorious a place, that I believe that it is almost impossible to procure respectable lodgers for the upstairs apartments'. John Fenwick may have found their lodgings at number 97 conveniently close to his work, but it was no place for a respectable family man to bring up teenage daughters.

THE DOMESTIC SERVANT

Significantly, John's eldest surviving daughter, Elizabeth, was not among the members of the Fenwick household listed in the 1841 or 1851 censuses. At seventeen, she had already left home to join a great women's army, perhaps 200,000 strong, working as domestic servants in London households. The demand for servants was highest in the West End, a region where some of the city's poorest households were 'placed in a peculiar position by their proximity to so large a number of their superiors in fortune'. The grand seigneurial establishments dramatised in television shows such as *Downton Abbey* and *Upstairs Downstairs* were more the exception than the rule: most servants, even in the West End, were distributed in ones and twos through a host of smaller households. In 1841, Elizabeth was the sole female servant in the home of James Edwards, a postmaster living in Kinnerton Street, near Belgrave Square. The Edwardses also employed an ostler, 50-year-old Josh Knight, to tend the postmaster's horse and coach. A 'maid of all work', or general servant, stood on the bottom rung of the ladder: poorly paid, hard worked, and 'usually taken from the industrious and labouring classes of the community, who are bred up with a view to the situation, having no other prospect or dependence'.

Most general servants were young women, in their teens and early twenties: less skilled, perhaps, than older women, but robust, pliable and cheap. Their only real prospect of escape from domestic service was marriage, although their long hours of work and the strict discipline exercised by their masters and mistresses ('no followers allowed') tended to limit the opportunities to meet prospective husbands. A woman who reached her mid-twenties without marrying was in danger of losing her job and falling into the lower ranks of industrial labour, or something worse. The economic downturn of the late 1840s tightened the market for domestic labour and drove many young Londoners to the brink of destitution.

In 1848, Europe's year of revolutions, economic distress seemed likely to foment a similar rising in England. During the spring, Chartists—supporters of a democratic People's Charter—drew enthusiastic meetings in Lambeth, Holborn and Trafalgar Square. The movement peaked in April when more than 20,000 protestors converged on Kennington Common in South London. Economic conditions eased in 1849, but the political mood remained tense. In the spring the city was visited by an epidemic of Asiatic cholera, a deadly disease spread—though people did not yet know it—through water supplies contaminated by human excrement. (A few years later, an observant physician, Dr John Snow, traced a concentration of cholera deaths to a single contaminated pump in Broad Street, near Soho Square.) The death toll was high in the ill-drained and crowded courts and tenements of the West End. Together, these crises left Londoners feeling chastened and uneasy. A chasm had suddenly opened beneath them, sapping public confidence in the previously unquestioned stability of the country's institutions.

THE NEEDLEWOMAN

In October 1849, the journalist Henry Mayhew, a 'special correspondent' for the *Morning Chronicle*, began a series of sensational articles on 'Labour and the Poor' in London. The rebellious son of a London solicitor, Mayhew had written for the popular theatre before turning to journalism, and he brought dramatic flair as well as a keen forensic intelligence to his investigations. At a moment when many feared that revolution could spread from Europe, his articles offered middle-class readers a disturbing glimpse into the cauldron of distress from which an English insurrection might spring. 'Do you devour those marvellous revelations of the inferno of misery, of

The image of the 'distressed needlewoman'—emaciated, careworn, vulnerable and exploited—came to personify the problem of poverty in London in the 1840s. (Punch, *22 December 1849*)

wretchedness, that is smouldering under our feet?' his father-in-law, the writer Douglas Jerrold, asked a friend.

The most sensational of Mayhew's revelations came in an article published on 13 November 1849 about the situation of poor needle-women living in the West End. The poor seamstress had long been an object of pity. Hundreds were employed as casual pieceworkers in the 'slop trade', making military uniforms or ready-to-wear shirts. Some were domestic servants who had been thrown out of work and were now homeless and indigent. In his novel *Little Dorrit* (1857), Dickens personified the problem of London poverty in the character of Amy, a young needlewoman. According to Mayhew and his fellow investigators, these women earned as little as three shillings a week for as much as eighty hours' employment. More serious still in the eyes of the *Morning Chronicle*'s respectable middle-class readers were the moral dangers to which the women were exposed. 'I had been so repeatedly assured that the young girls were mostly compelled to resort to prostitution to eke out their subsistence, that I was anxious to test the truth of the statement,' Mayhew reported. 'I had seen much want, but I had no idea of the intensity of the privations suffered by the needlewomen of London until I came to inquire into this part of the subject.'

His enquiries left him in no doubt about the truth of the matter. 'I am the daughter of a minister of the gospel,' one young woman confided.

My father was an Independent preacher, and I pledge my word, solemnly and sacredly, that it was the low price paid for my labour that drove me to prostitution. I often struggled against it, and many times have I taken my child into the streets to beg rather than I would bring shame upon myself and it any longer.

Others testified to the same experience: it was impossible to live on what they could earn from needlework, even though they worked from dawn till long beyond dusk.

By early 1850, my great-great-grandmother, 26-year-old Elizabeth Fenwick, was one of these 'distressed needlewomen'. She had lost her position as a servant and was earning a mere three shillings and sixpence a week from casual needlework. Her younger sister Alice, aged just seventeen, was in a similar predicament. This discovery disconcerted me at first. An English yeoman, even a dispossessed and impoverished one, was an ancestor one could revere. Even a convict forefather, a cunning thief or clever forger, would have added colour to one's lineage. But a 'distressed needlewoman', especially one who might be supplementing her earnings with prostitution, aroused more mixed feelings. I had no illusions that my pedigree was noble or distinguished, but the family's sense of itself, reinforced by several generations of Methodism, was of modest respectability. A hundred years ago, when people still feared the taint of 'bad blood' and hereditary moral failings, Elizabeth's identity as a needlewoman, a line of work only a short step from prostitution, was something she, and her descendants, may well have wanted to keep dark. Mr Mayhew may have regarded the needlewomen with compassion, but I wondered if even he would have wanted his son to marry one.

Mayhew is an old friend, in a way. As a historian of the nineteenth-century city, I had been bumping into him for years. He was the first and most influential of the great social investigators, the new breed of journalists and social scientists I call 'slummers'. I was a bit of a historical slummer myself, interested in how the other half lived, and Mayhew and his Australian imitators have often been my guides to the low life of Sydney and Melbourne. Like them, I was a middle-class outsider seeking entry to a plebeian world I perceived as alien. Ordinarily, I would see Elizabeth Fenwick and her sisters as Mayhew saw them, from above and from the outside. But knowing we were kin subtly changed my vantage point. Now I am wondering how my great-great-grandmother might have seen Mr Mayhew, the rotund, ruddy-faced inquisitor from Fleet Street, as he approached her for an interview.

Mayhew's articles shook some cherished beliefs. The Victorians believed in the dignity of Labour almost as much as they believed in the purity of Womanhood. But Mayhew revealed a world where both were imperilled. Here were some of Her Majesty's subjects, living within sight of Buckingham Palace, who were willing to work but unable to survive on their earnings alone, and compelled, through

Henry Mayhew

no fault of their own, to surrender their reputation. On 5 December, a young Conservative politician, Sidney Herbert, addressed a letter to the editor of the *Morning Chronicle*. 'These disclosures of the sufferings of the poor have excited a general and sincere sympathy,' he noted. He applauded the benevolence shown towards the needle-women. 'Theirs is the most helpless sex, the most intense poverty, the most fearful degradation.' But what was to happen to them when the funds and sympathy were exhausted? 'Cannot these alms be so applied that permanent good may be effected? Instead of palliating the symptoms, might we not trace the causes of the malady, and make a vigorous attempt to repress or diminish them?'

Herbert was an aristocrat and a devout Anglican. Like his friend the future prime minister William Gladstone, he had supported the repeal of the Corn Laws but was shaken by the social crisis that ensued. While reluctant to interfere with the 'laws of nature'—by which he meant the free market—he sought to address 'the peculiar circumstances' of the London poor. 'Why not give them the means of escape?' he asked. 'In the southern hemisphere is a vast continent, which is as much a part of the British Empire as Wales. It has been peopled partly by force, partly by voluntary emigration.' Just as London suffered from a surplus population of indigent women, so was the moral health of the colonies damaged by a deficit of females and the lack of their civilising influence. 'A redress of this inequality is the crying want of society there, just as the redress of the opposite inequality in this country is the necessity here. Any woman so emigrating is a woman saved.' Australia's need was England's opportunity. All that was needed was the money to transport the distressed needlewomen from the city of fog and poverty to a land of sun and opportunity. Once the surplus population had been removed, he reasoned, female wages would rise and the destitution would be relieved. 'If we can dig a channel, the water will flow through it ultimately without help of ours.'

THE COLONIAL SAFETY VALVE

Urged on by the *Morning Chronicle* and supported by the great and good, Sidney Herbert and his wife threw themselves into the organisation of their female emigration scheme. An impressive list of subscribers, headed by the Queen and Prince Albert, who contributed £500, raised over £22,000. Local clergymen headed committees in Holborn and Bloomsbury (the West End), Westminster and Pimlico (southwest), Southwark and Lambeth (south), St George's (the East End), and Shadwell and Limehouse (the Docks). An enthusiastic meeting in St Marylebone called upon the middle classes to join the aristocracy in supporting the cause. The Australian colonies, one speaker declared, were like a safety valve on a steam engine, relieving England of its surplus population. He warned, however, that 'they must have better women sent to these colonies than the sweepings of our convict ships, or the offshoots of our workhouses (hear, hear). They must be the honest, industrious, and virtuous women of England, who he was sorry to say obtained so scanty and miserable a living in their mother country.'

Sidney Herbert

Herbert's was not the first scheme to promote female emigration. Caroline Chisholm had of course designed her plan for family colonisation, launched almost simultaneously with Herbert's scheme, to avoid the moral hazards previously experienced by young unaccompanied women on poorly supervised ships. In December, as he finalised arrangements for the first contingent of emigrants, Herbert assured William Gladstone, a former secretary of state for the colonies, of his awareness of the difficulties. 'I believe that we can get excellent emigrants from among the needle-women,' he wrote.

They are not a separate class who can do that and nothing else, but rather they are young women of all classes who have been driven to live on that occupation exclusively as a last resort. They are industrious generally, and are used more or less to domestic service, and a little training before they go will do much for them. We intend sending out a small but well selected number next month, who will go with families who are themselves respectable and will undertake their care, messing [eating] and berthing with them . . . I think the preservation of the family tie is of the first importance. But many of these young women have no such ties, and we must place them under the care of respectable families going out. The more we can disperse them in the passage the better. I am against taking up ships and filling them with this one class of emigrants alone.

Reading this letter, it comes as no surprise to learn that Sidney Herbert, the friend of the distressed needlewomen, and Caroline Chisholm, the advocate of family colonisation, were in close collaboration. His female emigration scheme was being modified to incorporate some of the principles of her ideal of family colonisation, notably 'the preservation of the family tie' through the leavening influence of 'respectable families' as fellow passengers. 'The character of the emigration will be judged in the Colony from the first sample, and they must be carefully selected,' he noted. To ensure that they were of blameless character, Herbert instituted a rigorous system of selection. Each applicant was required to fill out a questionnaire, giving details of her age, address and place of birth; whether she could read and write; the employment of her parents, and whether they wished her to emigrate; the nature of her own employment and earnings; and the name and address of her last employer. Two respectable householders from her own neighbourhood had to testify to her 'character for sobriety, honesty etc', a medical practitioner to her good health, and a magistrate or clergyman to the veracity of the supporting documents.

Among the 38 successful applicants for the first voyage to Port Phillip were Elizabeth Fenwick and her sister Alice. After the most rigorous examination, it seems, my great-great-grandmother had proved to be not a harlot but a respectable educated woman and a model emigrant. This revelation, coming like the climax of a Victorian novel in which the heroine's virtue is vindicated despite the cruel aspersions of her rivals, left me unsure whether to feel more satisfied about the restoration of family honour than ashamed of having succumbed to the Victorian double-standard. To be sure, I believed that the unfortunate needlewomen had been forced onto the streets through sheer economic necessity. The moral blame was not theirs but that of a cruel society that treated poor women badly. But I was relieved, all the same, not to have to reveal my great-great-grandmother's shady past to her descendants, at least to the older members of the family.

In vetting applicants so rigorously and training them before they embarked, Herbert aimed to fail-proof his scheme. According to his political opponents, however, all this proved was that the women most in need were not actually suitable for employment in the colonies. 'The Committee [of the Female Emigration Fund Society] have almost entirely departed from their original intention, and . . . instead of distressed needlewomen, a perfectly different class of females have been selected,' a correspondent in the *Morning Post* asserted. He knew of young women employed on high wages as ladies' maids who were now ready to sail for Australia at the committee's expense. (Were Elizabeth and Alice recipients of middle-class welfare, I now wondered!) Herbert's contention that the emigration of a few thousand needlewomen would abolish destitution in the metropolis was 'as absurd as it would be to attempt to bale the Atlantic with his hat'. The real cause of the distress was the policy of free trade, 'of which Mr Herbert, under Peel, was an advocate and promoter'. Some advocates of free trade, on the other hand, attacked Herbert's scheme on the ground that by assisting the needlewomen to emigrate it simply made more room for Irish immigrants to rush in and take their places.

To combat some of these allegations, the committee published detailed information about the 38 young women selected for the voyage, identifying them only by initials. It is easy to link this data with the names recorded in passenger lists and other tabular information collected after their arrival in Port Phillip. From this information, together with the 1841 British census and parish registers, it is possible to draw a collective portrait of Elizabeth and her fellow voyagers.

To keep faith with the subscribers, preference was given to 'needlewomen', a somewhat elastic category. Almost all applicants gave their occupation as 'needlewoman' or something similar—'braider', 'collar stitcher', 'lace transferrer', 'fancy worker', 'shirtmaker' or 'tail-oress'—with just a few describing themselves as 'servants out of place'. As the committee explained, 'a large proportion of needlewomen are servants out of place', that is, girls who had resorted to needlework when they lost their jobs as domestics, as Elizabeth and Alice had done. By the time they got to Port Phillip, where there was little demand for needlewomen, almost all, including the Fenwick sisters, had mutated into 'general servants'.

Overwhelmingly the emigrants were young, averaging 22 years of age. The committee had set a maximum age of 35, but with the exception of two women selected to act as assistant matrons on the ship, both in their late twenties, they were almost all under the age of 25. Alice Fenwick, who gave her age as seventeen (she was actually sixteen), was among the youngest; Elizabeth, who gave her age as 24 (she was actually 26), was among the oldest. They were not the only sisters among the recruits: Eliza, Esther and Margaret Burney, Anne and Eliza Coates, Matilda and Ellen Walker (who will make a later appearance in this story), and the three daughters of the ship's matron, Hannah Hughan—Marion, Jessie and Bertha—were the others.

Supporters of the scheme often portrayed the needlewomen as young country girls lured into the snares of the metropolis. More than half the city's domestic servants did indeed originate from outside London. But almost two-thirds (21) of the first contingent of female emigrants whose birthplaces were known (35) were born in London, with only a scattering from Cornwall and Devon (3), Kent (2), Essex (2), Wales (1), Suffolk (2), Ireland (2), Jamaica (1) and India (1). Their parents, so far as they can be traced, were from the lower strata of the London working class: shoemakers, hairdressers, glass benders, porters, shipwrights and tailors. The preponderance of London-born women suggests that local committees favoured women who had been resident long enough to become known. More than half (21) of the women were recruited from Holborn and Westminster, parishes with high proportions of London-born residents; about one-third (12) from St George's; and the rest from Southwark (5) and Shadwell (2). The East End had been slower to mobilise than the well-heeled parishes of the West, and claimed with some justification that political clout, rather than need, had determined the allocation of places. If so, Elizabeth and Alice, whose parents were old residents of Westminster, may have enjoyed some inside running.

The committee had negotiated passages for the needlewomen aboard a small frigate, the *Culloden*, whose owner-captain, Henry Ferguson, was said to enjoy 'a well-established character, as a good officer and strict disciplinarian'. The surgeon, Dr John Thompson, who would attend to nutrition, hygiene and health, and the matron, Mrs Hannah Hughan, who would supervise the women's daily routine, came with similar reassuring testimonials. The young women would be sharing a deck with other passengers to Port Phillip, some travelling as assisted immigrants and others as private passengers.

A handbill kept by one of the intermediate passengers, William Strutt, read:

EMIGRATION
TO

PORT PHILLIP AND SYDNEY

**The cheapest and most commodious Passage is now offered to
Persons of respectability desirous of Emigrating
To PORT PHILLIP and SYDNEY**

By the remarkably fine Frigate–built Ship,

CULLODEN, A1.

1000 TONS BURTHEN   **HENRY FERGUSON, COMMANDER**

'Commodious and well-ventilated Cabins' for intermediate passengers were offered for £20 for adults and half-fares for children under fourteen, but the 'berth deck', where the needlewomen were to be accommodated, was to be shared with the 'respectable families' in whose moral influence Herbert had reposed such confidence. How these respectable families were recruited, and what—if anything—they were to pay for their passage is not clear. By 1849, emigrants under the Colonial Land and Emigration Commission either travelled for free, as with 'agricultural labourers' and 'approved country mechanics' between the ages of eighteen and 35, or paid a reduced fare, between five and nine pounds, according to age.

Herbert and his supporters, we also know, were in close touch with Caroline Chisholm, who had received thousands of letters from prospective recruits to her family colonisation scheme. Nothing would have been more convenient than for her to recommend a respectable family of young people, from sturdy farming stock, eager to begin a new life in Australia—like Jane Hewett and her children, for example. Hearing of Herbert's need of respectable families, and recognising the Hewetts' need of an affordable passage, did she intercede on their behalf? I do not know. We do know, however, that they did not travel as assisted emigrants under the government scheme but shared the same deck of the *Culloden* as the needlewomen, although in a separate compartment. However it came about, this conjunction was a fateful one, and the four months during which the Hampshire farmers and the London needlewomen were thrown together on the high seas would have fateful consequences for both—and for their descendants.

At the Female Emigration Society's Home in Hatton Garden the needlewomen made preparations for their long voyage. (Illustrated London News, *12 March 1853*)

CHAPTER THREE
The voyage of the Culloden

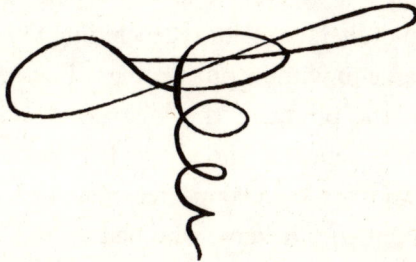

After a last English Christmas, Elizabeth and Alice Fenwick joined the other needlewomen in the Female Emigration Society's home at 76 Hatton Garden, Holborn. There the matron of the house, Mrs Baskin, assisted by Mrs Hughan, prepared them for useful employment in Australia. They were 'mustered' into groups and drilled in 'the habits of regularity and method' required for shipboard life. Most of their time was spent on lessons in domestic service and in making up an 'outfit' for the voyage: six shifts, two petticoats, six pairs of stockings, two pairs of shoes, two gowns, two pairs of sheets, sixteen towels, a cloak and a bonnet—to which were added ten pounds (four and a half kilograms) of soap. The women were scrutinised by the organisers to make sure no unsuitable applicant had survived the selection process. Denominational allegiances were not supposed to be taken into account in selecting the women, but the scheme was conducted under Church of England auspices and religious instruction was understood to be part of its ethos, so the emigrants were presented by the Society for Promoting Christian Knowledge with Bibles and prayer books as spiritual comforts for the voyage.

On 25 February, they arrived by appointment at Fenchurch Street station to be farewelled by the Female Emigration Society's committee. The party included the Right Honourable Sidney Herbert, the Honourable Arthur Kinnaird, the Honourable Mr Littleton, Sir Henry Verney, Mrs Herbert—who chaired the Ladies' Committee— and several clergy, led by Reverend Mr Quekett of St George's. 'Several gentlemen of literary celebrity', including the novelist William Thackeray, also came to witness proceedings. The *Morning Chronicle*, whose articles on the plight of the 'distressed needlewomen' had inspired the scheme, reported the event. Its 'special correspondent' Henry Mayhew, another keen supporter, may have been among the other literary gentlemen. Dickens, who had visited Mrs Herbert the day before, had arranged some days earlier with his friend, the Irish painter Daniel Maclise, to meet at Fenchurch Street station to visit an emigrant ship, perhaps the *Culloden*. I would love to think that Elizabeth shook hands with the authors of *David Copperfield* and *Vanity Fair*, or even with Mr Mayhew, if he missed her in his earlier journeys among the needlewomen. But the literary men, for all their great sentimental interest in the poor, may have been more interested in talking to each other than to the young women.

Or so I thought until I discovered that Thackeray had actually written up his visit, anonymously, in an article in *Punch*. 'It is rather a queer sensation to be in the same boat and the same station with a party that is going upon so prodigious a journey,' he wrote. He had found the 38 women, with bundles and baskets, waiting with remarkable composure to be taken to the ship. There were none of the wailings and sad farewells Mrs Chisholm had anticipated. 'They leave behind them little to weep for,' he concluded. 'Why should they be sorry to quit a mother who has been so hard to them as our country has been?' They had enjoyed none of the advantages of education, none of the arts and graces of life, and therefore, it seemed, experienced none of the refined feelings that Thackeray and his literary friends might have known on such a parting. If Mr Mayhew was a slummer, eager to identify with the down and almost out, Thackeray was a snob. Indeed, he had just published *The Book of Snobs*, a playful catalogue of the varieties of London snobbery. Now he was about to exercise his snobbery on my great-great-grandmother and her companions.

How would the distressed needlewomen be received in Melbourne? he wondered. Would a young gentleman living alone in the bush be likely to find a suitable mate from among them? Unlikely, he thought. 'There is no girl here to tempt you by her looks . . . no pretty, modest, red-cheeked rustic, no neat, trim, little grisette, such as . . . might find favour in the eyes of men about town.' All an English gentleman would see were her 'deficiencies of politeness', her 'outrages upon the Queen's English', her 'large hard hands and clumsy feet'. As I read these words, indignation rose on behalf of my slighted ancestor. If Elizabeth Fenwick had hard hands and clumsy feet, then it was through serving stuck-up people like you, I protested. Thackeray at last approached one of the needlewomen—was it Elizabeth or Alice?—who curtseyed, held down her head and spoke modestly, as became her station. Considering his disdain, you may feel she was too deferential, but with a free passage to Australia at stake, she could hardly be otherwise.

Thackeray conceded that London refinements might not count for much in the freer air of the colonies. 'The sun-burnt settler out of the bush,' he forecast, would not notice the female emigrant's rough manners, or worry that her hands were coarse or her ankles thick. 'He will take her back to his farm, where she will nurse his children, bake his dough, milk his cows and cook his kangaroo for him.' While their English-born mother might curtsey from old habit, her children would know nothing of that 'Gothic society with its ranks and hierarchies, its cumbrous ceremonies, its antique paraphernalia'. They would be 'bred up in the midst of plenty, freedom, manly brotherhood'. Democratic Australia, he grudgingly admitted, might be a better sort of place, at least for England's rejects. With such condescending goodwill, the great novelist blessed the poor needlewomen on their way.

EMBARKING

The farewell party set off by train to Blackwall, then by the *Satellite* steamer down the Thames estuary to Gravesend, where the *Culloden* lay at anchor off the Terrace Pier, 'her stout bulwarks dotted with anxiously peering heads, evidently watching with great interest for the advent of their *compagnons de voyage*'. I visualise four strapping, fresh-faced Hewett boys in fustian jackets leaning on the rail, gazing towards the approaching steamer, perhaps even picking out a prospective sweetheart as she stepped aboard. Were they repelled, like Mr Thackeray, by the Londoners' pallid complexions, rough hands and coarse speech? Or were the city girls perhaps amused by the young men's rustic garb and bashful manners? After four months at sea, the girls' cheeks would grow ruddier, their speech would become more familiar. Whatever inhibitions the young people felt at first sight would surely dissolve with time, proximity and the heat of a tropical sun.

The *Culloden* was 'a stout, bluff-built, and serviceable merchantman', with cabins for first-class passengers on the upper or poop deck and a lower or berth deck divided into separate quarters for single men fo'ard, single women aft and married couples with children amidships. The space in and below the launch on the upper deck doubled as pens for the sheep and pigs kept to provide meat on the long voyage. According to its owners, the ship was capable of accommodating up to one hundred passengers, but surprisingly, we do not know exactly how many were aboard the ship when it embarked. There were at

An artist's impression of the scene below decks as the needlewomen prepare to sail. Clad in the new outfits prepared for the voyage, some stand in the corridor where they will take their meals, while others make themselves at home in the narrow berths on either side. (Illustrated London News, *17 August 1850*)

least ten adult cabin passengers and 47 intermediate passengers apart from the 38 needlewomen. Among the intermediate passengers there were half a dozen or so family groups, two or three couples, and about 25 single men.

The cabin passengers were like a little wedding party-in-waiting, or rather the nucleus of several. Soon after their arrival in Melbourne, sisters Adelaide and Jane Munn, daughters of a Colchester surgeon, would marry merchants Samuel and Henry Bawtree, who awaited them in Melbourne. The young merchants' sisters, Lydia and Ellen Bawtree, occupying another cabin, were also intent on matrimony: Lydia would marry a young squatter, Benjamin Holmes, in 1851, while in 1853 Ellen would become the second wife of 45-year-old

Robert Tupholme of Wharparilla station. As gentlefolk and cabin passengers, they were elevated above the hoi polloi on the berth deck. Their interlocking marriage plans also reinforced their distinctness and created a kind of mutual chaperonage.

The intermediate passengers were a mixed bunch, with some who aspired to the status of gentleman sharing quarters with men and women whose status was at best respectable. 'Respectability' was one of the ruling ideas of the Victorian era. It stood for cleanliness, sobriety, independence, plainness in speech and living, and sexual continence. The sexual aspect was probably the one that most concerned Herbert and his committee. Groups of young single men and unchaperoned young females would be making a four-month voyage aboard a relatively small vessel. For most of the time they would be far from land. They would be living and sleeping in close proximity. There were only a captain, a surgeon and a matron to supervise them—the rest of the crew were likely to contribute as much to the problem as to the solution. The organisers were counting on the 'respectable families' selected to occupy the middle section of the berth deck of the *Culloden* to exercise a benign influence on the behaviour of the young people fore and aft.

The long sea voyage, in which strangers from different classes, regions and religions were thrown together for several months, has sometimes been seen as a nursery of Australian democracy. The word 'mate' and the Australian code of mateship, it is said, began in the experience of being shipmates, sharing the same boat and the perils of the voyage. But quite apart from the official class gradations, usually between cabin, second-class and steerage, passengers within these classes strove to maintain other no less important distinctions, between respectable and rough, English and Irish, Protestant and Catholic. In advertisements for the voyage, intermediate passages on the *Culloden* had been offered to 'persons of respectability desirous of emigrating'. William Strutt, a talented 24-year-old painter, with experience in France, was among the purchasers. 'I regret to say that I was very much disappointed in the society I had expected to meet on board,' he later confided to his mother. 'Most of the young men were very dissipated characters, indeed cursing, swearing, drunkenness & sometimes fighting were their general employments.' He clearly considered the agents had engaged in false advertising. Was he thinking of the Hewett brothers, I wondered, as among the drunks and brawlers? At present, I beg the reader to reserve judgement.

The journalists reporting on the embarkation took particular interest in the living and sleeping arrangements for the needlewomen. These offered more privacy than government emigration vessels, although less light and air. A 'dim shadowy corridor', illuminated only by thin streams of light from hatchways, ran the length of the ship. A long, narrow table, with wooden racks above for mugs and jugs, formed the dining/living room. A white-painted bulkhead running the length of the deck separated the central dining area from the sleeping quarters for the family groups, arranged in a series of cubicles, seven feet by five (two by one and a half metres), on each side of the ship and entered by sliding doors. Each cubicle contained five berths, snug shallow boxes lined with blankets; two double berths on each side and a single berth along the outer side of the ship. In the centre of this tiny room was a chest for clothes and a simple washstand with a tin basin. Imagine living in your bathroom with four other adults for four months, and you have some idea of the rigours of life afloat in the great age of sail. At the very rear of the boat, just under the stern windows and commanding a view of the wake, was a 'labyrinth' of berths arranged to form a large sleeping room, and laid out ingeniously so as to leave scarcely a square inch unoccupied. As crowded and uncomfortable as they appeared, these arrangements seemed to please the young passengers. 'It was pleasant to see . . . how fussily each girl arranged her parcels upon her bed, and with what innocent importance she announced to all querists that that was to be *her* bed.'

Around the time when the *Culloden* embarked, Dickens was writing the final chapters of his great semi-autobiographical novel, *David Copperfield*. As we know, he was an eager supporter of

Caroline Chisholm's and Sidney Herbert's schemes to transplant English domestic ideals to the Antipodes, and he was already making arrangements to publish articles about emigration in his new magazine, *Household Words*. He may have been one of the 'gentlemen of literary celebrity' who witnessed the departure of the *Culloden* in February 1850. Several of the principal characters in *David Copperfield*—the impecunious Mr Micawber and his family and Little Em'ly, a young woman in danger of falling into prostitution, and her uncle and protector Daniel Peggotty—find salvation from the ills of old England through emigration to Australia. In a scene from the novel perhaps inspired by his observations at Gravesend, or by contemporary accounts of the *Culloden*'s departure, Dickens makes the crowded conditions below decks an epitome of the entire migration experience.

> *Among the great beams, bulks, and ringbolts of the ship, and the emigrant-berths, and chests, and bundles, and barrels, and heaps of miscellaneous baggage—'lighted up, here and there, by dangling lanterns; and elsewhere by the yellow daylight straying down a windsail or a hatchway—were crowded groups of people, making new friendships, taking leave of one another, talking, laughing, crying, eating and drinking; some, already settled down into the possession of their few feet of space, with their little households arranged, and tiny children established on stools, or in dwarf elbow-chairs; others, despairing of a resting place, and wandering disconsolately. From babies who had but a week or two of life behind them, to crooked old men and women who seemed to have but a week or two of life before them; and from ploughmen bodily carrying out soil of England on their boots, to smiths taking away samples of its soot and smoke upon their skins; every age and occupation appeared to be crammed into the narrow compass of the 'tween decks.*

There are more contrasts of mood and social status in Dickens' fictional description than in the actual departure of the *Culloden*, but many of the details of the departure seem to have been drawn directly from life.

Above and below decks the vessel swarmed with visitors and passengers. As the time for departure drew near, the emigration authorities called the passengers' names, and the members of the emigration committee said farewell. Reverend Quekett offered a few words of advice and blessing, urging the girls to obey the rules of the ship and submit to the authority of the matron. A few began to cry openly and others quietly sobbed. As the steamer came alongside, there were handshakes all round, a shrill blast from the boatswain's whistle, three cheers for Old England, and they were on their way. A steam tug towed the vessel to Deal on the Kent coast, where it weighed anchor until the following morning. At last, with a favourable breeze, it set sail.

As the steamer comes alongside and the crew hoist the sails, the Culloden *prepares to set sail for Port Phillip.* (Illustrated London News, *17 August 1850*)

THE VOYAGE

For most of the voyage, the *Culloden* would be in open sea. After passing Porto Santo and Madeira, its passengers would not see land again until they sighted the Australian coast almost three months later. Strutt recorded the highlights of the long voyage in his 'autobiography' and in several sketches. In London his health had been poor and he was emigrating in the hope that a warmer climate would improve it. On the *Culloden*, he tended to keep to himself, communing with nature rather than with his uncouth fellow passengers. He recorded observations of turtles, flying fish, whales, porpoises, and especially the 'magnificent' albatrosses whose senseless slaughter by passing ships he lamented. 'It is agonising indeed to see one of these ocean monarchs, spread out lifeless on the ship's deck: and I seem to think that the wretches, who have been their captors, deserve to have a dip among the swarming sharks infesting these torrid waters.'

The passengers' main memory of the voyage was its tedium. 'An emigrant's life at sea must be monotonous—there was no variety,' Herbert warned as he farewelled a later contingent of female emigrants.

Pent up in a limited space, they would find it very wearisome if they did not employ themselves: and the thing for them to do therefore was to take advantage of the time to improve themselves . . . Idleness was the root of all evil, and especially on board ship; and therefore he hoped every one of them would be particular to conform strictly to all the rules as to the hours and different classes for receiving instruction in reading, writing, and in their religious duties; and that they would all endeavour to assist in maintaining harmony and regularity among themselves.

Two of the young women selected for the voyage, Margaret Landells and Jane White, had previously been employed as governesses and were perhaps expected to offer tuition, although there is little evidence that they did so. Supporters of the Female Emigration Society had supplied the *Culloden* with a quantity of calico and other materials so that the needlewomen could be employed in making clothes to be sold on their arrival, thus providing a little nest egg to launch them into colonial life, but the materials were not produced until the voyage was six weeks gone and the plan seems to have been a dead letter.

During the voyage, as Herbert correctly noted, 'they would have an excellent opportunity which they would never have again, because they were never likely to have so much leisure'. The opportunity he saw as offering the chance for self-improvement, and requiring 'regularity', however, may have been viewed by many of the young women as a welcome release from such demands. In a letter to her family later published in the Female Emigration Society's report, needlewoman Lucy Edwards from Islington conveyed a sense of how life aboard the *Culloden* appeared to a fun-loving seventeen-year-old.

> *we had a most beautiful voyage we were calmed a great deal but we never had a storm we had black and white squalls but nothing else and i have seen the waves wash over the mainmast and they have washed over me twice when i have been baking and then i have got laughed at for my pains at whatever i have been doing but the ship when it was rocking afforded me great pleasure for to see the things rattling about plates and dishes rattling the Children crying the girls a going into fits the Captain giving orders the Matron ordering the girls to be quiet because of the Captain we were all much happier than i expected to be for we were all like sisters for we waited on one another when we was ill which make things pass very comfortable.*

Women who had been on the brink of starvation a few months earlier may have relished three meals a day, plain and monotonous as the diet might seem to us. Even Strutt, accustomed to a middle-class diet and French cooking, considered the long voyage,

*though tedious, at least . . . health-giving. I left home considerably
troubled by dyspepsia, but arrived in Australia enjoying magnificent
health, notwithstanding a wretched fare and most indigestible food,
consisting mainly of salt beef commonly called 'junk', salt pork, and
for a change a tinned delicacy designated 'soup and bouilli', rice,
pease pudding, preserved potatoes and, in nautical terms, 'plum
duff', otherwise plum pudding.*

Strutt was a keen, if rather distant, observer of the volatile relationship between Captain Ferguson, 'a bluff good-hearted Scot', and
his crew and passengers. Soon after embarkation, a stowaway was
detected in the hold. After dressing him down, Ferguson set him
to work his passage as a member of the crew. One of the passengers
who trespassed on the ladder of the mainmast was tied hand and
foot as a punishment, while an insubordinate crewman was slapped
in irons. As would soon become evident, Ferguson's strict discipline
had begun to create resentment among some of the crew.

Early in April, in the south Atlantic, the *Culloden* was shadowed
by a suspicious-looking ship, low-rigged and rakish, which refused
to identify itself. Cabin passengers and emigrants were summoned
on deck, formed into companies and issued with guns and cutlasses
in preparation for a pirate attack. Ferguson directed 'a very powerful
man, a sturdy butcher we had amongst the emigrants', to drop a
heavy grindstone into the boat of any boarding party. Strutt recalled
'the resolute look' of the captain and his comrade-in-arms as they
tested the weight of the projectile, and the mingled disappointment
and relief when the feared attack did not materialise. Was the big
butcher my great-great-great-uncle John Hewett? As far as I know,
he was the only butcher on board. His brother Richard was five feet
six and a half inches (169 centimetres)—more than middle height at
that time—and 'strongly built'. Later generations of Hewetts, like
my grandfather and great-grandfather, were also big men, over six
feet tall. It sounds like him.

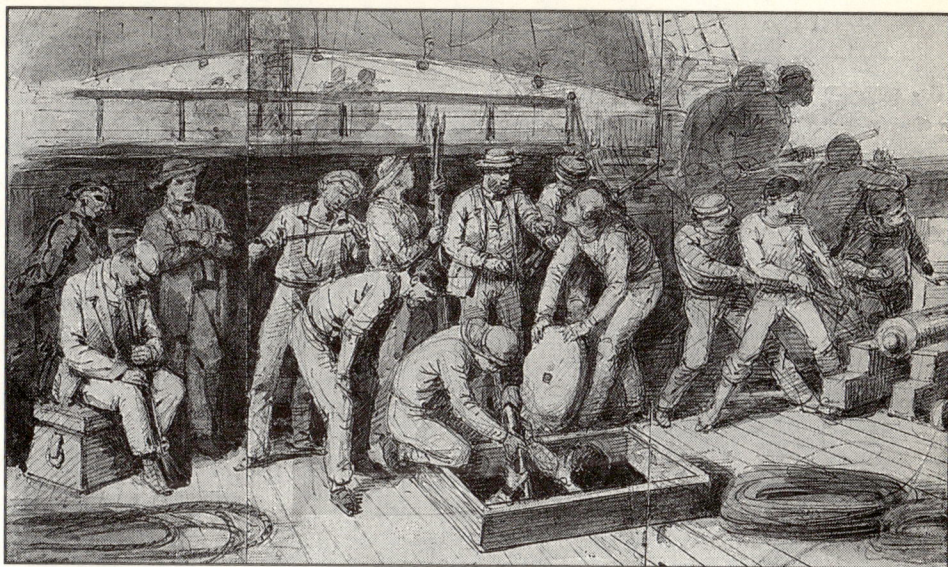

The Culloden's *company anticipates a threatened pirate attack. Beside the bearded Captain Ferguson, a strong young man (the butcher John Hewett?) prepares to cast a heavy millstone into the attackers' boat while crewmen ready the ship's only cannon. (From Sketchbook of William Strutt, Dixson Library)*

HIGH JINKS ON THE HIGH SEAS

On 13 April, as the *Culloden* approached the Equator, another altercation occurred between the captain and his crew. According to testimony later given in a Melbourne court, Ferguson, without provocation, had knocked down a seaman, who dashed his head against a davit. 'You will hear of this when you arrive at Port Phillip,' the seaman threatened. 'You vagabond, do you intend to police me?' the captain replied. Indeed he did. When the matter came to court, Ferguson explained that the seaman had been 'exceedingly ill-behaved and mutinous'. He had been found boring holes in the deck of the ship for the purpose of pouring bilge water into the female emigrants' berth. Perhaps the captain suspected the holes were designed for other mischievous purposes as well. The court was asked to judge whether the captain had exceeded his powers in using corporal punishment, rather than censure the motives of the seaman; but the testimony hints at an atmosphere of ribald jocularity between the crew and male passengers and the needlewomen, who may well have encouraged the attention. The court dismissed the seaman's allegation of assault, but later events would throw doubt on the captain's claim to be gallantly protecting the female emigrants.

Herbert's committee had stressed the need to protect the needlewomen by segregating their quarters from those of the other passengers. But as the surgeon later explained, on the berth deck there was no effective 'partition or separation whatever'. He had 'repeatedly to visit that part of the between decks in which the single women were berthed, twice and even three times during the night, to guard against any improper intrusion'. Ferguson agreed that 'he had much trouble in managing the single male passengers, both cabin and intermediate; that they tried all means to keep up intercourse with the single females; that he found them passing bottles of wine or beer (which they obtained by purchase aboard the ship) down through the ventilator to them'. The matron added that some of the females had 'contracted intimacy' with some of the crew. The captain's moral authority over the ship's company had been compromised by his decision to engage one of the needlewomen, Christina Tisdall, a 25-year-old widow from Southwark, as his personal 'stewardess'. It was known that he had persuaded her to stay aboard the *Culloden* as it proceeded to Sydney, rather than take up a position for which she had been engaged in Melbourne. This, as the Port Phillip immigration authorities later observed, appeared to be 'a very irregular and questionable proceeding on the part of the master'.

Between the decks of this nineteenth-century love boat, in the half-light between the ship's official code of regularity and respectability and its subculture of frank sexuality, Elizabeth Fenwick, London needlewoman, and Robert Hewett, country carpenter, fell in love. Robert's brothers John and Richard, and possibly his sister Lucy, also appear to have fallen in love with fellow passengers. How should we imagine these shipboard romances? Their courtship (if that is the word) was surely not governed by the precise calculations of social status, subtly coded emotional exchanges or small catastrophes of etiquette that shaped the world of *Pride and Prejudice*. But nor, judging by the few glimpses we have into the emotional lives of the needlewomen, was it just a matter of nocturnal assignations and furtive embraces amid the rigging or under the lifeboats of the *Culloden*, like the worlds of *Tom Jones* and *Moll Flanders*.

The female emigrants were well aware of their value in a colony where women were in short supply. Matrimony, rather than romantic love, was their objective. 'Comfortable'—a word that implies economic security together with at least a degree of emotional compatibility—was how they often described their ideal marriage. In contemporary parlance, a girl who lost her virginity was 'ruined', a term that had the double connotation of both moral and economic loss. Jane Hewett may have kept a tight rein on her daughters, especially 23-year-old Mary Ann, eighteen-year-old Jane and sixteen-year-old Susan, aware that any misstep in the closed gossipy environment of the ship could destroy their prospects when ashore. But her boys—28-year-old Henry, 27-year-old John, 22-year-old Robert and twenty-year-old Richard—were older and perhaps, after a decade without a father's discipline, harder to restrain. Significantly or not, while three of her sons developed liaisons with the needlewomen, only her eldest daughter, 26-year-old Lucy, appears to have developed a relationship with one of the young men aboard the *Culloden*.

LANDFALL

On 18 June, a cry from the masthead—'land ho'—announced the arrival of the *Culloden* on the Australian coast. On 1 July, when it passed Cape Otway and followed a little coasting schooner, *The Souvenir*, towards the Port Phillip Heads, the end of the long voyage came in view. Glimpsing the Union Jack flying from a flagpole on

Station Peak, Strutt hailed 'the magic emblem which seemed at once to bring Home thousands of miles nearer to us'. The ship dropped anchor in Hobson's Bay at 2.30 in the morning of 5 July.

On board, however, not all was well. Captain Ferguson had announced that, in view of their insubordination, he would not pay his crew the bonus for good behaviour promised at the beginning of the voyage. The crew then went on strike, refusing to assist in landing the passengers and their belongings. As Lucy Edwards recounted:

> *We came on shore at night on account of there a going to be a Mutiny with the Sailors and the Captain, because he would not give them there [sic] discharge when they came and asked him so they all struck and would not do any thing so he sent for the police Constables and he kept them on Bread and water until a great many of them run away and the rest he was very glad to give them 5s and let them go.*

So with the angry words of captain and crew still ringing in their ears, Jane Hewett and her children, along with the rest of the ship's company, climbed down the ship's ladder in the dark, tumbled into boats, and were rowed ashore onto Liardet's Beach (present-day Port Melbourne). After four months at sea, they stood on the shores of their Promised Land with nothing but the clothes on their backs. The local representatives of the Female Emigration Society later censured Ferguson for landing the emigrants without their baggage, although Charles La Trobe, superintendent of the Port Phillip District, believed he was right to protect them from the mutinous proceedings on board. Huddling together for warmth, the newcomers waited on the beach till dawn. Then they began a five-kilometre trek across the city's swampy outskirts towards Prince's Bridge. This was the traumatic landfall that lived so long in the memory of Jane's eighteen-year-old daughter and passed into family legend.

Word of the approach of the needlewomen had already arrived. The great and good of Melbourne, led by the Anglican bishop Charles Perry and Superintendent La Trobe, were eager to offer them succour. 'We feel that we need not plead to a Port Phillip public on their behalf, or suggest how strongly Christian charity demands that we should extend to these poor creatures a cordial and considerate welcome,' declared the Melbourne *Argus*. Knowing the high hopes of the scheme's powerful London supporters, everyone in Port Phillip from the superintendent down was eager to think well of it. Bishop Perry had hailed the needlewomen as 'by far the most promising company of females which had been landed here'. The *Argus* rushed to offer its congratulations to Captain Ferguson and Surgeon Thompson for their exemplary service: 'Greater kindness and attention under all circumstances it was not possible to experience than that received from both officers.' Satisfied that their charges had been landed in good condition, the local committee of the Female Emigration Society resolved to grant each man the gratuities promised by their London superiors.

La Trobe had written to Herbert assuring him of the success of his scheme before the shenanigans aboard the *Culloden* came to light. Because the vessel had sailed directly from London without putting in at another port where gossip could have passed to a faster ship, La Trobe and his officials had no way of knowing how the voyage had been conducted, beyond what Ferguson and Thompson told them. (Matron Hughan may well have been intimidated by the others, at least until subsequent events loosened her tongue.) In the resulting furore over the hurried landing, local officials had hastened to take the captain's part against the complaints of his crew. So far as anyone knew, the ship and its captain were returning with honour.

A SCANDALOUS EPISODE

About a month later, on the night before they were due to sail out of Port Phillip, Captain Ferguson and Dr Thompson called at the Immigration Depot to make onward travel arrangements with two of the needlewomen. Ellen Ellis, 'a good looking young woman', and 22-year-old Catherine Pain, were to continue on the *Culloden* to Sydney, where they had family awaiting them. Rather than proceeding to the ship, however, they stopped at the Club House Hotel in Flinders Street, where the landlord was asked to provide dinner for four. Despite the lateness of the hour, he complied, and when the meal was over, the two young women retired to the servants' room. At about eleven o'clock that night, Ferguson and Thompson began a furious argument. One of the waiters asked them to leave, assuring the two young women that they were welcome to stay the night without charge. Ferguson would hear none of this, and insisted on the girls dressing and leaving the house. Thompson proposed to return them to the Immigration Depot, but Ferguson said he would take Ellen with him and made off in another direction.

Towards midnight they arrived at the Bull and Mouth Tavern in Bourke Street, where the captain asked if he and his wife could be accommodated for the night. The proprietor, Mr Cantlon, noting the girl's age, refused. She would later claim to have objected that she was not Ferguson's wife, although Cantlon's recollection was that she was silent throughout the conversation. Was there another place that would accommodate them? the captain now enquired. The publican pointed to a nearby house. Ellen now attempted to escape and ran towards Swanston Street crying for help. The captain overtook her, struck her on the head, and clasped her around the throat. 'Oh you silly girl,' he remonstrated. Her strangled cries brought Sergeant Tucker of the City Police to her aid. Ferguson was subsequently charged with assault, while arrangements were made for Ellen to proceed to Sydney on another vessel. In the meantime, the gallant surgeon had apparently changed his mind about returning Catherine to the Immigration Depot and instead took her to the Rainbow Hotel in Fitzroy where, as La Trobe dolefully concluded, he 'effected the ruin of the . . . poor girl'. Concerned for Catherine's reputation—she was actually making her way to Sydney to get married—the authorities made strenuous efforts to conceal her identity, including removing her name from official documents.

This scandalous episode cast the previously unquestioned reputations of the captain and surgeon in an entirely new and dismal light. 'But for the unscrupulous and profligate outbreak ... both these officers would have left Port Phillip with characters which might have fully justified further employment in a service for which of all men they were most unfitted,' La Trobe ruefully observed. Others now began to speak more frankly. According to most witnesses, the officers' conduct during the voyage had been 'unexceptionable'. 'The Captain had never behaved in any way improperly to me before that night,' Ellen Ellis admitted. But sometime after their disembarkation in Port Phillip, they appear to have singled out the two young passengers to Sydney for their attentions. Two weeks before the *Culloden* was due to sail, Catherine Pain had visited the ship in order to get some clothes from her trunk. On her return, she told another of the female migrants, Margaret Burney, that the captain had behaved very improperly, inviting her to sleep in his cuddy (cabin) and using 'disgusting language'. In the aftermath, Dr Thompson, who had previously appeared to be 'a most pleasing and kind person', came to be regarded as 'even more profligate and infamous' than the captain.

La Trobe was obliged to write a penitent postscript, detailing the captain's and surgeon's misdeeds, retracting his first rosy estimate of the success of the voyage and recommending that the Female Emigration Society adopt the more rigorous regulations of the government's own emigration scheme. News of the scandal reached Herbert some months later. 'I received a short note from Capt F a few days back which your letter now explains,' he wrote in reply. 'I fear it is a bad business & I will have [to see] what steps we can take in the matter.'

It was by no means the last scandal to dog the female emigration scheme, but the revelation of events aboard the *Culloden*, the first and most publicised voyage, inevitably tainted the reputations of the female passengers as well as the main culprits, the captain and surgeon. In her book *A Lady's Visit to the Gold Diggings* (1854), Mrs Ellen Clacy noted:

> '*Sydney* [sic] *Herbert's needlewomen' bear but a bad name; and the worst recommendation a young girl applying for a situation can give, is to say she came out in that manner—not because the colonists look down on anyone coming out by the assistance of others, but because it is imagined her female associates on the voyage cannot have been such as to improve her morality, even if she were good for anything before.*

The *Culloden* had no sooner arrived in Port Phillip than a second contingent, of 67 women, arrived in Adelaide aboard the *Duke of Portland*. An indignant Adelaidian wrote anonymously to Herbert describing many of the new arrivals as 'utterly reckless and profligate, obscene in their language and demeanor . . . accustomed to the habits of the London streetwalker'.

In their after-life in the colonies, immigrants often continued to identify themselves by the name of the ship on which they came. Henceforward, the *Culloden*, which had embarked as a symbol of hope, would be remembered as a ship of shame. It is no wonder that Jane Hewett omitted its name from her account of the family's Australian landfall.

Once his true character was revealed, Captain Ferguson attempted to flee Port Phillip as quickly as possible. Before his case came to court, he called at his agent's office to pick up the ship's register, also carrying off that of another vessel, the *Iris*. The *Culloden* was nineteen kilometres down the bay before officials caught up, boarded the vessel and compelled him to hand over the misappropriated document. He sailed on to Sydney, still a step ahead of his accusers, where on 10 August he disembarked the remaining fourteen passengers. After two months in port, still without a cargo, he sailed back empty via Ceylon to England.

The *Culloden* would never again enter Australian waters. On 13 November 1854, carrying troops during the Crimean War, it sank in the Black Sea. The entire ship's company, master and crew, together with 35 Ottoman soldiers, was captured by the Russians, but its owner, Mr Ferguson of Glasgow, no longer its master, was fully compensated by his insurer, Lloyd's of London.

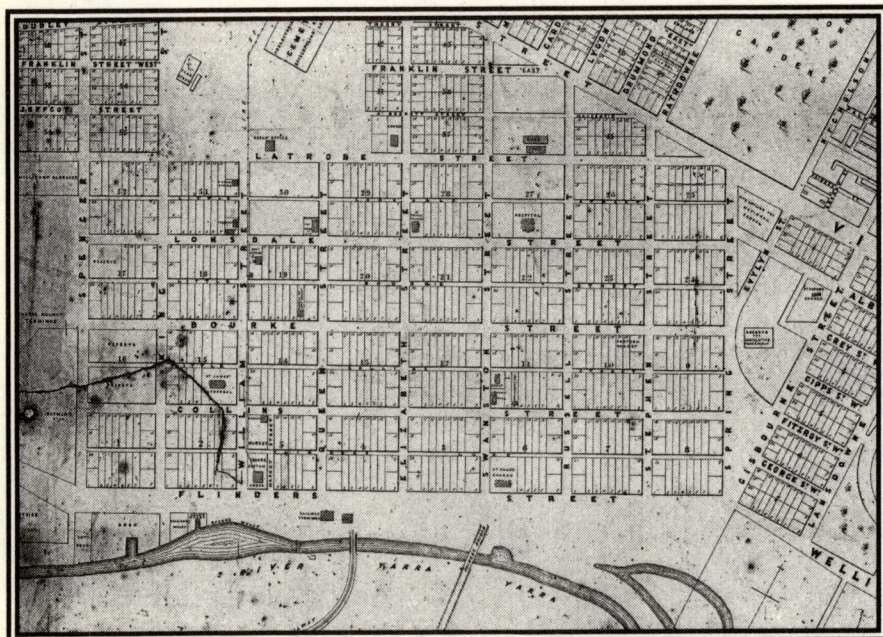

The Golden Mile in the early 1850s. Most of Melbourne's residents lived within the rectangular grid of streets laid out by Surveyor Robert Hoddle in the late 1830s. The Immigration Depot, where the needlewomen were accommodated, is located on a government reserve at the west end of town. Jane Hewett and her family lived in Russell Street, in the more respectable eastern end. (Plan of the City of Melbourne published by Campbell and Ferguson, Melbourne 1853? (detail), State Library of Victoria)

CHAPTER FOUR
Five weddings and a funeral

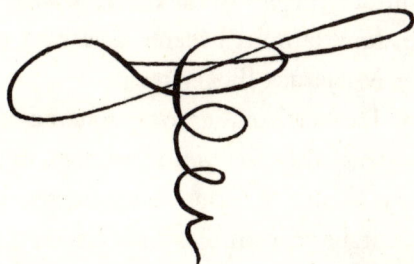

When the *Culloden* dropped anchor in Port Phillip Bay, Melbourne was a frontier town of less than 30,000 people, about the size of present-day Warrnambool or Wodonga. Almost all its inhabitants lived within the rectangular grid of streets we now call the Golden Mile. It was small enough for most people to recognise each other in the streets. Most of its houses were little more than shacks and its streets muddy tracks. It had grown fast from recent beginnings and was about to explode under the influence of gold. The frontier town would become an 'instant city'.

Its population was young and largely masculine, with all the rugged virtues and rough vices that tend to go with such frontier settlements. Males outnumbered females by 60 to 40, and among young adults the disproportion was higher still. For young women seeking marriage, Melbourne was a seller's market. Sidney Herbert's first objective had been to rid England of its surplus of indigent females, but he also hoped that the *Culloden*'s cargo would fill a void in the colony by providing eligible partners, good mothers and moral guardians in a society badly in need of their civilising influence.

The Female Emigration Society had delegated the task of receiving the migrants and finding them employment to the government's Immigration Depot, a squat, anonymous building at the intersection of Collins and Spencer streets. But because of the chaos surrounding the ship's arrival, and the liaisons that had developed during the voyage, it had taken 'no small degree of good management, temper and patience' to prevent a number of the young women from running off. A few of the 36 women who landed in Melbourne were offered positions by respectable families travelling on the *Culloden*: twenty-year-old Elizabeth Ireland, for example, became a servant in the household of cabin passenger Mr James Bickerton.

The success of Herbert's emigration scheme as a 'safety valve' depended on how smoothly the young women were absorbed into Port Phillip society. Would London seamstresses, used to the ways of a big city, be suitable for employment as servants in a frontier colony? Would locals be prepared to engage them? A fortnight after their arrival, the *Daily News* reported that only four of the female immigrants remained unemployed: 'There has been a great demand for them. We believe if there had been 100 instead of 36 they would all have found places by the end of the week. The wages given have been the highest for some months.' These results seemed to vindicate the scheme, although privately, in letters to Herbert, La Trobe expressed misgivings about the unrealistic expectations of an easy life some of the young women had brought with them.

The high demand for their services was partly contrived by the organisers, who solicited places in the homes of their friends on what looks like a semi-charitable basis. While their wages may have been generous by contemporary standards—usually about twelve to fifteen pounds per annum with full board—the term of employment was usually short, just three or six months, suggesting the jobs were essentially probationary. Elizabeth Fenwick became a general servant in the Richmond home of Mr Edward Bell, La Trobe's secretary, while her young sister Alice was offered a six-month appointment on the property of a squatter Captain W.F. Langdon on the Loddon River. Did the organisers decide to separate the Fenwick sisters for their own good? Perhaps they thought that sixteen-year-old Alice was better off in the country, away from the temptations of the metropolis and the rapidly evolving matrimonial plans of her sister and her other older shipmates. Other sisters, however, were kept together: Matilda Walker, for example, aged in her late twenties, was employed in the Richmond home of the barrister and judge Robert Pohlman, who promised to find a situation close by for her younger sister Ellen.

The satirical magazine Punch *contrasts the prosperous and virtuous life of the London needlewoman as the wife of an Australian bushman with the poverty and moral hazards of single life in London.* (Punch, *12 January 1850*)

'I am in a very comfortable situation in Melbourne at £12 [a year] to begin with,' seventeen-year-old Lucy Edwards wrote to her father in London. She was employed in the home of the merchant Alexander Fyffe on a probationary term of employment.

I am to have £14 when my quarter is up I am very happy to say
i was engaged 3 days after i came ashore and am much happier
than some of them are as three of them talk about running away
from their situations which will not be very well i doubt for them
for they have signed for six month and they are bound to serve it
Ruf or smooth or else go to prison. I have a young friend who only
signed for 3 months because she is a going to get married and I am
to be the brides maid which will be a good bit of pleasure for me
as i am very attached to them and so are they to me.

Lucy herself would also marry within the year, to seaman Edward Camplin, possibly one of the crew of the *Culloden*, bearing three children and then emigrating to Canada in the 1860s.

THE COLONIAL MARRIAGE MARKET

The *Culloden* had no sooner berthed than several couples tied the knot. Caroline Dennis, daughter of a shoemaker from Shoreditch, was wed to Mr Walford, an intermediate passenger, and departed with him to Hobart. Others met their partners soon after arriving. 'A great many of the girls who came out with us are married to working men here, and seem to do tolerably well,' 22-year-old Mathilda Read wrote to her family in May 1851. 'I am living now with my husband [Charles Servante, brother of one of the other needlewomen who had travelled on the *Culloden*], at a place called Collingwood, about two miles from Melbourne, which is the chief city of Port Phillip.' Another needlewoman, identified in the semi-anonymised version of her letter published by the Female Emigration Society by the initials

E.M. (Elizabeth Madgely?), detailed the matrimonial triumphs of several of her sisters.

> *M-J- is married, and has gone to live up the bush; please tell her mother that she has got a very good husband and she is very comfortable. My husband was at the wedding; she was married about a fortnight before me. M-A-B [Margaret Burney] was married to a clergyman on Christmas and is very comfortable indeed; she is at Port Adelaide.*

As rash as these hasty marriages may seem to us, the authorities generally smiled on them. After all, the female emigration scheme aimed to supply wives as much as domestic servants, the one being a sanctified version of the other in the eyes of some colonists. Getting them married was a step towards ensuring they did not fall back into the same poverty trap they had emigrated to escape. There is little evidence, however, to support the suspicion that they were all marrying in haste, or because they were already pregnant. Of 36 women, at least 29 would marry in Victoria; one appears to have remained single, and six could not be traced. Six were married in 1850, seven in 1851, eight in 1852, and eight in later years. Like Lucy Edwards' friend, they seem to have been eager to marry in their own time and with at least some ceremony. Their partners, by and large, were from the same level of society as themselves: labourers, tradesmen, seamen and occasionally small businessmen. Until 1852, the bridegrooms were likely to be assisted immigrants; afterwards, when the population was transformed by an influx of gold seekers, the balance swung towards free or unassisted immigrants. There were few genteel Jane Eyres, and even fewer gentlemanly Mr Rochesters.

How did the Hewett family fare in this overheated colonial marriage market? 'It is a good place for all maids to come as they are sure to get a husband,' twenty-year-old Fanny Hickmott from Southwark reported to her mother.

I am not married yet, but I shall be before long—before you get this—to a young man who came out on the same ship. There was a mother and four sons and four daughters, and this is one of the sons that I am to have, and —— is to have another and —— is to have a third. If you can, prevail on my sisters to come to me and all shall be done by both me and Richard that can be done to make them happy.

The mother with four sons was, of course, the widow Jane Hewett. By 1851, she was living at 7 Russell Street, Melbourne, possibly running a boarding house. The unnamed women were Matilda Walker and Elizabeth Fenwick, both needlewomen aboard the *Culloden*. Matilda had been born in Scotland, the daughter of silversmith Daniel Walker, but the family had later moved to London. Matilda and Elizabeth had lived in the same district of London, along with their younger sisters, Ellen Walker and Alice Fenwick, both in their late teens. Matilda Walker was now engaged to butcher John Hewett, while Elizabeth Fenwick was promised to carpenter Robert Hewett. Fanny's own intended was the youngest Hewett son, twenty-year-old Richard.

These marriage plans, forming so soon after the Hewetts' arrival in Port Phillip, must have both pleased and disconcerted Jane and her family. In forming new partnerships, the young people were laying the foundations of independent lives in the colony. But the departure of some members of the family, at the very moment when they were all still finding their feet in a turbulent frontier town, may well have unsettled those who were left behind. The Hewetts had been a family unit all their lives, knit together by the shared enterprise of Hook Farm. Whether it was a happy family or not, it had been a fixture in their lives. Now, for the first time, the members of the family were about to part ways, dispersing to the four corners of the colony. As the boys departed, they left their mother and sisters alone.

Emigration is a risky enterprise, and the risks are greatest at the beginning, when the migrants are still finding their way in the new land. They are multiplied when the migrants come, like the needlewomen, without the protection and support of family, and sometimes still experiencing the trauma of separation. They become greater still when conditions in the new land are also unsettled, as they were in 1850s Victoria. Each generation of newcomers, from the English and Irish of the nineteenth century to the Calabrians, Greeks, Vietnamese and Lebanese of our own time, experiences heightened levels of hardship and psychological stress. Their struggle to adjust may be accompanied by poverty, friction, crime and family breakdown. Some simply don't make it. This uncomfortable fact rubs hard against the cherished national myth that migration is a success story, that Australia is a welcoming society, and that newcomers generally make good. Like most descendants of migrants, I cherish these myths myself, so it has been sobering to find that some of my own forebears were not the morally upright, upward-striving, modestly successful folk I had always imagined them to be. A good proportion were families that social workers would today describe as 'dysfunctional', 'multi-problem' or 'at risk'. The mixed fortunes of the Hewett children in Victoria's golden age reveal the intense pressures of adaptation to life in the fast-changing colony.

JOHN AND MATILDA

On 19 November 1850, in the first of the Hewett weddings, 27-year-old John Hewett married 29-year-old Matilda Walker. Matilda had barely completed her probationary three months with the Pohlmans, but as her thirtieth birthday approached, she was evidently eager to delay matrimony no longer. The wedding took place in the residence of Alexander Morison, minister of the Independent Church in Collins Street, with John 'solemnly declaring' that he held communion with the denomination. Morison was a vigorous and popular figure in Melbourne although the Hewetts' choice of a minister may also have been a matter of convenience—the Independent Church was just a hundred metres or so from the Hewetts' new home. At the time of the wedding Matilda was living in Richmond, probably still with the Pohlmans. Robert Hewett and Elizabeth Fenwick, now also engaged, were the only recorded witnesses.

Ten months later, the couple's first children, twins—a girl, Alice, and a boy, Frank—were born, but only Alice survived infancy. When their third child, Fanny, was born in 1853, John was trying his luck on the goldfields. They later moved to Warrnambool, where John resumed his old trade, opening a butcher's shop with an attached abattoir in rented premises in the main street. Warrnambool was still very much a frontier settlement, surrounded by bush—it had been threatened by fire in 1851—and in an era when transport by land was more costly and difficult than by sea, its river port made it a strategic gateway to one of the colony's richest regions, the Western District. It exported wool, wheat and, from the late 1850s, salted pork, a trade in which John may have played a part. But it remained a small, secluded settlement of barely a thousand people, as far from the thriving metropolis of London as one can imagine, and perhaps further than Matilda found congenial. As a small-town butcher, John seems to have enjoyed modest prosperity, but as the children approached adulthood, the marriage ran into trouble. Sometime in the 1870s, the couple separated and Matilda moved to Melbourne, where she resumed her old trade as a dressmaker, living in a succession of rented houses in Prahran and Collingwood.

We do not know exactly what precipitated the split and drew Matilda back to the city, but other family troubles may have played a part. In 1853, Matilda's younger sister Ellen, another of Herbert's needlewomen, had married Thomas Arthur, a Cornishman. They settled in Collingwood, where Thomas conducted his business as a drayman from their owner-occupied cottage off Johnston Street. Over the next fifteen years, Ellen gave birth to nine children, of whom six, however, did not survive even to their second birthday: John, born in 1855, died the following year; Sarah (born 1859), after ten months, William (1861), after a month; Harriet (1865), after a year; Charlotte (1867), after a year, and Thomas (1871), after seven months. Two children survived infancy but died before reaching adulthood: Ellen (born 1870), died at the age of twelve, and Alice (1863), a domestic servant, died of phthisis (tuberculosis) at eighteen. All eight are buried in a common plot in the Melbourne General Cemetery. Elizabeth (born 1856) was the only child to reach adulthood and to survive her parents. Ellen herself died in 1883, aged 49, from a 'pharyngeal abscess', an acute throat infection that spread to the brain. When Thomas died six years later, aged 52, his daughter Elizabeth and son-in-law Reuben Auty, a Collingwood boot warehouseman, were the only heirs to his modest fortune of £300.

Even in an era when child mortality was high, this was a truly catastrophic record of death and misery. It must have weighed heavily on the physical and mental health of the parents, surviving family and extended kin. Historian Janet McCalman, who has studied the birth histories of Melbourne working-class mothers and their children, notes a small but significant number of mothers with large numbers of offspring who all, or nearly all, died in infancy. One local doctor of Malthusian outlook even suggested that such calamities were a wise provision of nature in operating as a brake on population growth. It is unlikely that the parents were themselves so philosophical. As McCalman notes, 'just because [infant death] was common does not mean it was endurable'. Every child was named, and several lived long enough to smile, speak and respond to their parents and siblings.

Some early deaths were caused by congenital syphilis, the life-threatening infection passed in utero or at birth from the mother who had previously contracted the disease. This possibility cannot be entirely discounted, although the diverse recorded causes of her babies' deaths—'dysentery', 'diarrhoea', 'congestion of brain', 'strangulated hernia', 'diphtheria', 'exhaustion from measles and pertussis' (whooping cough) and 'dentition and hydrocephalus'—do not match the classic symptoms of congenital syphilis.

In any case, it is unlikely that Ellen's misfortunes had come entirely from her past. The Arthur family was living through a dangerous time, when epidemic diseases were rife and knowledge of their causes was rudimentary. In the aftermath of the gold rush, just when Ellen was having her first babies, Victoria was visited by epidemics of measles, scarlet fever and diphtheria. The danger was greatest in summer, when high temperatures, combined with the effects of contaminated milk and water, almost doubled the rate of infant mortality. It was not the times alone but also the place where the Arthurs lived that heightened the danger. Since the 1850s, doctors and public health officials had identified Collingwood, a crowded, unsewered suburb of cheap timber cottages interspersed with tanneries, slaughter yards, boot factories and warehouses, as the most dangerous, as well as the poorest, in the metropolis. When disease was still associated (falsely) with the influence of 'miasmas', or the noxious vapours emanating from bad drains and sewers, the 'suburb with bad breath' had a bad reputation which, for other reasons, was well deserved. Next to Carlton, whose infant death rate was swollen by the presence of the Lying-In Hospital (later Royal Women's Hospital), it led the metropolitan table for infant deaths as well as general mortality.

There may have been more, however, to the high toll of babies and children in Ellen Arthur's family than just foul drains and bad smells. Ellen was herself a product of poverty, in London and Australia, and her capacity to bear and rear healthy children may well have been compromised by poor nutrition or an inability to effectively breastfeed her offspring. Babies with low birth weights born into low-income families were less likely to thrive than those from more secure households. As McCalman notes, 'there was a fatal reciprocity between failure of a household at birth and the prospects of reproducing a next generation'. While several of the Arthur children died in the first months of life, it is surely significant that even those children who survived into their teens died early, as did the parents themselves. Tom Arthur's work as a drayman or carter was low paid and irregular, and although they owned their own house, the family was probably living hand to mouth much of the time. They were unable to save, to look ahead or to minimise risk. The diseases that

Cure for cancer

The discovery consists in applying to the sore; Chloride of Chromium — a new salt of this rare metal incorporated into stramonium ointment. This preparation converts the tumour into perfect carbon and it crumbles away in a few hours.

Good cheap beer

Pour ten gallons of boiling water upon 1 peck of malt in a tub, stir it about well with a stick, let it stand about half an hour, and then draw off the wort: pour ten gallons more of boiling water upon the malt, letting it remain half an hour, stir it occasionally, then draw it off and put it to the former wort when this is done mix 4 oz of hops with it, and boil well then strain the hops from it and when the wort becomes milk warm, put some yeast to it to make it ferment: when it have done fermenting put the liquor into a cask and as soon as it have done working over bung it close down the beer is then fit for use.

killed them were diseases of poverty, like tuberculosis and other bacterial infections.

In an era before antibiotics, or even effective antiseptics, infection could spread rapidly within families and between them, especially if they were unwilling or unable to practise the simple rules of hygiene— washing hands, sterilising milk, isolating infectious members of the family. The poorer, more harried and unwell the mother was herself, the more likely disease would become rampant in the household. Some Collingwood mothers, if they had trouble breastfeeding or simply had to work to support their families, 'farmed out' their babies to wet nurses, a practice that notoriously endangered the infants' lives. One cannot dismiss the possibility that the parents themselves, through either negligence or ignorance, were compounding the problem.

By the time Matilda arrived back in Melbourne, her own eldest daughter had become a fellow sufferer in this cycle of poverty, sickness and premature death. In 1873, 22-year-old Alice Jenetta Hewett married 26-year-old Robert Jerrome, a carter like Tom Arthur, living nearby in Ryrie Street, Collingwood. A year later she was a widow. Jerrome's fellow members of the United Excelsior Lodge of the Order of Oddfellows, the friendly society that probably paid for his funeral, followed his coffin from the couple's home in Easey Street, Collingwood, to the Melbourne General Cemetery. Six weeks later, their seven-month-old daughter Jenetta was also dead. This double tragedy could well have been the shock that precipitated Matilda's decision to leave Warrnambool and her husband for the metropolis. How it affected Alice herself we can only imagine. In 1877, she sailed alone to New Zealand, and a few months later married 27-year-old Fred Litchfield in Christchurch. Litchfield was a Melbourne man—his father was a furniture dealer in Chapel Street, Prahran—who had left for New Zealand in 1874, not long before the death of Jerrome. The circumstances suggest the couple already knew each other, and possibly had an understanding before Alice embarked for New Zealand. Was Fred an old admirer who came to her rescue? Or could an old friend of her husband's have taken pity on his widow?

In the absence of evidence, I invite readers to invent whatever romantic scenario appeals to them. In 1878, the couple returned to Melbourne via Sydney. The birthplaces of their children—Balmain, South Yarra, Footscray, Hotham and Oakleigh—suggest a rather peripatetic life, although by 1890 they had settled in Melbourne's eastern suburbs, where Fred had become an optician.

Meanwhile, in 1876, Alice's younger sister Fanny had married a local Warrnambool boy, Thomas Benson, a butcher in her father's shop. A daughter, Florence, was born in 1880, and as John grew older, Thomas took over the running of the shop. By the time John died in 1888, the breach with his wife and elder daughter was evidently unbridgeable. In his will he made small bequests of £50 to his maiden sister Jane, to his younger daughter Fanny and to his 'dear grand-daughter Florence', and left the residue of the estate and business, valued at about £300, to his son-in-law Thomas. His wife Matilda and first daughter, Alice, were nowhere mentioned. By now Alice was seriously ill with rheumatoid arthritis, a progressive disease that gradually disabled her. When she died six years later, aged only 43, in the Austin Hospital, her mother was living in Moor Street, Fitzroy. The old lady survived only a few more years, dying of 'senile debility and exhaustion' in the Melbourne Hospital in 1899, just short of the fiftieth anniversary of her arrival aboard the *Culloden*, and was buried in the Melbourne General Cemetery. Her daughter Alice shares a nearby plot with her first and second husbands and her firstborn child, a poignant testament to the fragility of life and human affection in the age before modern antibiotics and sanitation.

ROBERT AND ELIZABETH

Robert, the third of the Hewett brothers, was only 22, and the London needlewoman Elizabeth Fenwick 26 when the *Culloden* arrived in Port Phillip in 1850. While John and Matilda were old enough to know their own minds, Robert's mother Jane may have hoped that the younger couple would wait a little longer before rushing to the altar. But on 29 March 1851, just eight months after their arrival, they were married in the residence of Reverend Morison, in a simple ceremony witnessed by Robert's elder brother Henry and sister Mary Ann.

How should we imagine this match between a Hampshire farmer's son and a London tradesman's daughter? In his great comic novel *Vanity Fair*, William Thackeray, who speculated on the marriage prospects of the needlewomen as they assembled on Fenchurch Street station, presented contrasting images of contemporary femininity in its two heroines. Was our Elizabeth Fenwick a Becky Sharp, a cunning little adventuress, or an Amelia Sedley, soft, pretty and helpless? And what of Robert Hewett: was he a guileless country boy, unable to resist the wiles of a city girl, or was he, as William Strutt's observation on his shipmates suggested, a hard-drinking, roughly spoken, hard-living yokel?

Two weeks before the wedding, an interesting item appeared in the Melbourne *Argus* under the heading 'Blackguard Conduct'. On the previous Sunday afternoon, 'a man named Robert Hewett' had forced his way into the Catholic chapel, 'he being in a state of drunkenness, and having his person exposed, at the same time making use of blasphemous language'. In recognition of the 'gross nature of the offences', the magistrate imposed the heaviest penalty the law allowed, a five-pound fine, or if it was unpaid, two months' imprisonment.

I admit this discovery shook me. It looked as though my great-great-grandfather was not just a drunk (a bad enough offence in the eyes of my Methodist forebears), but also a Sabbath breaker, a bigot, a blasphemer and a sexual pervert. If anything was to be admired in his conduct it was the economy with which he had managed to break every commandment in a single afternoon. I began to look for explanations and excuses. Perhaps a buck's party had gone terribly wrong? But Robert was apparently alone, and it was Sunday afternoon, not Saturday night. Had he been seized by the temporary madness that sometimes overcomes a young man as he feels the bonds of matrimony settling on him? But if so, how to explain the blasphemy and the exposure? Could this really be the same person who would one day be 'mourned and respected by all who knew him'? Many a respected older man, I reminded myself, could look back on a reckless youth.

Why should this matter to me? I wondered. After all, there were four generations between us. I was only one-sixteenth Robert's descendant. Plenty of other people had drunks, criminals and even deviants in their family tree: why not me? Would I think less of a friend whose escutcheon was similarly stained? Even to ask the question, I realised, was to acknowledge the obstinate influence of heredity on my sense of identity. There seemed to be a contradiction between my liberal convictions and some vague anxiety that Robert's sins could somehow taint his descendants. If we can draw strength from the virtue of our good ancestors, surely we must be diminished by the sins of our bad ones?

Since Robert had duly appeared to be married, I assumed he paid the fine, making a big hole in the couple's savings, rather than spending his honeymoon in the clink. But just to be sure, I checked the Central Register of Male Prisoners. And there, to my surprise and relief, I found *another* Robert Hewett. Born in 1829, Robert Hewett, Prisoner 3639, was just a year younger than my great-great-grandfather. A fresh-faced, semi-literate tinsmith, he was a Protestant, born in Belfast—that nursery of bigotry—and was sentenced in 1857 to two years in a road gang on a charge of 'cutting and stabbing'. Maybe I'm profiling him, but he looks a more likely 'blackguard' than the village carpenter from Hampshire. I did not know whether to feel pleased or sorry about this new development. Having reconciled myself to a blemished pedigree, I began to regret the loss of a colourful character.

What happened to Robert and Elizabeth after their wedding is the subject of the next chapter. But, on the whole, I am glad to send them on their way with Robert's reputation intact. When they married early in 1851, nobody expected the whirlwind that ensued when news of the discovery of gold hit Melbourne a few months later. They probably anticipated staying on in Melbourne, already a prosperous town where carpenters were in short supply and wages were high. Perhaps they would have built or bought a cottage in one of its suburbs. Elizabeth can hardly have anticipated, when she left Gravesend, that she would exchange life on the mean streets of the world's metropolis for life in a tent on the richest alluvial goldfield in the world.

RICHARD AND NANCY

When Fanny Hickmott wrote early in 1851 encouraging her sisters to join her in Melbourne, she was looking forward to her own wedding. But when her sister Ann arrived in Melbourne, she was in for a surprise: the anticipated union with Richard Hewett had fallen through. Early in 1853, Fanny placed an advertisement in the *Argus* advising that 'Ann Hickmott, who left London about two years since will hear of her sister Fanny, now Mrs Veever, who arrived here by the Culloden' by contacting her through Sayce and Cheetham, Staffordshire House, Elizabeth Street.' Had Richard got cold feet and decided that marriage was not yet for him? Or had Fanny found a better prospect in John Veevers, a grocer, soon to own his own freehold property in South Yarra? The couple would eventually have three daughters and try their luck on the goldfields before moving back to Melbourne, where Fanny died in Hawthorn in 1908.

So what had happened to Richard? According to his sister, he had gone to New Zealand and lost touch with the rest of the family. I looked for him there and found no trace. In fact, like his eldest brother, Henry, Richard had actually headed north into New South Wales. He was living in Maitland and working in one of the several flour mills along the Hunter River. In 1859, he married 23-year-old Nancy Maria Hawkins, a local girl, and in 1860 a son, Richard

Edward, was born, who died when he was barely two years old. A tombstone in the Campbell's Hill cemetery registered the grief of the parents and maternal grandparents. Two more children, John and Alice, were born in 1862 and 1863. In 1865, Richard was arrested in Sydney attempting to pass a forged cheque, sent back to Maitland for trial, convicted and sentenced to three years in Maitland Gaol, a term reduced in consideration of his previous good character. The record of his release provides the fullest physical description of any of the Hewett children. He was 37 years old, five feet six and a half inches (169 centimetres) in height, strongly built, with blue eyes, brown hair and a sallow complexion, and had a mole on his lower left arm. He gave his religion as C of E and his occupation as miller. He got out in just over two years, with remission for good behaviour.

Richard seems to have spent the rest of his life knocking around at various places within the Maitland–Wollombi–Cessnock area. Three more children, Edward, Alfred and Caroline, were born, in 1868, 1870 and 1872 respectively. In 1879, he was called as a witness in a case brought by the police against William Sweetman, the keeper of a notorious wine saloon on the Wollombi–Maitland Road, for Sunday trading. The circumstances suggest he was well acquainted with the place. Two years later, he was dead at the age of 51, from injuries sustained in an accident at Cessnock. Another of his children, John, had already died at the age of twelve, but four others, ranging in age from nine to eighteen, remained for his widow to support. Once again the head of a Hewett household, a 'native of Hampshire, England', had died young, with 'a wife and large family to mourn their loss'. 'Melbourne papers please copy,' the announcement in the *Maitland Mercury* added.

Was this request, a common practice at the time, the family's way of informing Richard's brothers and sisters of his death? It suggests that Richard was no longer in regular contact with his family in Victoria. As a black sheep, he may well have wished to keep word of his brush with the law a secret from his family south of the border. And in a day before telephone books, it was much harder to track people down, especially if they wanted to lie low. Now, thanks to Ancestry.com and Trove, I can go where his family could not. I have pursued their brother down the digital highways and byways, like Sergeant Bloodhound, bringing his shameful past into the light. I have pursued him through birth and marriage registers, directories, newspapers and court records right to the gate of Maitland Gaol.

Having found him out, I am worried that I may also have misrepresented him. Family historians rely largely on sources created by the state, or earlier by the church. Our narratives are hung on the skeleton created by legally defined events—births, marriages, deaths, bequests, leases, taxes, property transactions, crimes, censuses and the like. But little of what matters most in our lives is captured by such documents. If we are lucky, a few old letters, like that precious fragment from Fanny Hickmott's, or bits of oral testimony like Jane's conversation with my grandfather, may have survived. Otherwise we are left to reconstruct the most intimate, precious, fragile, irreducibly personal part of our lives from the outside in, relying on materials that are cold, standardised and impersonal. Like the prophet, the family historian sometimes seems to inhabit a valley of dry bones, inert and meaningless until they are clothed with flesh and the spirit is somehow breathed into them.

LUCY AND JAMES, SUSAN AND ROBERT

According to Jane, five of her siblings married shipmates; at least that is what my grandfather wrote in his notebook. We now know that this cannot be true, for only five of the children married at all, and at least one, Richard, did not marry a shipmate. What about the others?

In July 1851, Lucy, the eldest daughter, married James Maxfield, a miller from Herefordshire, once again at the Independent Chapel, in the presence of her mother Jane, and siblings Robert, Richard and Susan. Maxfield had also arrived in the colony in 1850, but his name does not appear on the official list of assisted immigrants on the *Culloden*, nor on the less complete lists of paying passengers in contemporary newspapers. Neither does it appear on any of the other lists of passengers entering Port Phillip by sea in this period. While we cannot be sure that he accompanied the Hewetts on the *Culloden*, it is likely that he came as a paying intermediate passenger, like William Strutt.

James and Lucy had more than a little in common, and it is easy to imagine how they may have drawn closer as they chatted on the long voyage. Both were elder children of widowed mothers. Both had grown up within the intimate worlds of the village and the family business. And both had seen their inherited way of life transformed by new technologies and market forces. Thirty-one-year-old James had grown up in Llangarron, a tiny village tucked away in the foothills of the Cambrian Mountains, close to the Welsh border. His family's business, Langstone Mill, harnessed the waters of Garron Brook, a tributary of the Wye River, to turn the wheat and barley grown by local farmers into flour.

Curious to know if Langstone Mill survived, I recently drove from Gloucester, where my wife and I were staying with friends, to Ross-on-Wye. We paused in the old market square, where James may have sold his flour, to buy an ordnance survey map of the district before driving a few kilometres southwest. From the parish church of St Dienst, the centre of the village, a narrow lane rises towards Langstone Court, an imposing Palladian mansion still inhabited by descendants of the Maxfields' landlord, Reverend Mr Jones, before descending into the valley of the Garron where it meanders across a lush floodplain. At the end of the road, next to a substantial farmhouse and stables, we found the sturdy three-storey stone mill, now bereft of its waterwheel but lovingly restored into a cosy house and office. We introduced ourselves to the owners, who produced a family Bible inscribed with the names, alas not of the Maxfields, but of one of the several successors. Surveying this apparently idyllic scene—with horses quietly grazing knee deep in summer pasture, and the Garron gushing beneath a quaint stone bridge—it was hard to imagine how James could ever have contemplated abandoning Hereford for the rigours of life in a hot dry land half a world away.

The Maxfields had lived in Llangarron since at least the mid-eighteenth century. Along with his six brothers and sisters, James had grown up into a traditional family enterprise, much like Hook Farm, where it was difficult to say where family ended and business began. When James was a boy, his father, Edward, and mother, Mary, ran the mill and an adjoining farm. Historians have counted the physical remains of more than three hundred such small mills scattered across the Hereford landscape. The ruins of a medieval mill, part of an abbey, lie within sight of Langstone Mill. These mills were the legacy of an era of subsistence farming when small communities produced most of what they ate and wore. By the 1840s, however, the distance that had previously insulated them from the metropolitan economy was lessening. Flour milling, like brewing, cider making and weaving, was gravitating towards larger centres of population linked by canals, railways and navigable rivers to London and the coast. By the time Edward died in 1847, aged 72, the capacity of the mill to support his children was in doubt. James's mother, now about to enter her sixties, could not run it forever. George came home from nearby Tretire, where he had been assisting his uncle Robert, to help her. James, now in his late twenties, was no longer needed at home. All around him other young men were forsaking the villages for larger cities and towns. The signs were clear: he would have to find a future elsewhere. By the mid-1850s, his younger brother Edward was running Langstone Mill in tandem with another at Lucton, but by 1861, when the census taker called again, his mother was dead, the mill had passed to William Banton, a local farmer, and Edward was working as a journeyman miller at St Briavels on the lower reaches of the Wye.

When James decided to emigrate to Port Phillip is unknown, but he appears to have acted in accordance with a definite plan. He either paid his own way to Port Phillip or it was paid for him, perhaps by his family, or perhaps by Robert Allan, proprietor of a large mill at Kilmore, north of Melbourne, the oldest in the colony, with whom James soon formed a partnership. He was already living in Kilmore at the time of his wedding to Lucy. By 1853, he had bought out Allan and embarked on a rapid expansion of the business. The widow Jane Hewett must surely have been pleased with this match, for, as time would show, her son-in-law was a kind, well-liked and public-spirited man, as well as an enterprising businessman.

Encouraged by James's success, his brother Robert, thirteen years his junior, who had previously tended the family farm in Llangarron, came out to join him in 1852. In 1857, the alliance between the Hewetts and Maxfields was consolidated when Robert married Susan, the youngest of Jane's daughters. In later life Jane seems to have looked to her daughters and sons-in-law more than to her sons for her support, as did her two still-unmarried daughters, Mary Ann and Jane. That the daughters stayed closest to their mother and sisters hardly needs explanation, but the link may have been stronger because the Maxfields also had the houseroom and money to accommodate their extended kin. I will return to their story in Chapter 6.

As they scattered to different points of the compass, the Hewett children took up different stations in society. Their prospects in the new land were governed by many factors, including their native intelligence, skills, capital (if any) and personal charm, but making a new life also depended on the kind of marriage they made. A good marriage could make a man or woman, as a bad one could undo them. Whom they married was influenced, in part at least, by their relative bargaining power in a colonial marriage market where women were in shorter supply than men. While the Hewett boys John, Robert and Richard, who had been born into the middling ranks of rural society, married down into the unskilled urban working class, Lucy and Susan married into their own stratum of society, even perhaps a shade higher.

Why, in a colony where women were in short supply, and the overwhelming majority married, did two of Jane's daughters, Mary

Ann and Jane, not do so? Were they too plain? Did they simply fail to meet men they found congenial or of their own class? Was there even, perhaps, some psychological residue of the voyage of the *Culloden*, and the unwanted attentions of fellow passengers and crew, that put them off matrimony for life? It is intriguing that Jane, who was eighteen when she disembarked, gave her age as fourteen to my grandfather: did she prefer to think of herself arriving as an innocent child rather than as a young woman? There is no answer to these questions. The sisters' long spinsterhood in a society of couples is one of the many voids the sources regrettably do not permit us to fill.

HENRY

One other member of the family was conspicuously absent from all these marriage plans—Henry Hewett, Jane's eldest child. As a farmer accustomed to English agricultural methods and to running things his own way, he may have faced the biggest challenge of all the Hewett children in adapting to life in a colony of big squatting runs. He was present as a witness to his brother Robert's wedding in Melbourne in March 1851 but not at his sister Lucy's four months later. By 1855, he was apparently living near Beechworth, a mining area in northeast Victoria, but working some sixty kilometres away at Little Billabong near Holbrook in southern New South Wales. It was shearing season, and he may have been working on the large station recently purchased by a big squatter, William Henry Williams. On 5 August 1855, he died, aged only 32, in mysterious circumstances. An inquest found that, like his father, he had died of 'apoplexy'. He was the third of the Hewetts' male heirs to die prematurely, but not the last member of the family to die of the disease, which may have been hereditary. He appears to have died suddenly and alone. Reverend Henry Elliott of Albury, a parish with a radius of over a hundred miles, rode out to bury him the next day.

His younger sister Jane later recalled that Henry had gone 'on the land', and his burial certificate described him as a 'settler', yet the circumstances suggest an unsettled life. The swagman, camping by a billabong and dying mysteriously far from home, is a legendary figure immortalised in Banjo Paterson's famous song 'Waltzing Matilda'. Years ago, in a study of the patterns of geographical mobility in colonial Australia, I was struck by the hundreds of inquests into the deaths of men who died alone in the bush—a 'lonely tribe of rogues, runaways and rolling stones who wandered by choice', as I called them. Some, I speculated, had been unlucky in love, while others were black sheep, alcoholics or psychological cripples. I little thought that one of my own relations was among them.

I wonder how news of this tragedy affected his mother, Jane, and her other children. In an age before railways and the overland telegraph, when the Southern Highway was no more than a dusty track and letters from rural New South Wales had to make their way back circuitously through Sydney and by coastal vessel to Melbourne, word of his death may not have reached his family for weeks, too late to permit anyone to attend his funeral. In happier circumstances, Henry would have taken over the lease of Hook Farm, tilling the land his father and grandfather had tilled before him. Jane must surely have wished that Australia had offered her firstborn the chance of a farm and family of his own. Henry died six years before the passage of the Robertson Land Act challenged the stranglehold of the squatters and opened up land for free selection in New South Wales; the land around Little Billabong would then become one of the hotspots of conflict between squatters and selectors. As well as missing the chance to farm his own land, Henry had not enjoyed the stability of marriage and a family. In the busy marriage market of Melbourne, willing brides were still outnumbered by would-be husbands, and in the bush the balance was even less favourable. His was a sad and lonely fate, although not an unusual one.

Reflecting on its pathos, I recently detoured from the Hume Highway just northeast of Holbrook in search of Billabong, the place where he had died and perhaps was buried. This is some of the richest and most beautiful pastoral country in the land, drained by the Lachlan River and within sight of the foothills of the Australian Alps. Banjo Paterson knew and loved it well. It pleased me to think of Henry lying at peace in such a beautiful place. I found the gate to Little Billabong Station, crossed Little Billabong Creek, drove along Little Billabong Road, passed Little Billabong Community Hall and even glimpsed a real billabong, a few hundred metres off the road, but found no obvious grave or cemetery. Only when I got home and googled Little Billabong did I discover Henry's probable resting place. According to an environmental impact study carried out after the duplication of the highway, the former Little Billabong cemetery lies in the median strip between the north- and southbound carriageways of the Hume, invisible save for one or two headstones, a mound of tussocky grass and a rusted wire fence. There, within a few metres of the roaring cavalcade of semi-trailers and road trains, unknown to the thousands of drivers who speed by every hour, my kinsman reposes in an unquiet grave.

BAD BLOOD

Lurking in the shadows of this story is the ghost of an ancient superstition: the dread of bad blood. Family historians may no longer hunt for noble or famous ancestors, but they remain nervous of the discovery of bad ones, especially if they fear that their moral or biological failings could be passed on. Perhaps that was why I was relieved when Elizabeth Fenwick, the poor needlewoman, passed the respectability test. And why I was glad that her husband Robert was not the 'blackguard' I first feared him to be. On the other hand, I was a little embarrassed by Richard's spell in Maitland Gaol for forgery. The fear of bad blood surfaced in a different way in the story of Matilda, John's wife, and her sister Ellen, whose catastrophic experiences of infant death raised questions about their genetic propensity to produce unhealthy babies, just as the apoplexy that killed John Hewett, as well as his own father and eldest son, suggested an inherited strain of circulatory disease.

Our continuing fear of bad blood is evidence of a surprising turn in contemporary culture. Democratic societies like Australia were strongly shaped by the struggle against the idea of inheritance. Since convict times, Australians believed that individuals could shape their lives, free from whatever disabilities they suffered because of their parentage. This was the conviction that underlay contemporary arguments on behalf of emancipists—convicts who had paid for their crimes—and native-born Australians, who were generally believed to have escaped the physical or moral defects of their convict parents. English observers, more deeply attached to ideas of tradition and inheritance, liked to remind Australians of their bad blood, as Winston Churchill did in 1942 when he attributed their insistence on withdrawing troops from the Middle East to defend their own shores to 'bad stocks'.

In rejecting the influence of heredity, Australians were convinced that history was on their side. While Robert and Elizabeth were preparing to marry, educated people in England were debating the ideas of the philosopher John Stuart Mill, a strong critic of hereditary institutions. Radicals fought for inheritance taxes to limit the perpetuation of inherited privilege. Inspired by the French and American revolutions, they embraced ideals of fraternity that made fellow citizens brothers and sisters in a larger national family. In eugenic debates about the relative effects of heredity and environment, Australians leaned to the environmental side, confident that Australian sun and economic prosperity corrected whatever bad characteristics their forebears acquired from living in the slums of Europe.

In the early twentieth century it looked as though the democratic principle, in its liberal or socialist forms, would overtake outmoded notions of blood and inheritance. Yet in a way that would have surprised democrats of an earlier generation, ancestry has made a comeback. Inheritance taxes have been repealed. The attempt to redress inherited disadvantage through education has faltered as religious and ethnic communities, and the principle of parental 'choice', have prevailed over the secular state schools. Aboriginal children and others separated from their mothers for adoption have fought and won campaigns to be reunited with their natural parents. In all these ways, ancestry has re-emerged as the basis for new political and social rights and as a core component of personal identity.

The question 'Who do you think you are?' (the title of the popular family history television program) was once asked indignantly, by superiors rebuffing democratic upstarts. Now everyone asks it, but of themselves and pensively, and expects the answer to be found in a family past. As our attachment to larger civic, class or national identities has shrunk, so we cling to the more intimate and enduring world of family. We take refuge from a world dominated by impersonal market forces in our families, 'havens in a heartless world'. The confidence that democratic ideals would prevail over ethnic and family loyalties has receded, along with the grand narratives of liberation that propelled them. 'With the decline of grand narratives has come a more atomised sense of ourselves,' argues the British historian Peter Claus. 'The whole enterprise of genealogy has arguably emerged from a reduced confidence in the ability to reduce the past to a simple universal story.'

Genealogy offers a gateway into an extended family, linked vertically through time rather than horizontally in the present. In a world of confused and multiple identities, it promises a deeper sense of who we are. Going online multiplies these linkages, although with effects we have yet to understand fully. By reuniting us with our kin, across time and space, it extends our family, but the bonds between its members may be emotionally thinner, rather like those between 'friends' on Facebook.

A television advertisement for Ancestry.com soliloquises: 'I typed my name and date of birth and, step by step, decades were crossed. When I was lost, my ancestry tree showed me the way that led to you. And I saw you—coming home.' In a few keystrokes, the narrator, once 'lost', has come home. She has been delivered from something more than the technical pitfalls of genealogical research. Her 'ancestry tree' has reunited her with an intimate but unspecified 'you'—perhaps a beloved forebear, or that other self who emerges in response to the question 'Who do you think you are?' The family one meets online is a virtual family in two senses: it belongs in cyberspace, not physical space, and in the past, not the present. It invites us to share the triumphs and tragedies of our forebears but without the emotional vulnerability it would entail in real life. Knowledge of their lives may elicit pride, pity, curiosity or shame but none of the anxiety, remorse, jealousy, anger and irritation that bedevil family relationships in the present.

If identity is a kind of conversation with our forebears, then it is often only a one-way conversation. We tend to draw from the family past only as much of their story as we find confirming of our own sense of self. So Australians may boast of their convict ancestors, but only because they have managed to turn them into political rebels, victims of social injustice and 'founders of the nation' rather than the career criminals they often were. Family history has been largely purged of the patriarchal assumptions and eugenic concerns that once shaped it, but its sympathies often remain narrow. Questions of shame and honour may have receded, but they have not entirely disappeared. In an age when traditional family structures are in radical dissolution, the family historian may now be more pleased than sorry to find forebears with matrimonial disasters of their own, but may flinch from a more radical questioning of the role of the family in society. By situating our families in the throes of history, and viewing their individual experiences against the background of their times, we take a first step towards making family history something more than a private hobby. It is here that genealogy, memory and history may become partners in a shared civic endeavour.

Wesley Hill took its name from the Wesleyan Church, the first on the goldfields, planted above the reefs and gullies of Forest Creek in 1852. Robert Hewett 'pitched his tent' on Sailors' Flat (right) in 1852 and later purchased a double block of land on the top of the hill at the point where the road deviates opposite the Welsh Calvinist Church where he built a simple cottage. Other significant features of the landscape are Little Bendigo, home of the Hewetts' kinsmen the Swallings, the Melbourne and Murray River Railway, and the cemetery reserve at Pennyweight Flat (top). (Map of Castlemaine, Victorian Mines Department, 1861 (detail), State Library of Victoria)

CHAPTER FIVE
Wesley Hill

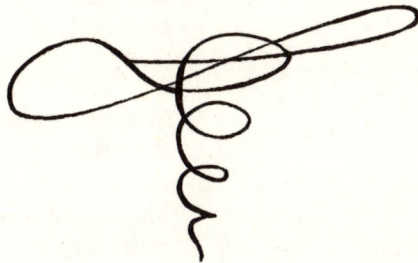

At Elphinstone, about a hundred kilometres north of Melbourne, the Calder Highway divides. One branch heads north towards Bendigo, while the other, the Pyrenees Highway, winds west along the valley of Forest Creek towards Castlemaine. Near the village of Chewton, the woodland thins into clumps of spindly eucalypt, and you enter one of the most remarkable manmade landscapes in Australia. This is not a country patiently moulded over centuries to human needs and desires, like Hampshire or Tuscany, or like the land the Aboriginal people carefully tended before the Europeans came. It is the product of a sudden assault. Historian Geoffrey Blainey calls such places 'pummelled landscapes'. Over the years, the scars of the attack have faded, but they are still easily visible. The skin of precious topsoil has been broken and its flesh exposed and bruised. Along the valley,

THE HEWETTS OF WESLEY HILL

Robert Hewett
1828–1894
m.
Elizabeth Fenwick
1824–1879

Annie Mary
1852–1924
m.
John Newbury Swalling
1848–1941
8 children

Clara Jane
1853–1942

Elizabeth Jane
1855–1945
m.
Thomas Morecroft
1860–1894
3 children

Robert Henry
1859–1933
m. **Susan Stephens**
1856–1918
4 children

Edward John
1862–1862

Francis Deacon
1863–1954
m.
Keziah Burrows
1857–1940
1 child

hillocks of raw clay and jagged gullies filled with gorse mark the pitiless advance of the attacker.

These are the ruins of what was once the largest alluvial goldfield in the world. In 1852, about 30,000 people—almost as many as had recently lived in Melbourne itself—camped along Forest Creek. Men in dungarees and cabbage-tree hats laboured for up to eighteen hours a day, covered from head to foot in yellowish clay. They burrowed into the creek's banks, shovelled its sandy bottom into cradles, sank shafts deep into its underground tributaries, and polluted its waters with their dishwater and excrement. The air was filled with the sound of pick and shovel on rock, and the rhythmic rattle and swish of cradles. Observers likened the scene to a burial ground, with mounds of fresh earth interspersed with open graves. The landscape the miners left was a work of sheer muscle power almost unaided by horses or steam engines. The pummelling was mostly human. It would be pummelled again later in the century by steam-powered water jets and sluices, but its contours had been set by 1860.

According to family tradition, in 1852 Robert Hewett 'pitched his tent' in Sailor's Gully, in the midst of this manmade desert. The phrase 'pitched his tent' echoes the Genesis story of Abraham who 'pitched his tent in Bethel', and so casts Robert as our colonial patriarch. Sailor's Gully closely adjoins Englishman's Gully and was named, it was said, in memory of a sailor who died after a bout of heavy drinking. Names like 'Englishman's Gully', 'German Gully', 'Scotchman's Gully', 'New Chum Gully', 'Manchester Flat', 'Adelaide Flat' and the 'Welsh Village' evoke the 'clannish spirit' among the first parties of alluvial miners. Exactly when Robert pitched his tent and who joined him there we do not know. Robert and Elizabeth's first child, Annie Mary, had been born in Richmond on 29 February 1852, and mother and baby may have stayed on in Melbourne before joining Robert later in the year. His elder brother John and other members of the family may also have tried their luck at Forest Creek during this first hectic phase of the rush.

I wonder how the boy from Hook Farm, accustomed to the soft green fields, brown loam and gurgling brooks of the Hampshire countryside, viewed his new home. 'We came a long way to make a fortune,' one digger recalled. 'Our longing eyes at length obtained a view of the Eldorado—Forest Creek . . . The whole scene to a new chum was one of unspeakable squalor.' Instead of the rustic charm of Wood Plain, Ash Coppice and Wild Herons, Robert found himself in a landscape, at once intimate and harsh, of 'hills' and 'flats', 'points' and 'gullies' shaped by the fickle fortunes of gold-digging. Good luck left its mark on Golden Point—on several of them, in fact—while misfortune was inscribed on Poverty Gully, Hard Hill, Shicer Gully ('shicer' meaning an unproductive mine) and Pennyweight Flat. Murderer's Hill, Deadman's Gully and Cemetery Gully alluded to an even grimmer feature of goldfields life, the possibility of violent death.

LOVE IN A TENT

Writers and artists converged on the valley to record what everyone realised was an epochal event. In 1851–52, the artist David Tulloch made a series of delightful sketches of 'The Gold Diggings at Mount Alexander' that were later published by the Melbourne engraver and printer Thomas Ham. A set of these pictures, inherited from my grandfather Vic Hewett, now hangs in our dining room. Vic was born in nearby Campbell's Creek and often returned to Castlemaine throughout his life. When his grandfather Robert died in 1894, Vic was twelve, old enough to have heard him reminisce about the gold era.

To our eye, Tulloch's images are static and stilted. The artist seems to be trying, against the odds, to make chaos picturesque. Yet they remain an illuminating record of Forest Creek in the summer of 1851–52, about the time Robert pitched his tent in Sailor's Gully. In one, *Golden Point, Mt Alexander*, a party of diggers is captured in the act of pitching a tent. Tulloch collapses the stages of the operation—cutting tent poles from the surrounding bush, lashing them together, hammering posts into the ground, covering the frame with canvas, and making tea after the job has been done—into a single composite image. In the background, hundreds of diggers swarm across the land, each within a small patch of ground, digging, pushing wheelbarrows, chatting, lounging. One fires a rifle into the surrounding bush—perhaps aiming at a wallaby or parrot, both prized as game in the early days of the rush. In the far distance, the flag of the Gold Commissioner's tent announces the arrival of authority.

A party of miners erects a tent while a woman and her children look on. Men outnumbered women three to one on the Castlemaine goldfield, not quite as much as this sketch suggests. Golden Point, the field depicted here, was the scene of the first major protest against the hated licence fee in December 1851. (Engraving by Thomas Ham from a sketch by David Tulloch (detail), author's collection)

On the far right of the picture, overlooking the diggings, a solitary woman stands outside her tent. Wearing an apron and kerchief, she is nursing a baby and holding hands with a little girl. It could be Elizabeth Hewett, who arrived at Forest Creek with a babe in arms, and gave birth to two more daughters, Clara Jane in October 1853 and Elizabeth Jane in June 1855, while the family was still living under canvas. Men far outnumbered women on the goldfields, especially during the first phase of the rush, but not as much as Tulloch's engraving suggests. 'It is now getting the fashion for good housewives to follow their lords to the mines,' the teacher and writer James Bonwick noted in 1852. 'The filth, disorder, the domestic misery give place at the presence of a female to cleanliness, regularity and comfort.' The solitary woman in Tulloch's sketch is as a symbol of maternity and domesticity, values jettisoned for the moment in the headlong pursuit of gold but at the heart of the diggers' aspirations for the time beyond the rush. These yearnings did not take long to assume material form. 'Everywhere tents may be seen enclosed within bush fences, and a "wee bit o' garden" under process of cultivation,' the *Mount Alexander Mail* observed in 1854. 'Few of the tents are without that appendage which betokens permanence—a stone or mud chimney,' it later reported.

Keeping house in a tent and caring for small children amid the hazards of the diggings must have taxed Elizabeth's vigilance, domestic skills and sheer stamina. Until piped water arrived from the dammed-up waters of the Coliban River, miners depended on often-polluted nearby creeks or expensive supplies carted by horse or bullock. For mothers and especially children, the diggings were also a potential death trap. A few hundred metres from Sailor's Gully was the Pennyweight Flat cemetery, now often called the Children's Cemetery because of the large number of children buried there in the early 1850s. The causes of death recorded in its register are a dismal catalogue of the hazards of childhood on the diggings: accidental drowning, dysentery, diarrhoea, convulsions, slow fever, measles, inflammation of the lungs, accidentally killed, accidentally shot, accidentally burnt, falling into a waterhole.

The dangers of life on the diggings became a lively theme in the recollections of Castlemaine's pioneers. Years later, Clara Jane, the second of the Hewett children, recalled that during the family's years under canvas her father had slept with a pistol under his pillow. She lived on in Castlemaine until 1942 and told the story to her niece Millie Morecroft. Millie, who grew up in the same household as Clara, relayed it to John Boothroyd when he interviewed her in 1983, and John, in turn, to me. Did Clara really remember seeing the pistol under the pillow herself? She was only four or five when the family ceased to live under canvas. It is just as likely that the story was told and retold by the parents, and then by their children, to reinforce their pioneering credentials and Robert's image as the strong father and protector. Who was he protecting them against? In Millie's recollections, Clara's memories of the pistol are mingled with talk of thieves, of Chinese immigrants working over the mullock left by earlier diggers, and of Aboriginals loitering on the edge of the fields.

Robert and Elizabeth's tent was as close as the Hewetts came to a home of their own in the 1850s. In April 1853, other members of the family gathered there when Reverend John Cheyne, the only Church of England clergyman on the diggings, celebrated the wedding of Elizabeth's nineteen-year-old sister Alice Fenwick to James Wyatt, a 27-year-old baker from Dover. Alice had worked as a servant on the property of the wealthy squatter Captain Langdon on the nearby Loddon River. When she married, however, she and Wyatt were both living in Forest Creek. They would move away from Castlemaine, have four children, and live in several places, mainly in the goldfields, before Alice died, aged only 39, in 1873.

Among the other wedding guests was 37-year-old Elizabeth Whiting, who had recently emigrated to Victoria with her husband Joseph, Alice and Elizabeth's 50-year-old uncle. Her presence is the first evidence that the Hewetts had an extended colonial family beyond the company of the *Culloden*. Joseph was a widower with six grown-up children when he married Elizabeth in 1850, but, lured by gold and the prospect of a fresh start, they set off to the Antipodes, leaving most of his old family behind. They tried their luck in Forest Creek before moving to Ballarat, where Joseph had mixed fortunes as a blacksmith. They also began a new family. Their first child, Robert Whiting, born on Forest Creek in 1855, would become rich far beyond the dreams of his parents. He qualified as a lawyer, married into a prosperous Bendigo family, acquired pastoral properties in Victoria and Queensland, as well as rubber and cocoa plantations in Papua and residences in South Yarra and Mount Macedon. He had accumulated a fortune of £90,000 by the time he died on the eve of the Great Depression. By then his humble origins had been left behind: his obituary says he was born in Melbourne, not Forest Creek.

SETTLING

By the mid-1850s, as the alluvial phase of the gold rush subsided, the camps began to merge into a town. At the junction between Forest Creek and its tributaries, government surveyors laid out the town of Castlemaine on the standard rectangular plan. Beyond the grid, however, the settlement sprawled along the spindly network of camps and tracks created by the diggers themselves. Even today the logic of its evolution is plainly visible. From Chewton to Castlemaine, the highway winds along a narrow isthmus between old mine workings. Tiny brick and timber cottages, interspersed with pubs, a mechanics' institute, the world's smallest 'town hall', and several disused churches, mostly of the Methodist persuasion, line the route. Near Castlemaine, you reach Wesley Hill, named after the founder of Methodism, John Wesley, whose followers erected a chapel on the rise overlooking Pennyweight Flat in 1852. By the 1860s, this humble building had already become a shrine. 'While Batman's Hill [in Melbourne] was the first place in Victoria where the gospel was preached, Wesley

Hill was the first place on the "goldfields" on which a Methodist or any other place of worship was erected,' the *Wesleyan Chronicle* noted in 1864.

As children, we sometimes accompanied my mother on nostalgic journeys 'back to Castlemaine'. As we approached the crest of Wesley Hill, she would point out a red-stuccoed two-storey house, its gable end clearly visible from afar. 'The Ranch', as it was known in the family, was a converted pub where Mum's grandfather, Robert Henry Hewett, son of the patriarch, spent his retirement. A picturesque building with a narrow veranda, it would not have been out of place in a Drysdale painting.

Only years later, and almost as an afterthought, did she point to a humbler cottage, about a hundred metres back along Duke Street, shielded by a high paling fence and unruly hedge. Located next to what is now the Bold Café, and opposite the Welsh Calvinist Church—now the site of a popular Saturday market—it was Robert Hewett's first permanent home, a four-room brick cottage built by the carpenter himself. It sits well forward on and to one side of its wide allotment, with a doorless façade to the street, leaving a large backyard and side garden. It is one of the oddest houses I know—a clumsy, almost illegible testament to one man's valiant effort to create a home in a new land. When my mother first pointed it out, the owners kindly invited us in to look about our ancestral home. 'When did you come here?' I asked as we were about to leave. 'Just a few years ago,' they replied. 'Oh well,' I responded, 'if you should ever think of selling, let me know.' 'Why did you say that?' my wife Barbara remonstrated when we got in the car. 'It wouldn't suit us at all.' She was right, of course, but at that moment I wasn't looking for a suitable weekender; I was imaginatively reclaiming my patrimony.

Robert had bought the allotment at a public auction of 'suburban lands' on 22 December 1856, paying three pounds, nine shillings and five pence for about one-eighth of an acre. In December 1851, Forest Creek had become the first flashpoint in the wave of digger protests against the hated gold licence that culminated in the Eureka rebellion three years later. From the beginning, the political grievances of the miners were rooted in the demand for political and social rights, including the right to land. Even before the formation of the Land Convention and its demand to 'unlock the lands' of the squatters, miners were demanding freer access to land on the goldfields. As the camp became a town, its inhabitants sought the permanence and security of their own homes. In many gold towns, miners were able to exercise the miner's right to build houses on the land they mined, but in Castlemaine, where the alluvial phase of mining quickly passed, land was more often purchased as freehold.

'Extensive suburban land-sales are anticipated,' the local correspondent for the *Argus* reported in June 1856. On the three days preceding Christmas, more than a hundred allotments of town and suburban land bordering the road from Chewton to Castlemaine and in the neighbouring villages of Fryerstown, Guildford and Campbell's Creek were put up for sale. Robert purchased his lot at the 'upset' or reserve price of £30 an acre, a bargain in our eyes, although higher than the prices prevailing only a few months earlier. Robert joined the lucky half of Castlemaine householders who owned their own home, a lower proportion than in the larger mining towns like Ballarat and Bendigo, where home ownership reached 80 per cent, but higher than in the capital cities, and incomparably higher than in England.

When Robert began building, more than two-thirds of Castlemaine families were still living in tents. Most of them were alluvial miners, still the largest proportion of the population. The houses of the rest were very modest, usually of no more than two rooms, so Robert's house was substantial by local standards. With the birth of his fourth child and first son, Robert Henry, in 1859, his family's need of living space was growing. He had already gone back to his old trade as a carpenter. With the Scottish contractor David Borland, he helped construct some of the public and private buildings that began to give the town a more permanent and dignified character in the later 1850s. As the alluvial rush came to an end, however, many diggers departed for new fields, and Castlemaine began a slow decline. Its population would more than halve over the following two decades, and the busting of the speculative mining boom around 1859–60 hit it hard. In October 1861, Robert was declared bankrupt, with debts of £96 19s and assets of only £57 10s. 'Depression and losses in trade, together with pressure of a creditor' were the causes given to the Insolvency Court.

For the next twenty years, Robert's livelihood, and the fortunes of his family, relied on the uneven flow of contracts for government offices, railway stations, gaols, factories, hospitals, schools and commercial buildings. 'Mr Hewett was an excellent tradesman and was often sought for when good work had to be done,' one of his acquaintances recalled. His fine joinery is probably to be seen, if only one could identify it, in many of the buildings that helped to endow Castlemaine with a solidity and dignity that visitors now recognise in its covered market and imposing town hall. Surrounded by a pummelled landscape stripped bare of nature's adornments, the gold-rush generation did penance for their vandalism by creating elegant streets, parks and civic buildings.

THE HOUSE THAT ROBERT BUILT

If the house Robert built on Wesley Hill now strikes us as odd it is probably because it had to be improvised in response to the needs of his growing family, using whatever spare hours and materials he could salvage from his working days. Most of the joinery in the house is made from imported timber, some—like the French window that appears in an early photograph—probably salvaged from other building projects. The house was probably built in stages, with new sections being added as the family grew and its economic circumstances changed. It was a product of 'sweat equity' and barter, with Robert possibly offering his own labour as a carpenter in return for the services of a local bricklayer.

The typical miner's cottage was a wooden box with a gabled roof, a chimney at one end, and a lean-to kitchen at the back. As the family grew, they simply added more boxes, each with its own gable, creating a characteristic zigzag roofline. In his classic book *Australia's Home* (1952), architect Robin Boyd identifies the 'primitive cottage' as the first and most popular of the five principal plans followed by colonial Australian homebuilders. But Robert Hewett's house seems to follow none of these sensible plans. It consists of two rectangular hip-roofed brick rooms, each about five metres by four, and five metres high, separated by a low, skillion-roofed timber section consisting of two smaller rooms.

Exactly how, and in what sequence, the rooms were built remains something of a mystery. Did Robert build the two larger brick rooms intending to link them with an intermediate brick section of similar generous proportions, only to be forced, perhaps by his financial straits around 1861, to complete the house on a more modest scale? Or were the substantial brick sections constructed as wings to an earlier and more modest two-room cottage? Perhaps the cottage succeeded an earlier tent: Robert Henry, born three years after the purchase of the allotment on Wesley Hill, claimed to have been born under canvas.

To try to solve the puzzle, I returned to the house, now owned by Dugald McLellan, an art historian. I brought along my friend Tony Dingle, an economic historian who has restored a miner's cottage in nearby Maldon. He noticed features of the house I had missed, like the irregular shape of the handmade bricks in the central 'cottage' section compared with the more regular manufactured bricks used in the wings. We climbed down a ladder into a large cellar under the kitchen, from where we could view the stone footings and see under the floor of what we now decided was the first part of the house to be built, the two-room cottage. Originally the cottage would have had a gable roof, just like that on other nearby miner's cottages; but once the wings were added, the top of the gable would have projected above the gutter of the wing. So the roof was re-pitched as a skillion and now projects low over the entrance. Like a cap pulled low over its face, the new roofline obscures the original façade. As we investigated the house, I was on the lookout for some mark, however small, of the builder and the lives of its original inhabitants. In the cellar, Tony pointed out the precise mortice and tenon joints in the hardwood floor joists, surely the work of an English craftsman builder like Robert Hewett rather than a rough Australian bush carpenter.

How the Hewetts lived in the house is another puzzle. When Robert began to build, he had just three small children, all girls, but with the birth of two sons, Robert Henry in 1859 and Francis Deacon in 1863, the family grew to seven. This was a modest household by Castlemaine standards (the average size of completed families in Castlemaine in 1861 was almost eight children). Like other contemporary working-class families, the Hewetts would probably have used rooms flexibly, for both living and sleeping space. The age of the separate bathroom and laundry, let alone the lounge and dining room, was a long way off. The four rooms were arranged one behind the other, so that three were essentially corridors, leaving little privacy except in the large high-ceilinged room at the rear—probably the parents' bedroom. To us, the house looks small and inconvenient, but the Hewetts were much better housed than many working people of the time. Nevertheless, when we think of the Victorian family we need to think of it living under physical circumstances as straitened as Victorian morality.

'A STUPENDOUS UNDERTAKING'

On 15 October 1862, the people of Wesley Hill greeted the railway age. It is difficult now to recapture the extraordinary imaginative impact of what Charles Dickens aptly called 'railway dreaming'. The ease and rapidity with which people could now travel from place to place seemed to induce a novel mental state. At a blow, the expense and fatigue of the two- or three-day road journey to the goldfields were eliminated. A train carrying the Governor, Sir Henry Barkly, and other distinguished visitors had set off from Melbourne at 9.15 and passed through Kyneton in the mid-morning. Shortly before noon it emerged from a long tunnel at Elphinstone, crossed Forest Creek at Chewton, and chugged along the valley. It passed through Wesley Hill in a cutting just a hundred metres or so behind Robert's house before beginning a long, looping descent over a twelve-metre-high brick viaduct to Castlemaine station. Along the line, crowds of excited townsfolk gathered under the triumphal arches erected at each bridge, tunnel and viaduct.

Robert was just ten years old when the London and Southampton Railway arrived in Hook, an event almost coinciding with his father's death, the first in the chain of circumstances that led to his family's eviction and emigration. But the coming of the Murray River Railway, the most expensive public project completed in Australia to that time, would shape his family's life in more benign ways. Castlemaine had fought hard to persuade the government to divert the line through the town. Its leaders knew that if the railway bypassed it, the town was doomed. There was general rejoicing when the contractor for the new line, John Bruce, announced that he would live in Castlemaine and build a large foundry to supply rails, girders and other components of the 'stupendous undertaking'. 'It is not unreasonable to conclude that a large proportion of that money will find its way into Castlemaine. There's a good time coming,' the *Mount Alexander Mail* exulted.

Overnight, the mining town got an industrial base. Almost two thousand men were employed locally in construction activity, eight hundred as quarrymen and navvies, and about half that number as blacksmiths, metal founders and engineers. For local boys like Robert Hewett's sons, Robert Henry and Frank, the tall chimney on Cornish and Bruce's foundry heralded a new era of opportunity. The new jobs called for more brain than brawn, more precision than force, more punctuality than perseverance, more prudence than risk, more literacy, numeracy and knowledge of the wider world. 'The making of Australian railways . . . needed trained and systematic thought,' historian Alan Atkinson noted. Better than anything else, the locomotive symbolised 'the newly independent power of colonial peoples'.

MIDDLE AGE

I have followed the journey of Robert and Elizabeth from England to Australia, and from infancy to middle age, without finding so much as a word in their own handwriting or a glimpse of their appearance. Only in solid middle age, in a pair of portraits taken in T.D. Ferris's Bendigo photographic studio, which operated from 1866 to 1872, do we at last discover what they actually looked like. The face, it is said, is a mirror of the soul. These days we are used to the pocket camera or mobile phone, capable of instantly capturing our unguarded moods and expressions. But photography in the 1860s and 1870s was a more formal and contrived process. The subjects posed in the artificial setting of a photographic studio and were required to hold a set unsmiling pose for the two or three seconds that it took for their negative image to be fixed on the glass plate from which a print was made. They usually wore their best attire, and the photographer took trouble to ensure that they turned their best side to the camera.

Robert Hewett looks to have been a shy, even reluctant, subject. He sits awkwardly across the chair as though to avoid looking into the camera, legs astride and feet splayed, one hand resting on the back of the chair, the other tightly clenched. He wears an ill-fitting lounge or smoking jacket (a prop supplied by the photographer perhaps?) over a plain woollen vest and trousers. (The lounge jacket, an item of fashionable working-class attire in the 1870s, was the prototype of the modern lounge suit.) His slicked-down hair and bushy beard frame a face whose most striking feature, a strong aquiline beak, his descendants will dub 'the Hewett nose'. Is this, I wonder, the face and deportment of a shy country boy, robbed of a father when he was only ten years old, uprooted from his home and village in his early twenties, and now trying to accommodate himself to a fate he had never chosen?

Elizabeth, on the other hand, appears more at ease: was she the instigator of this photographic expedition? A plain, matronly woman, she is determined, nonetheless, to make the most of herself. Her hair is carefully and elaborately braided, and her ample girth is swathed in yards of rumpled satin. She wears a brooch and pendant earrings. Her arm rests comfortably on a pedestal, and the hint of a smile plays around her lips. In her late forties, she is, to be blunt, overweight. Faced with the photographic evidence, I am compelled to admit that Thackeray, who doubted the physical charms of the *Culloden*'s female emigrants, may have had a point. Reared in poverty and sometimes close to starvation, Elizabeth had evidently taken with relish to the colonial diet of bread, meat three times a day, and perhaps strong drink. The handwritten 'Collection of Valuable Recipes by Mrs Hewett' found among the contents of the Duke Street house contained more than a dozen recipes for wine and 'good cheap beer', made from elderberry, parsnip, grape, raisin, ginger, barley, gooseberry, damson and currant, as well as hops.

The photographic expedition had a sad sequel. In June 1879, the little community at Wesley Hill was shocked by news of Elizabeth's sudden death. She had been unwell for some time but was 'able to go about'. She had made an expedition into town and returned with a cold for which she had taken 'the ordinary domestic remedies'. But on the twenty-fourth her condition worsened. Her son—probably twenty-year-old Robert Henry—ran for Dr Malcolm, a long-serving and respected local doctor, but by the time he arrived it was too late. An autopsy found 'that the body of the deceased was loaded with fat and that the liver was enormously large'. 'Fatty degeneration of the heart' was the coroner's finding. The commonest causes of fatty degeneration of the heart and liver were alcoholism and obesity. We know, from her photograph, that Elizabeth was obese; whether she was also a heavy drinker is less clear. According to the fiction she had

Elderberry wine

Take of cold soft water 16 gallons
Malaga raisins, 50 lb
Elderberries, 4 gallons
red tarter, in fine powder, 4 oz
Mix ginger in power, 5 oz
cinnamon, cloves, and mace of each 2 oz
3 oranges or lemons, peel and juice then add
1 gallon of brandy.
This will make 18 gallons.

maintained for her 29 years in the colony, now inscribed on her death certificate, she was 51 years of age—although we know that she was actually almost four years older. Over-indulgence was probably only half the story: the combined effects of a decade of domestic service, emigration, separation from her family, childbirth and the rigours of keeping house under canvas had also taken their toll. Two days later, her husband Robert, his family and a little company of mourners left the house at Wesley Hill to follow the body of his 'late beloved wife' to the Congregational section of Campbell's Creek cemetery.

LEAVING HOME

By the time Elizabeth died, her children were almost off her hands. The eldest, Annie Mary, was only nineteen when she married 23-year-old John Newbury Swalling from nearby Little Bendigo in 1871. Swalling was a stalwart member of the Wesley Hill Wesleyan church, just a few doors from the Hewetts'. During the 1870s, the Swallings' first children, William, Barbara and Bertha—the Hewetts' first grandchildren—arrived, reinforcing the bond between the two families. John Swalling, a decade older than Robert Henry and Frank, assumed the role of a kindly elder brother. He was a patternmaker by trade, and an employee of Thompson's Engineering Works (which had succeeded Cornish and Bruce as the town's largest industrial employer), as well as an enthusiastic inventor—he patented a metal clothes peg of his own design. John may have spoken for Robert Henry when he too was apprenticed to the metal trades as an engineer, perhaps at Thompson's. An enthusiasm for things mechanical and a respect for good craftsmanship seem to have been qualities fostered in both households. After his death, Robert, the English carpenter, was praised for his 'kind heartedness and willingness to help [younger members of the trade] in difficult work, and as a result many of them became good tradesmen'. His own younger son, Frank, was among his pupils, learning his trade as a carpenter from his father before winning a government appointment as an inspector of public works at the age of only 23.

These family influences were probably more important than formal schooling in shaping the futures of Robert and Elizabeth's children. In the 1850s, when their daughters reached school age, Forest Creek was an educational wilderness. There were almost no schools, and little interest for the moment in building them. 'The absence of education amongst so large a portion of the Colonists could not but be contemplated with apprehension,' A.B. Orbelar, a school inspector, noted in 1853. Three years later, when the foundation stone of the first National School building (later State School number 119) was laid, more than one thousand townsfolk attended the ceremonies. It was gratifying, the presiding officer observed, 'to have laid the foundations of a building to promote education where not long ago there was nothing but nomadic barbarism'. But the town's educational ambitions far exceeded its grasp: for each of the seventy or eighty children enrolled in the school there were four or five others of primary school age apparently unprovided for. It was probably not until the mid-1860s, when Robert Henry and Frank reached school age, that educational places and school-age population approached equilibrium.

The Hewett children sat in overcrowded classrooms where over-burdened teachers marched them through the Three Rs, with only occasional detours into History, Geography and other branches of Useful Knowledge. Attendance was low: teachers waged an unceasing battle against truancy, unpunctuality, untidiness and inattention. Few pupils emerged without being able to read, write and count, but fewer still with a basis for higher learning. How you got on after school depended on whether your family had a business or trade, whether a friend of the family offered you a job or an apprenticeship, or whether a local politician found you a government job.

Robert Henry had been fortunate enough to get an engineering apprenticeship, but his prospects depended very much on Castlemaine's precarious future as an industrial centre. In the early 1870s, as the mining industry continued to decline and the first phase of railway development came to a close, local politicians began to lobby the Victorian government to create a regional railway workshop in the town, perhaps utilising the buildings recently vacated by Cornish and Bruce. By the early 1880s, as Melbourne boomed, the exodus of young people from the mining towns became a flood. Remembering the 'good time' that followed the town's first railway boom, Castlemaine's city fathers fastened their hopes of stemming the outflow on the plan for a local railway workshop. 'The townspeople of Castlemaine would not rest until railway workshops were established in the town,' Mayor J.A. James declared. Robert Henry and his family may have been among those sharing his hope.

In 1880, the 21-year-old engineer married 24-year-old Susan Stephens from Campbell's Creek. It was a quiet wedding in the manse of the Independent Church. Robert's mother had only recently died, and Susan's mother, herself a widow, may have been happy to be spared the expense and fuss of a larger celebration. The couple lived, for the time being, with the bride's family at Campbell's Creek, where their first son, my grandfather Victor, was born in 1882. By 1883, with the appointment of a new railways administration, it was already clear that the town's prospects of industrial revival were remote. If the railways workshop would not come to Castlemaine, young men like Robert Henry would have to go to Melbourne, where the railways, like everything else, were rapidly being centralised.

But the railways were a division of the public service, subject to the vagaries of political patronage. If you wanted a job in the railways, you asked your local member, who might intercede with a political ally or, if he happened to be a minister, appoint you himself. James Patterson, an English-born immigrant, had arrived in Castlemaine in 1852, the same year as the Hewetts. A butcher by trade, his slaughter yards were just down the road from Wesley Hill at Chewton. In a small community with relatively few long stayers, he and Robert senior were probably at least nodding acquaintances. Patterson became mayor of Chewton in the 1860s, before entering the Victorian Parliament

Lychgate of the churchyard of St Nicholas Church, Newnham Green, Hampshire, the last resting place of the yeoman farmer John Hewett. His widow, Jane, emigrated with her eight children to Port Phillip in 1850.

The White Hart Inn (now Hotel), established in the eighteenth century, operated as a staging post for coaches on the road from London to Portsmouth and Southampton. Publican James Hewett looked across the road to Hook Farm, home of his sister-in-law Jane.

Jane Hewett was in her early eighties when the German-born photographer Herman Moser took this image between 1871 and 1874. Found among images of other members of the family in the house at Wesley Hill, it is most likely the matriarch herself.

'A Collection of Valuable Recipes by Mrs Hewett', copied by several hands into an 1858 cashbook and left among the relics of the house at Wesley Hill, gathers the family's stock of household lore from the old country and the new.

The carpenter Robert Hewett (Jane's third son) and his wife, Elizabeth (née Fenwick), the former needlewoman, visited a Bendigo photographer sometime in the late 1860s to pose for these companion portraits.

Pioneer photographer Richard Daintree captured the manmade devastation of the Forest Creek diggings in this view of Golden Point in 1858. The taller buildings on the horizon line the highway where Robert Hewett began to build his house in this year. (State Library of Victoria)

Robert Hewett's house at Wesley Hill viewed from the side garden. The low-slung central section, constructed with hand-made bricks, was probably the first to be built, but the original gable was replaced with a skillion roof when the kitchen and bedroom wings were added.

The house at Wesley Hill viewed from Duke Street, c. 1900. The children are Robert Hewett's grandchildren, Agnes, Millie and Clara Morecroft, who shared the house with their widowed mother, Elizabeth, and maiden aunt, Clara. They are photographed with a neighbour, Mr Smith.

Interior of the kitchen at Wesley Hill today. With its underground cellar, the room appears to have been designed as a kitchen, but was later used by Robert's daughter Clara as a bedroom.

Kitchen garden at 'The Ranch', 1920s. In retirement, Robert Henry Hewett, Robert's son, returned to Wesley Hill, buying this former pub a few doors from the house his father built; he spent his time growing vegetables and entertaining his grandchildren. His sisters still lived in the family home.

Langstone Mill, the childhood home of James and Robert Maxfield, is situated on the swift-flowing Garron, a tributary of the Wye, near the village of Llangarron in Herefordshire. The low circular window indicates where the axle of the waterwheel, now removed, penetrated the wall.

James Maxfield's mill once dominated the town of Kilmore. Maxfield took it over from its original owner, James Allan, in the early 1850s and carried out improvements valued at over £5000 later in the decade. (State Library of Victoria)

*Lucy Maxfield (née Hewett) (1824–1912).
(Euroa Historical Society)*

*James Maxfield, miller (1819–1887).
(Euroa Historical Society)*

*James Edward Maxfield, son of James and
Lucy (1860–1931). (Euroa Historical
Society)*

*Jeannie Maxfield (née Macdonald)
(1859–1919). (Euroa Historical Society)*

Box Brownie snaps of life at 'Woodstock' (centre right) on Upper Flynn's Creek, c. 1904. Edward (Ted) Maxfield sits astride his horse and inspects a prize bull, while his wife Martha and daughter Kitty prepare to drive to town. Kitty coaxes their dog to jump for a bone and ties the shoes of sister Florrie after paddling in the creek. (Collection of Colin Maxfield)

Miner Samuel Stephens, depicted here as a bandsman in the Castlemaine Volunteer Rifles (c. late 1860s), was born in Cornwall, where tin mining, band music and Methodism were strong. In Campbell's Creek he became proprietor of a hay and corn store and served on the local council.

Born in Carmarthen, Wales, Martha Lloyd met and married Samuel Stephens in Cornwall before emigrating with him to Burra in South Australia and later to Victoria. This photograph, found among other Stephens photographs, is almost certainly of her.

Susan Stephens (1856–1919), youngest child of Samuel and Martha, married Robert Henry Hewett in 1880.

Robert Henry Hewett (1859–1931), eldest son of Robert and Elizabeth, followed his trade as a railway engineer from Castlemaine to Melbourne in the mid-1880s.

Campbell's Creek viewed from the northwest in the 1870s. The pitched roof of Samuel Stephens' house and adjoining hay and corn store appear midway between the Primitive Methodist (left) and Wesleyan Methodist churches. (Castlemaine Historical Society)

Newport Railway Workshops. During the railway boom of the 1880s the workshops became Victoria's largest industrial complex, employing more than 1500 men, including Robert Hewett. (Public Records Office of Victoria)

Taken in 1883 shortly before the workshops moved from Williamstown to Newport, this photograph of railway fitters captures the dignity of a trade that attracted the elite of the railway's industrial workforce. (Public Records Office of Victoria)

The respectable Methodist family, c. 1905. From left, Frank, Robert (John), Susan, Victor, Robert Henry and Reuben (Bob) Hewett.

Electra Street Wesleyan Church. Opened in 1876, its imposing interior, with pipe organ, choir stalls and central pulpit, reflected the prosperity of the industrial suburb and the confidence of the 'Forward Movement' in contemporary Methodism. (State Library of Victoria)

The author's grandfather, Victor Hewett (foreground), worked as a compositor in a Christchurch printing shop during his time in New Zealand (1906–07). Printing would become his entrée into the wider worlds of literature, art and book collecting.

Victor Hewett (in bowler hat, centre front row) among young Methodists, c. 1905. Combining evangelical zeal and social uplift, Methodism also accommodated many features of contemporary youth culture such as fashionable dress and cycling.

Jane Hewett, last survivor of the family that emigrated in 1850, now resident in the Old Colonist's Homes, posed for this photograph around 1920. Her great-nephew Reuben (Bob), the photographer, stands at the rear, while his father, Robert Henry, nurses the youngest male heir, also Robert Henry ('Harry') (born 1914).

Aunt Jane Hewett and a female lineage. On the left, Nell, Bob's wife, baby Meryl and older children Glad and Harry; on the right, May, Frank's wife, with baby Ruth and daughter Olive.

Victor and Emma Hewett with their first child, the author's mother, Emma May (born 1909). The family had recently moved to Essendon and Vic would shortly become deputy overseer at Varley Brothers Printery.

The Brothers Hewett: motor engineer Reuben (Bob) (left), tug captain Frank (centre back), and printer Victor (right), farewell their younger brother, John, as he departs on one of his overseas trips with the Church Missionary Society.

as member for Castlemaine in 1870. A man of the people, easy in manner though rough in speech, Patterson became a virtuoso in the art of political patronage. As Commissioner for Public Works and later as Minister for Railways (the two departments with the biggest payrolls), he supplied hundreds of jobs to his Castlemaine constituents. Rumours circulated of Castlemaine lads turning up in the wilds of Gippsland to claim government jobs that locals understandably considered ought to be theirs. Eventually the clamour for his favours became too much even for Patterson. In 1881, he abruptly announced his intention of abolishing patronage completely. 'It was not that he did not like the exercise of it,' he protested,

> *for he liked to serve his friends as well as any man did . . . But he found the thing an abominable nuisance . . . It was said that he only took that step after all the young people of Castlemaine had been appointed, but that was a little story manufactured by people who were not pleased with the action he had taken.*

Patterson had decreed the death of patronage, but it took many years to finish it off. He had resigned any hope of bringing a railway workshop to Castlemaine but was eager to throw out a lifeline to his local supporters while he could. During this time, Robert Henry was able to secure a job as a fitter in the Victorian Railways workshops at Williamstown, possibly as a so-called 'supernumerary', or casual employee, before the position was made permanent in 1885. The family lived for a while in Kensington, where their second son, Reuben (later known as Robert), was born in 1883, before moving to Parker Street, Williamstown.

Robert Henry's was the first in a series of departures from Castlemaine. In 1887, his younger brother Frank won an appointment (under the new examination system, not patronage) as an inspector in the public works department, a job that took him all over the colony. And in 1886, their sister Elizabeth Jane, then aged 31, married Tom Morecroft, son of a local railway ganger, Charles Morecroft. Only

Clara, the second eldest of the Hewett children, still single in her thirties, remained at home, keeping house for her father.

In his sixties, Robert had the patriarchal appearance befitting a Castlemaine pioneer. His full head of white hair and bushy beard, dark eyebrows and kind brown eyes made him a well-known identity among the little community of Wesley Hill, 'beloved and respected by all who knew him'. Around 1892 he seems to have suffered a stroke, and two years later, in May 1894, he was dead. His last years had evidently been hard, and the memorial card sent to acknowledge the condolences of his friends portrayed his death as a sweet release.

> *There is rest from care and labour,*
> *There is rest for friend and neighbour;*
> *In the shadow of His wings.*

In his will, executed in the mid-1880s, he left the family house to Clara, in the expectation that his other children would be provided for. Sadly, on New Year's Day 1894, his 33-year-old son-in-law Tom Morecroft died of dysentery, leaving Elizabeth Jane and her three daughters without a breadwinner. There had apparently been no opportunity to alter Robert's will, perhaps because he was already incapacitated.

Once again, the loss of a male breadwinner in the midst of hard times threw the family into crisis. The widow and her children, Agnes, Millie and Clara, returned to Castlemaine, and for another generation shared the house on Wesley Hill with her sister Clara. Elizabeth and her children occupied the middle section of the house, and Clara the front room, while the back room was used as a kitchen and bathroom. The family was squeezed physically and economically. Long after town gas supplies reached the area, their house was lit only by kerosene lamps and candles. Clara described herself as a needleworker, and Elizabeth Jane as a dressmaker: fifty years after their mother, a 'distressed needlewoman', left London, they had yet to escape her fate.

132

Their all-female household was a stark contrast to the overwhelmingly male population of Wesley Hill forty years earlier, but was consistent with the rapid feminisation that overtook the goldfields as the young men departed. In the only photograph we have of the house in its original form, Elizabeth Jane's three girls, dressed in white pinafores, stand in front of its picket fence together with an elderly neighbour, Mr Smith. Millie left school at thirteen to learn dressmaking at Niebuhr's Drapery before joining her mother and older sister Aggie in a shop in Mostyn Street, Castlemaine. Each girl earned five shillings a *week* at a time when the famous Harvester Judgment had awarded workingmen a 'basic wage' of seven shillings a *day*. The women later moved to another shop, in Hargreaves Street, where they subdivided their labour, Millie making skirts and Aggie bodices, often working late into the night and sleeping in a bedroom behind the shop.

By the outbreak of the First World War, Aggie and Millie had both married and moved away from Castlemaine. In 1919, Clara, the youngest, married Alf Mussett, a Chewton boy and former railway fireman, who had recently returned 'permanently unfit' after active service as a driver on the Western Front. He 'had not enlisted for money or for an overseas bride, but simply from a spirit of loyalty to his country', the local paper noted proudly on his return. Soon afterwards, he went into business with a well-known local identity, Morton van Heurick, who owned the bakery next door to the Hewetts' house in Duke Street. (The shop is now a popular eatery, the Bold Café.) Eventually Alf and young Clara took over the shop and began a family of their own.

The two sisters, her aunt Clara and mother Elizabeth, entered their sixties in the early years of the twentieth century. Each fortnight they walked together from Wesley Hill to the Castlemaine post office to collect their old age pension, the frugal allowance that finally broke their bondage to the thimble and the sewing machine. The house that Robert built passed on Clara's death in 1942 to her sister Elizabeth, and then, on her death three years later, to Robert's great-grandson Roy Mussett. It had housed four generations of Hewetts over almost a century.

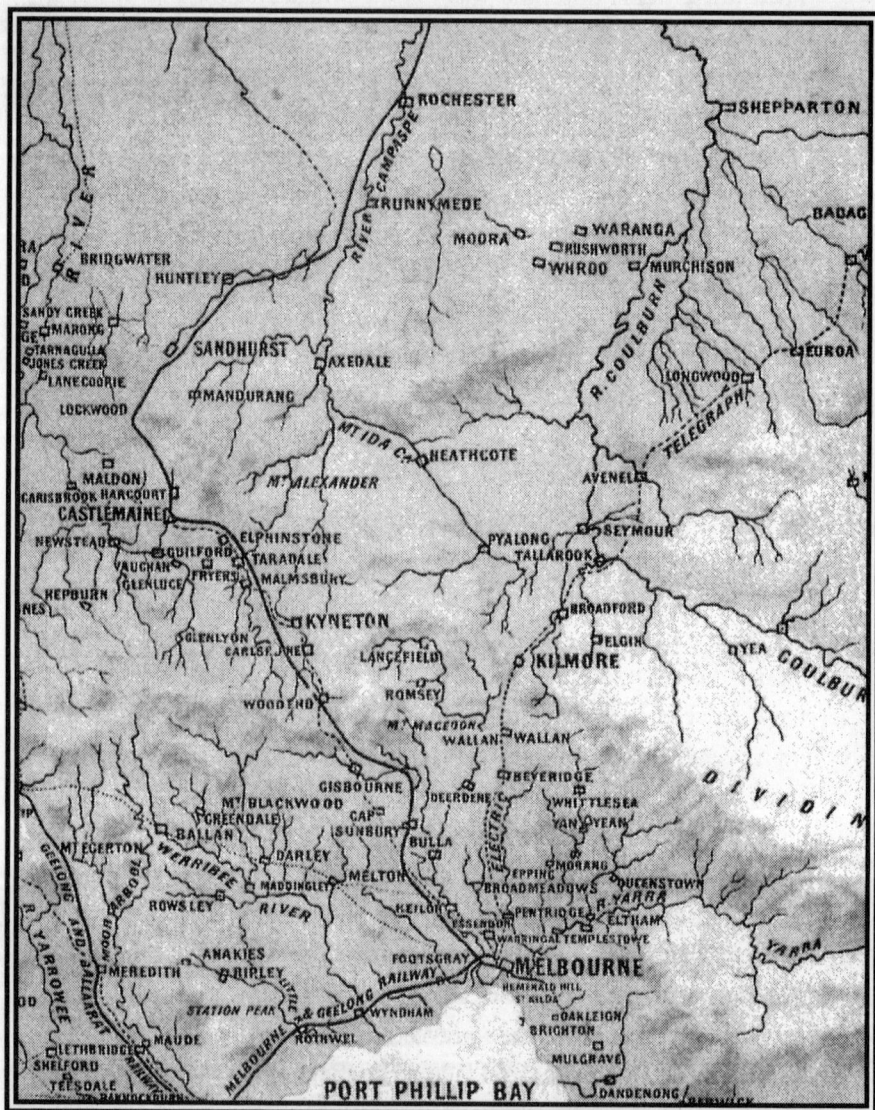

Gold was not the only maker of fortunes in gold-rush Victoria. Between the early 1850s and the 1870s the miller James Maxfield and his family migrated by stages along the Sydney Road from Kilmore to Broadford and then to Longwood. As the wheat frontier moved to the northwest, and the railway supplanted the ox and horse teams, Maxfield's mills were marooned from the main corridors of commerce. (Tulloch and Brown's Map of the Colony of Victoria, 1856 (detail), State Library of Victoria)

CHAPTER SIX
The millers' tale

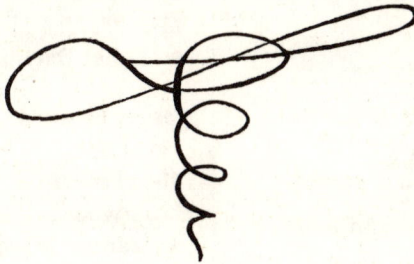

Gold made Victoria rich, but where the wealth went nobody knew. Some of it travelled with the lucky few who returned to spend it in Britain, or was despatched in remittances to appreciative families. A handful of prospectors became rich, but most made no more than wages and, like Robert Hewett, soon returned to their old occupations. 'I have never yet met with that man who has made a fortune by gold-digging,' claimed writer William Howitt, an acute observer of goldfields life. The biggest fortunes were made not in digging for gold but in feeding, clothing, housing and transporting diggers. When they married the flour millers James and Robert Maxfield, Robert's sisters Lucy and Susan Hewett hitched their fortunes to one of the most lucrative businesses of the day.

THE MAXFIELDS OF LLANGARRON, LONGWOOD AND FLYNN'S CREEK

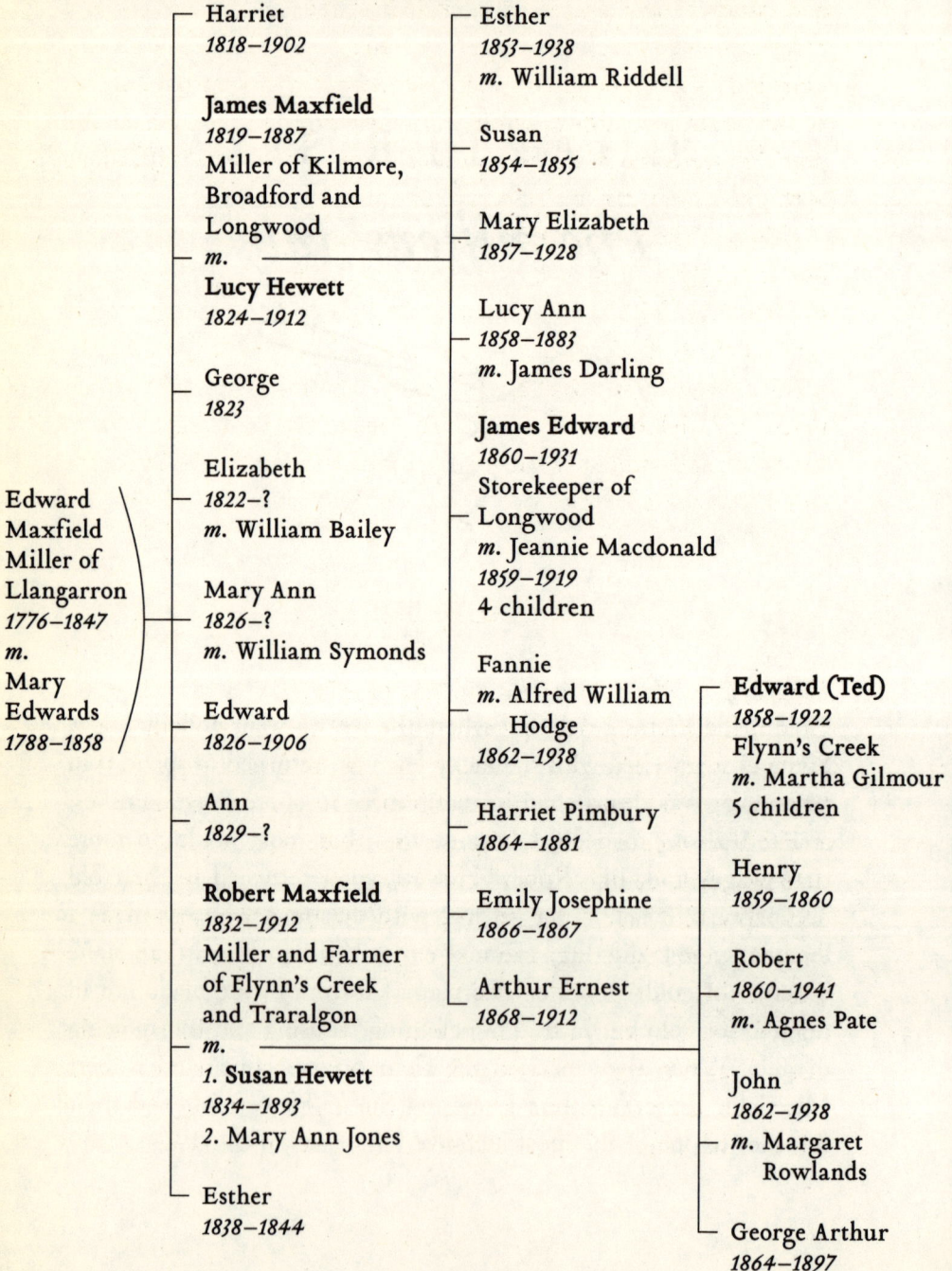

Edward Maxfield Miller of Llangarron
1776–1847
m.
Mary Edwards
1788–1858

Harriet
1818–1902

James Maxfield
1819–1887
Miller of Kilmore, Broadford and Longwood
m.
Lucy Hewett
1824–1912

George
1823

Elizabeth
1822–?
m. William Bailey

Mary Ann
1826–?
m. William Symonds

Edward
1826–1906

Ann
1829–?

Robert Maxfield
1832–1912
Miller and Farmer of Flynn's Creek and Traralgon
m.
1. **Susan Hewett**
1834–1893
2. Mary Ann Jones

Esther
1838–1844

Esther
1853–1938
m. William Riddell

Susan
1854–1855

Mary Elizabeth
1857–1928

Lucy Ann
1858–1883
m. James Darling

James Edward
1860–1931
Storekeeper of Longwood
m. Jeannie Macdonald
1859–1919
4 children

Fannie
m. Alfred William Hodge
1862–1938

Harriet Pimbury
1864–1881

Emily Josephine
1866–1867

Arthur Ernest
1868–1912

Edward (Ted)
1858–1922
Flynn's Creek
m. Martha Gilmour
5 children

Henry
1859–1860

Robert
1860–1941
m. Agnes Pate

John
1862–1938
m. Margaret Rowlands

George Arthur
1864–1897

A working miner consumes about 4500 calories a day, more than twice the intake of workers in more sedentary occupations. Lamb chops cooked in a frying pan, billy tea sweetened with sugar, and damper—the simple wheaten loaf cooked in the embers of a campfire—were the almost universal diet of Victorian goldminers. Ours is a society powered by petrol and electricity, but until the arrival of the steam locomotive, colonial Victoria ran on grain. Bread and porridge were the main human fuels; oats and wheat chaff, along with grass, were the main sources of animal power.

Most of the cost of the diggers' supplies was eaten up in transportation. By the time a bag of flour had travelled from Melbourne to Forest Creek it had more than doubled its price. 'In this, the third year [of the gold rush], many well-informed persons seriously dread a famine at the principal gold-fields, solely in consequence of bad roads,' the Melbourne *Argus* warned. Anyone who could get flour to the goldfields without having to carry it all the way from Melbourne stood to make a fortune.

KILMORE

When James Maxfield arrived in Melbourne in 1850, he had little idea that such a golden prospect awaited him. He became the manager of a large steam-powered flour mill owned by Scotsman Robert Allan at Kilmore, 60 kilometres north of Melbourne. Allan had arrived in Port Phillip in the early 1840s, and by the early 1850s his industry and frugality, combined with the strong demand for his produce, had made him rich. By the time James arrived, Allan was thinking of retirement; the engagement of the younger man may have been part of a succession plan.

Kilmore was known as 'the granary of Victoria'. In the age of the horse-drawn plough and the bullock wagon, more than two-thirds of the colony's grain was grown within a hundred kilometres of Melbourne, much of it near Kilmore. The town took its name from

To make common buns

Rub 4 oz of butter into 2 lbs of flour, a little salt, 4 oz of sugar, a dessert spoonful of carraways, and a tea spoonful of ginger: put some warm milk or cream to 4 table spoonfuls of yeast, mix all together into a past, but not too stiff, cover it over and set it before the fire an hour to rise, then make it into buns, put them on a tin, set them before the fire for a quarter of an hour cover over with flannel, then brush them with warm milk, and bake them of a nice brown in a moderate oven.

the hometown of William Rutledge, an Irish capitalist who had taken advantage of a provision in the colonial land regulations for Special Surveys to create a settlement for Irish tenant farmers. Kilmore became the most Irish town in Victoria, perhaps in all Australia. The farmers who brought their grain to Allan's mill were mostly smallholders, sowing their crops by hand and harvesting them with scythes and sickles, just as the Hewetts had done on Hook Farm. An old-timer later recalled the sight of bullock drays, sometimes sixteen or twenty in a team, slowly descending the surrounding hills to the Kilmore mills.

Kilmore stood at a fork in the northern road, just beyond Pretty Sally, the lowest crossing point on the Great Dividing Range. From there, roads radiated westwards behind Mount Macedon towards Heathcote, northeast along the route pioneered by Hume and Hovell towards the Ovens Valley, and south to Melbourne. When the gold rush began, it was ideally placed to act as a conduit between the wheat-growing areas and the main markets for flour and fodder.

Six months after James's arrival, on Thursday, 6 February 1851, devastating fires encircled the town. Harvest was almost over, and most farmers had already burned off the stubble on their properties. On the Wednesday, however, as temperatures rose, one laggard was still burning off when the wind swung round to the northwest. 'The tongues of flame, driven by the gale, glided through the stubble like the fiery serpents of old, utterly consuming and melting away whatever opposed their onward course,' an eloquent local correspondent reported. A bullock dray from Benalla bound for Allan's mill to pick up flour was destroyed save for the ironwork. After nightfall, the townsfolk looked towards the surrounding hills, where the glowing trunks of trees resembled 'the lights of a mighty but distant city'. Fifteen farmers on the Special Survey, all with Irish names, were burnt out, losing very nearly everything they possessed. Despite the impact of the fire on his own business, Allan allowed the farmers to continue drawing funds to pay their harvest labourers, and offered bags of flour to the most destitute.

A few months later, James Maxfield travelled to Melbourne for his wedding to Lucy Hewett. The ceremony took place on 26 July, just a fortnight after the announcement of the first gold discoveries at Clunes. The newlyweds returned to Kilmore to meet a gold-induced fuel crisis, as the demand for flour and fodder strained supplies. Kilmore boasted that it was 'the cheapest market to buy flour in'. When gold was discovered in the Ovens Valley, the town's location became even more advantageous. 'Parties proceeding to the Ovens Diggings, can always be supplied with flour of first rate quality and fresh, at the same retail prices of Melbourne, which saves 40 miles of the very worst of the road.'

At the beginning of 1853, Allan retired to Buninyong and handed the business over to James. 'Mr Maxfield has managed my business the last two years, and from my confidence in his integrity I feel assured he will do justice to any order entrusted to him,' Allan assured his old customers. In a town where class and ethnic tensions lay just below the surface, Allan's reputation for integrity and kindness was a precious asset James vowed to maintain. While still in his thirties, he became a leading figure in the locality: treasurer of the local hospital board (1854), vice-president of the mechanics' institute (1854), treasurer of the Kilmore Agricultural Society (1858) and a municipal councillor (1856). These were eventful years for the Maxfield family too. Every upward step in James's career seemed to be marked by the birth of another child: four girls—Esther (1853), Susan (1854 d. 1855), Mary (1857) and Lucy (1858)—before a son and heir, James Edward, in 1860. At the beginning, Lucy could count on the help of her sisters Mary Ann and Susan, but in 1857 Susan married James's younger brother Robert, who had come out from Hereford to join him in the business. Their first children, Edward (1858) and Henry (1859 d. 1860), were also born in Kilmore.

By the end of the decade, James had made enough money to 'retire on a competency'. Retirement, however, was not in his nature. 'Mr Maxfield was a man of a speculative turn of mind,' a contemporary noted. When gold was discovered at the McIvor (Heathcote) diggings, he considered opening a new mill there, but eventually resolved to expand the Kilmore mill. He rebuilt it in brick and stone, commissioned the Melbourne engineer Thomas Fulton to install a powerful new steam engine, grinding stones and dressing machines, and added workmen's cottages, stables and a coach house. All told, the improvements cost over £5000, a considerable sum. The opening of the new building was a gala occasion, with a public viewing of the new engine and a feast for the locals, both Aboriginals and settlers.

WHIRLED INTO POLITICS

In August 1859, James was persuaded to stand for the Victorian Legislative Assembly against the sitting member and premier, John O'Shanassy. Australian democracy was very young—the first Victorian Parliament, elected under manhood suffrage, was only three years old—and James was a political novice. Victoria had only recently adopted the secret ballot, and many of the customs that surrounded the old regime of open elections, such as vigorous canvassing and lavish hospitality, were still well alive. James had come forward 'very reluctantly' but because he believed that Kilmore deserved to be represented by a local man. (As everyone knew, O'Shanassy lived in Melbourne, in a mansion called 'Tara' in the city's eastern suburbs.) As the proprietor of one of the town's most important businesses, James had 'the honour of a personal acquaintance with nearly every elector in the district'. His policies were those of a colonial liberal: free selection, secular education, strong local representation, opposition to patronage and corruption. He looked a strong contender.

His opponent, O'Shanassy, was a formidable foe. A Tipperary man, broad of face and accent, he was the acknowledged tribal leader of Victoria's Catholics. *The Age* called him 'a low, scheming, shortsighted peasant', but the Kilmore Irish adored him. He spoke their language, identified with their grievances, and defended their interests. He was also a tenacious fighter, not bound by gentlemanly rules of fair play. In daring to oppose him, Maxfield, a Protestant, had unwittingly roused a virulent source of discord in colonial society, religious sectarianism.

By election day, Kilmore was abuzz with threats and rumours. Business began early at the town's three pubs, where the sitting member offered free beer to all comers. Asking a neighbour why there were so many strangers in town, a local was told: 'The boys come to put in Mr O'Shanassy.' Crowds of excited and sometimes drunken partisans surrounded the mechanics' institute, jostling and jeering voters as they approached the polling booth. Some were armed with sticks, whips and stones.

Inside the booth, voters who refused to show their ballot papers were intimidated and abused. Many of the names on the voters' roll, it was later alleged, were fictitious or ineligible, while some registered voters turned up only to be told that their vote had already been cast. Late in the afternoon, Reverend William Singleton, the Anglican vicar, was driving down Sydney Street with his three young children when he was intercepted by drunks shouting, 'Down with the Protestants.' 'The amount of rowdyism, threatening, violence to persons and property was perhaps never before instanced in the history of the civilised world,' an outraged spectator protested.

At the declaration of the poll, O'Shanassy was returned with a clear majority—437 votes to Maxfield's 270. For his rival it had been a searing experience. 'Mr Maxfield's windows were smashed to atoms, and threats of direct vengeance held out against himself and family for daring to oppose Mr O'Shanassy.' The very electors whose personal acquaintance he had counted on for votes had turned violently against him.

To compound his troubles, the wheat frontier was moving away from Kilmore. With the opening of the Melbourne to Sandhurst railway, the main centres of grain production had moved closer to the goldfields. 'The property upon which a vast outlay had taken place became almost valueless for the purpose intended,' the *Kilmore Free Press* noted soberly. In 1860, James had purchased a second steam

Melbourne Punch's *view of the 1859 Kilmore election. The violent and drunken behaviour of the supporters of James Maxfield's political opponent, John O'Shanassy, confirmed the paper's strong anti-Irish prejudices. (Monash University Library)*

mill at Kalkallo, 33 kilometres from Melbourne on the south side of the range, and installed his brother Robert as manager. Robert and Susan's sons Robert (1860) and John (1862) were born there. But only two years later, James seems to have completely revised his thinking. People had already begun to agitate for the construction of a railway to the northeast, linking Melbourne to the Ovens Valley, through Kilmore and Seymour. James's sights turned northwards.

LANGSTONE REBORN

In February 1862, James engaged the Kilmore architect James Fleury to design a new water-powered mill on the Sunday Creek at

Broadford, 90 kilometres north of Melbourne. 'The cost will be about £6000 and the waterwheel is one of the largest in the colony,' it was reported. He leased the Kalkallo mill and sold his Kilmore property to Patrick O'Dea, a local grazier with strong links in the local Irish community. In choosing waterpower, James was returning to his roots. The depletion of forests for fuel and mine timber had driven up the cost of firewood. Water was cheap, renewable and available on the spot. But Broadford was not Llangarron. In a land of droughts and flooding rains, where harvest time was also the driest time of year, a water-powered mill could be hostage to the weather. Twelve months after its completion, James constructed an overflow dam to supplement his supply. He had bet on waterpower at the beginning of a drought; before it was over, other water millers had installed steam engines to see them through.

Always a dreamer, James was attempting to realise two conflicting visions. One was the desire to return to the intimate world of his Hereford childhood with its water-powered family mill, swiftly running stream, lush surrounding farmland, and tight-knit rural community. Broadford was an antipodean version of Langstone Mill. After the excitement and stress of his short political career he may have yearned for a quieter rural life. For Lucy, too, the mill may have represented something like a return to Hook Farm. During the next decade, they would have four more children, three girls and a boy, and settle into the Broadford community. Public-spirited, trustworthy and gregarious, James quickly won the confidence of his neighbours, becoming a member of the Roads Board and the local school committee, and sitting on the bench of the local magistrates' court as a justice of the peace.

But there was always another James Maxfield—the railway dreamer, eager to ride the locomotive of industrial progress. He had no sooner completed the Broadford mill than he embarked on the construction of a new steam-powered mill, designed by the Melbourne architects Crouch and Wilson, at Seymour, 25 kilometres further up the line. Perhaps the returns on his expensive venture into waterpower had been disappointing and he hoped to offset his losses with the more assured returns of a steam-powered mill at Seymour. Or perhaps his entrepreneurial drive was simply unstoppable.

Outwardly, James Maxfield was a success, but his business rested on shaky foundations. He had pushed further into the northeast just as the wheat frontier was shifting westward, towards the dry flat lands of the Wimmera, where farmers could exploit new technologies like the stump-jump plough and the harvester. Yields were declining in the older agricultural regions. Over the next decade, grain production in the Broadford district would halve while it grew more than tenfold in the Wimmera. Soon there was 'an insufficient supply of wheat' to support his mills. It wasn't long before creditors were knocking on his door. In October 1870, the stock and station agents William Sloane and Company put the Broadford and Seymour properties up for sale. Their description of the Broadford mill reveals something of the mind of its proprietor and his way of life.

Reading this lovingly detailed description of Maxfield's estate, one can feel the pain of relinquishing a beautiful dream. A silent witness to these proceedings was James's wife Lucy, now in her forties, mother of a family of seven surviving children ranging in age from two to seventeen. Her own mother, Jane, had been about the same age, also with a family of eight, when Hook Farm was put up for sale, setting in train the events that brought the Hewetts to Australia.

LONGWOOD

The Seymour mill sold quickly, but almost five years passed before 'Broadford Park' at last found a buyer. Meanwhile, James, never lost for a plan, decided to move his family and business 60 kilometres further up the line to Longwood. The route selected for the northeast railway diverged from the highway, cutting the old coaching station of Longwood adrift from the line. James seized the opportunity to become the king of New Longwood, the new town beside the

All that very valuable freehold property, situated in the centre of the township of Broadford and known as

BROADFORD FLOUR-MILL,

together with about

40 ACRES of LAND,

Intersected by the Sunday Creek, and subdivided into paddocks. The building is a most substantial one, the lower storey of stone, and the upper one of brick. The ground floor is 9ft. high, the second and third 8ft., with commodious storeroom and offices.

The mill dam is constructed in a most substantial way, the water-wheel is perfect, and the working plant is most complete, consisting of three pairs of stones 3ft. 4in., large silk-dressing machine, patent wire flour-dresser, smutting machine, elevators, hoisting tackle, &c. The miller's dwelling is situated at the entrance of the property, and comprises comfortable weatherboard house with five rooms, kitchen, and first class cellar; also, two good three-roomed weatherboard cottages, extensive piggeries, garden of two acres well stocked with vines, fruit trees, &c. The land has an extensive frontage to the Sydney road and Sunday Creek, suitable for building and other purposes. There is an entrance on each side of the tollgate, and farmers and others can thus avoid paying tolls. The North-eastern Railway line now constructing passes directly through the township.

railway station. He bought several adjoining allotments in what became Maxfield Street, and built a new flour mill, a poor man's version of his old ones, in rough timber. Beside it, he erected a general store—'Maxfield's Stores'—combining separate grocery, drapery and hardware shops and a four-bedroom residential section. It was a comedown from his glory days, but the new businesses offered employment for his children, and the railway dreamer could always hope that his business would grow along with the town. For a while, however, it seemed that even this cut-price kingdom might be lost. In October 1874, the assignees of his estate also put the Longwood property on the market. It was not until the end of 1875, when the Broadford property was sold and James's creditors reached an agreement with the trustees, that the spectre of insolvency finally disappeared.

In the early 1880s, the family's fortunes slowly began to recover. Longwood was no boomtown, and the trade generated by the surrounding community of farmers, sawmillers and rabbiters was never more than modest. James opened another store at Reedy Creek near Kilmore, designed to take advantage of a brief upswing in goldmining in the district, but by 1883 he had sold up and left the town. Financial stress and family tragedies had taken a toll. The Maxfields' seventeen-year-old daughter Harriet died in 1881, and two years later her newly married elder sister Lucy was also dead, aged only 25.

By the mid-1880s, James himself had succumbed to a 'long and lingering illness', probably tuberculosis. His elder son, James Edward, took over the family business. He was a popular, sociable, public-spirited man who seemed destined to fill his father's shoes. In 1884, he mobilised the townsfolk to erect a mechanics' institute as a venue for public meetings and social events, such as amateur theatricals. He had taken one of the principal roles in Longwood's recent production of *Aurora Floyd*, a sensational melodrama exploring themes of bigamy, murder and elopement. 'With practice Mr Maxfield will make a really good actor,' the *Euroa Advertiser* wrote encouragingly. Among the other performers was Jeannie Macdonald, youngest daughter of a local station manager, whose 'brilliancy and dash' on the pianoforte had already won James Edward's admiration. They were married just over a year later, at the bride's home, and their first child, Albert, was born later that year; sadly, he died soon after birth.

James Maxfield senior died in August 1887. He was 68 years old. The next Sunday, the day after his burial, his family and friends assembled in the New Longwood hall. 'Men should not exhaust their whole energies in money getting and money spending,' declared Reverend Fitzgerald, the vicar of St Andrew's, but should regard their lives as 'a probation time for eternity'. That was how James Maxfield had lived. By his example 'as a husband, as a father, as a neighbour, a citizen, a friend', he had won treasure beyond earthly riches. As everyone in the congregation knew, James had once known earthly riches too, but by the time he died, his fortune had shrunk to about £900, most of it sunk in the stock and goodwill of the Longwood general store. Admiration for James' virtues was mixed with pity for his sad decline. Perhaps his widow and children would have settled for less admiration if there had been less reason for the pity.

In 1887, Victoria was enjoying boom conditions, but the Maxfields would soon encounter tougher times. Hard upon the 1890s banking crash came the 'Federation drought'. A storekeeper, like a miller, occupied a pivotal position in the local community. James Maxfield junior's universal popularity was an asset in good times when customers could easily pay, but a potential liability in hard times when debtors sometimes had to be hounded or further credit refused. In 1900, he suddenly announced that he was selling up and moving to Cobden in the Western District. Everything in the Longwood store, and the business itself, was to be auctioned, as well as his household furniture, books, carpenter's tools, weights and measures, carriage and mare, along with 50 acres of land adjoining the township. Surprised and distressed by his decision, the community gathered in the hall he had helped to build to present him with a 'weighty purse of sovereigns' and thank 'one who has proved himself a worthy citizen, public man and friend to all'. Rising to respond, the guest of honour could hardly bring himself to speak. 'It was at once the saddest and proudest moment of his life,' he said.

> *Some 25 years ago he had come to Longwood, where he had lost his father, had married, and his children had been born and buried, and he felt sad at severing the associations that had become so dear to him. But it was also a proud moment, because he went away a rich man . . . rich in friends and loving hearts.*

This was not just young James speaking; it was also his father, whose example, as erratic businessman and inspiring community leader, he seemed fated to follow.

A NEW FRONTIER

When the elder James Maxfield began his push to the north, his younger brother Robert was part of the dream. The bond between the two brothers was strengthened by their marriages to the Hewett sisters, who may have hoped that their children would grow up together. Robert was involved in the building of the Broadford mill, but when the Seymour mill opened, James engaged two of his old Kilmore employees to manage it. After getting a taste of independence, Robert may have wanted to run his own show. There was a thirteen-year gap between them (ten between the Hewett sisters), and the younger brother may have wanted to make his own way in life. By 1864, Robert and Susan had departed for Victoria's newest frontier, Gippsland, east of Melbourne.

They settled in Sale, where Robert became the manager of the Aurora Mill, newly established in the main street close to the riverfront. He had arrived at a moment of opportunity, as graziers settled along the banks of the Latrobe and Thomson rivers. Some had begun to grow small quantities of grain but were frustrated by the lack of transport and modern milling. 'What am I to do with my wheat?' one farmer cried in exasperation. A local entrepreneur, Phillip McArdell, had opened the Wattle Mill in 1859 and purchased a steam vessel with the aim of transporting grain and flour along the Latrobe River, but snags and sandbanks impeded navigation and there was no connection to the sea. Even when the farmer got his grain to the mill, the product was often inferior. 'Gippsland flour is no good,' one bluntly remarked. Many customers bought South Australian flour transported by road from Port Albert rather than the local product. In a bid to win their custom, the Aurora Mill installed new machinery capable of producing fine white flour rather than the despised coarse wholemeal.

Milling was a seasonal occupation, and flour millers often combined it with farming, as Robert had done back in Llangarron. Talking with local farmers in Sale, he would have gained a good idea of farming prospects in the hinterland. And like many other gold-rush immigrants, he nursed an ambition to secure a farm of his own. 'The great object of a land law in this country should be to settle a yeoman class upon the land,' a supporter of the 1869 Grant Land Act declared, using language calculated to appeal to dispossessed English farming folk like the Maxfields. Under this measure, almost five million acres of previously unsettled country was thrown open for selection by smallholders. Squatters had already seized the best land on the central plain of Gippsland, so the selectors turned to the more heavily wooded country along the creeks that flowed, or trickled, into the Latrobe and Thomson rivers.

In 1871, Robert applied for a 160-acre allotment close to Flynn's Creek, about fifteen kilometres southwest of Rosedale. He later enlarged his claim to 320 acres. While remaining a foreman at Holdein's mill, he spent the winters clearing and fencing his land. By 1874, when he applied for a lease, he had erected a four-room weatherboard house with a bark roof, two sheds, a bark and slab pighouse, and about 240 chains of fencing. The land, he noted, was 'heavily timbered' and 'unfit for cultivation': grazing was all it was good for. In the next two and a half years, he cleared dead wood off 150 acres, grubbed ten acres and sowed 45 or 50 acres with grass. It was a beginning, nothing more.

As a solo part-time farmer, it would have been an uphill battle. From the beginning, however, the Maxfield farm was a family concern. Robert's sister-in-law Mary Ann Hewett selected the adjoining 320-acre block. What Mary Ann had done in the twenty years since the Hewetts' arrival in Port Phillip is unknown. In her application, she described herself as a 'monthly nurse', a woman employed for the first month or so after the birth of a baby to assist the new mother. She had probably performed a similar role for her sisters Lucy and Susan when their babies were born, and now offered the same service for payment to other families in the district. As soon as they left school, Robert's sons Edward (Ted) and Robert also came to live on the property and assisted with the work of clearing and fencing; Mary Ann probably cooked and kept house for them until Robert and Susan and the other children joined them in the mid-1870s. Described as a 'dairywoman', she apparently took charge of milking and tending the small herd while the boys continued clearing and fencing. By 1874, with Robert senior's assistance, they had erected 200 chains of fencing, a four-room dwelling, stockyard, milking shed, garden and orchard.

By combining his sister-in-law's farm with his own, and employing his sons' labour, Robert overcame two of the main obstacles to success as a free selector: insufficient land and insufficient labour. As soon as he turned eighteen, in 1876, Ted selected a block on Upper Flynn's Creek, adding to it over the next few years. In 1882, when he married Martha Gilmour, the daughter of a neighbouring farmer, he had built up a viable holding. Over the next two decades, Ted and Martha had five children—two girls and three boys—who would follow them onto the land. As neighbours failed or retired from the land, the Maxfields took the opportunity to expand their holding. To finance these acquisitions, Maxfield needed the security of freehold, so as soon as each lease was granted, Robert immediately applied to have it converted into a grant. By 1890, the family had managed to consolidate most of its holdings in contiguous strips of well-watered pasture, over one thousand acres in all, along both sides of Upper Flynn's Creek. Robert named his homestead 'Woodstock', while his son Robert junior called his 'Langstone'.

FLYNN'S CREEK

In February 2014, I visited Flynn's Creek in company with Robert's great-grandson, Colin Maxfield, a retired butter factory employee. Heading east from Traralgon, the Hyland Highway skirts the Loy Yang open-cut mine and power station, its massive chimneys and cooling towers looming over the countryside, before dipping into the valley of Flynn's Creek. Just across the bridge, you turn south along a dirt track, Maxfield Road, and after about three kilometres, a well-weathered California bungalow surrounded by abandoned cow yards and milking sheds, appears at the end of the road. This is 'Woodstock', the successor to the original four-roomed cottage erected by Ted Maxfield in the 1870s. From its porch, you look back across a well-grassed valley. A reporter who visited the farm in 1901 noted the 'prolific growth of herbage, so high that the backs of the cattle can just be seen grazing in the marshy land'. Even today, the present owners say, the winter rains often inundate the flat, stimulating the growth of spring pasture. It may have been the nearest thing Victoria afforded to the lush pastures of Llangarron.

In 1879, the first train on the new Gippsland railway, connecting Melbourne with Sale, ran along the Latrobe Valley about ten kilometres south of the Maxfields' property. It marked the beginning of a new era for the dairy farmers of Flynn's Creek. Gippsland farmers could now send their butter and cheese speedily to Melbourne markets. By the end of the 1880s, regular milk trains were also running from as far as Warragul to the city. When the Maxfields first took up their selections, Mary Ann and Susan made butter

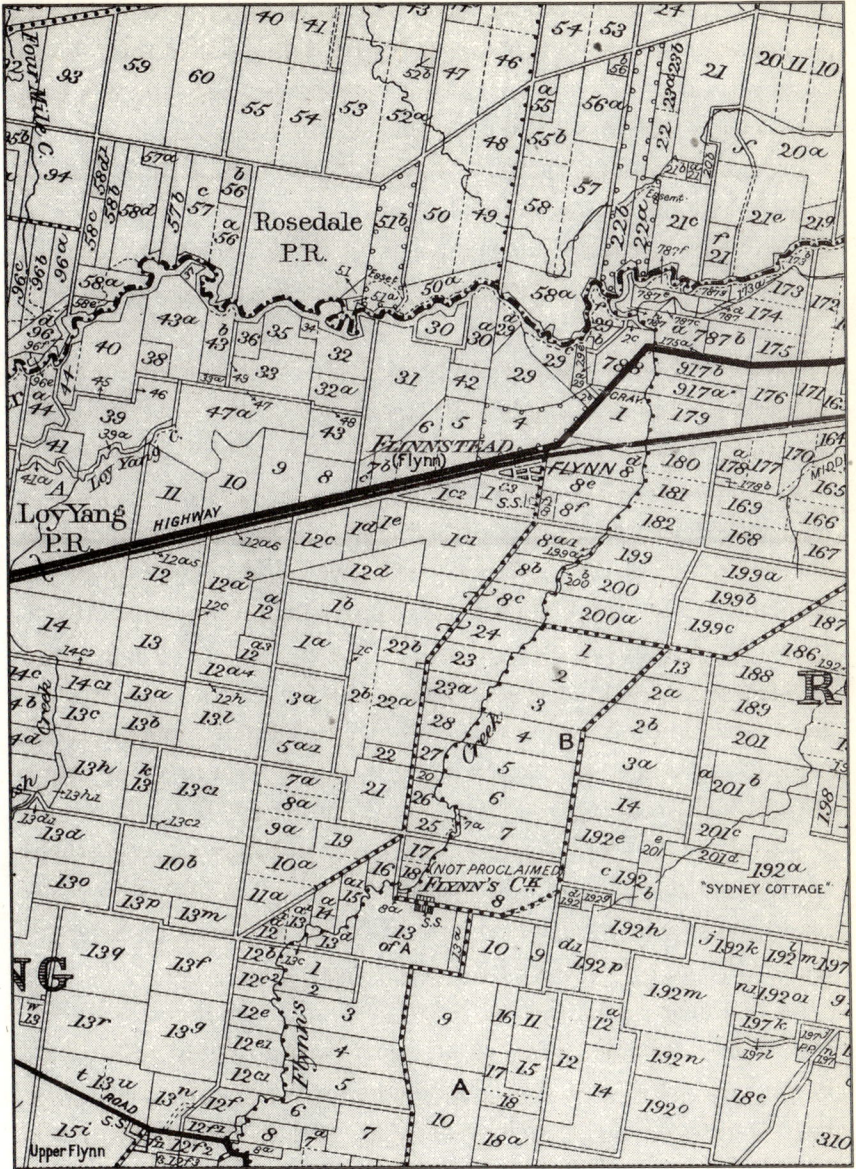

The Maxfields took up their selections on the upper reaches of Flynn's Creek, a tributary of the Latrobe River, in the 1870s after the first phase of pastoral settlement along the river itself. The well-watered pastures along the creek, within reach of the Gippsland railway, were well suited for dairy farming. (Cadastral Survey, Rosedale, Victorian Department of Crown Lands and Survey, 1938, State Library of Victoria)

in the old-fashioned way, by warming whole milk to separate the cream before churning it by hand. Hard on the heels of the railway, however, came the De Laval cream separator, a simple and relatively inexpensive machine that enabled farmers to make their own butter more quickly and efficiently. 'I have heard of two or three persons who are about to invest in De Lavall's [*sic*] cream separator,' a Flynn's Creek correspondent reported in 1886. 'The old fashioned and slow methods of labour must give way to the advances of science and machinery.'

Ted Maxfield, a keen agricultural improver, was almost certainly one of the purchasers. In 1889, he was elected chairman of the Upper Flynn's Creek and Tong Bong Railway League, formed to agitate for a branch line from Traralgon to Yarram via Upper Flynn's Creek. The 'extraordinary fertility' of the surrounding country was bound to make the line a success, he argued. The railways commissioners, beset by similar demands from all over the colony, thought otherwise. In the following year, Ted helped launch the Traralgon Butter Factory and became one of its first shareholders. When a vacancy occurred on the Traralgon Shire Council in 1895, he was elected unopposed, and served for the next six years. Among the dairy farming community, 'Woodstock' was regarded as a model property. Ted's Plymouth Rock hens were regular prize-winners at local shows, and his herd of Ayrshire cattle, the product of careful culling and breeding, was regarded as the finest in the district. Like his cousin James Edward, he was becoming a pillar of the community.

As he entered his sixties, Robert senior gradually relinquished control of the family farms to his sons. He transferred his interest in the land at Flynn's Creek and bought a new property, Loch Park, near Traralgon. The shadow of mortality was encroaching. In April 1892, 'after a long illness', Mary Ann Hewett, the indispensable maiden aunt, died at Loch Park. Then, nine months later, her sister Susan was making her way home from afternoon tea with a friend when she suddenly collapsed in the street and died. Stroke—the hereditary affliction of the Hewetts—had struck again. In 1902,

Robert married the twice-widowed Mary Ann Jones, and moved into the town.

Despite recent losses, he could look back on his life in Gippsland with satisfaction. After a slow start, his family had become moderately prosperous farmers. Robert was almost forty and his children were in their teens before he was able to give up wage labour and devote himself entirely to farming. In contrast to his elder brother James, whose fortunes peaked in the 1850s then declined as he tried unsuccessfully to expand his milling empire, Robert had proceeded slowly and cautiously, extending and improving his property, consolidating his debt, and modernising his farming methods. Slow and steady, he seemed to have won the race.

Historians of Australian land settlement long regarded the nineteenth-century free-selection acts as a failure. The reformers' dream of creating an Australian yeomanry, they say, was thwarted from the start by a harsh climate, insufficient capital, uneconomically small farms, and the vested interests of squatters and other large landholders. Their view may be too severe: recent historians have shown that while many selectors failed, a considerable number actually achieved 'modest but comfortable fortunes'. Why did the Maxfields succeed while many others failed? The pastures of Gippsland may have been better suited to small-scale agriculture than some other regions. New forms of transport and technologies, like the railway and the cream separator, enabled small dairy farms to become viable businesses. More important than any of these, however, were the human resources of the farming family itself. Without the agricultural and domestic skills that Robert and Susan brought from England; without Mary Ann Hewett's contribution as housekeeper, dairywoman and landholder; without the muscle power and ambition of four strong sons, eager and willing to become farmers; and—above all—without the readiness of every member to subordinate their individual ambitions to the family's interests, the Maxfields would surely never have prospered as they did.

All that survives to evoke the Maxfields' life on Upper Flynn's Creek is an album of curled and faded photographs kept by Colin Maxfield. These tiny two-and-a-quarter-inch-square images were taken sometime around 1904 when the cheap, mass-produced Box Brownie camera suddenly made every family its own photographer. 'You push the button, we do the rest' was Kodak's catchy advertising slogan. The Maxfields pushed the button of their Box Brownie with alacrity, capturing candid shots of their everyday lives.

Their home, 'Woodstock', a simple timber cottage, stands in a paddock surrounded by the forest. Nearby, a milking shed, pig pens and stables fashioned from local timber and corrugated iron and fenced with split palings comprise the engine room of the farm. Ted himself, a tall middle-aged man with a drooping moustache and a wide-brimmed hat, is snapped astride his white horse and, in another image, standing among a crowd of dairy farmers admiring a prize bull. Martha, his wife, and her daughters, Susan, or Kitty as she was called, and Flossie, are dressed for town as they depart in the family buggy. The young men, Jack and young Ted, with their horses and dogs, round up the cows and pose with their bicycles, hats pushed nonchalantly back on their heads, trousers tucked into their socks. Fourteen-year-old Arthur strides manfully through the muddy cow yard in boots and sou'wester. Kitty, dressed in a wide hat, white blouse and ankle-length skirt, bends to tie the shoelaces of her handicapped younger sister Flossie beside the creek. It seems to be mid-summer, for the stream merely trickles between its steep banks. Above her, a felled tree forms an improvised bridge. Kitty reappears in the farmyard, dressed now in a white pinafore, coaxing one of the dogs to leap for a bone while one of Ted's prize hens can be glimpsed in the background. The heads of two swimmers bob above the waters of the creek in flood, and tennis players pose on a grass court roughly marked out in a paddock—proof that life on the farm was not all hard work.

There is a cheerful innocence, a Dad and Dave simplicity, about these images. They capture a way of life soon to be extinguished by the machines and mod cons of the twentieth century. Of course, there were facets of farm life that escaped the camera's gaze—the pioneering work of clearing and fencing, the daily ritual of rising in the cold and dark before there was enough light for photographs to milk the cows, and the scenes inside the house, too dark for the Brownie's film, where the women made fires, cooked, washed, cleaned and sewed.

Gippsland was emerging from a testing time. Depression and drought had strained the local economy, as they had at Longwood, where Ted's cousin James Edward had recently quit town. A new generation of Maxfield boys was approaching adulthood, hoping to get farms of their own. In 1901, Ted sold off three hundred of his best cows, ostensibly because 'he feels he needs a change', but probably to recapitalise the farm after a period of poor returns. Soon afterwards he became the first farmer in the district to adopt milking machines, and in 1907 he purchased a further 1100 acres on Flynn's Creek, perhaps with his son Jack's approaching marriage in mind. On the surface it looked as though the Maxfields were going from strength to strength.

Then, quite suddenly, the sky fell in. As his grandson Colin relates, Ted was persuaded by a friend to invest in 'a good thing', a goldmining venture that then went bad. Rather than renege on his debts, Ted honourably insisted on paying them in full, even though it meant surrendering 'Woodstock'. In December 1909, the entire estate, 'the best dairy farm in the district', was put up for auction. Everything—478 acres of prime pasture, 350 cows, horses, bullocks, milking machines, cream separators, wagonette, sideboard and chiffonier, even a phonograph and fifty records—went under the hammer. When it was all over, the family moved, first to a leased farm in Jeeralang, and later to Drouin, where they began all over again.

Ted's father Robert, the Hereford miller, was still alive when 'Woodstock' was sold. He died three years later, aged 79. 'He was a fine specimen of the English yeomanry,' the *Gippsland Times* noted. The yeoman ideal had been the lodestar of many Australian pioneers. Robert Maxfield had witnessed the gradual extinction of the Hereford yeomanry but had hoped to revive the idea, as much as conditions allowed, in his adopted country. For a time the Maxfields made a fair go of it. What sustained them, one suspects, was not an economic ideal but a domestic one: a belief in the virtues of the self-reliant, cohesive, community-minded rural family.

FAMILY TRADITION

Like all histories, family history is selective. In choosing a path into the past, it follows some branches and prunes others. I had never heard of the Maxfields until I traced my great-great-grandparents, Robert and Elizabeth Hewett, back to the voyage of the *Culloden*. This prompted me to wonder about the fate of their brothers and sisters. Going back to their arrival, and looking forwards, encouraged me to think about my own branch of the family in a different way, as just one path among several. In marrying the Maxfield brothers, Lucy and Susan Hewett chose partners from rural origins much like their own. In Victoria, they remained farmers, millers and country storekeepers (even today the Maxfields' descendants mostly live outside the capital cities) and displayed cultural characteristics redolent of their village origins. Perhaps the Maxfields were more like the people the Hewetts had been before they left England than my own branch.

The more I discovered about the Maxfields, the more I liked them. Through all their ups and downs, they displayed resilience, a love of life, and a commitment to their friends and neighbours that inspired admiration and affection wherever they went. Reviewing the parallel, but largely separate, histories of James and Lucy, Robert and Susan, and their families, one is struck by similarities of outlook and orientation that seem much more than coincidental, and lead us to ponder that most elusive of questions: the influence of what may be called, for lack of a better word, family tradition.

Well beyond the first Australian generation, the Maxfields remained gregarious, popular, public-spirited people. James Edward had no sooner arrived in Cobden than he was again throwing himself into community affairs, chairing the local tennis club, the library and debating institute, and beginning a campaign to build another mechanics' institute. He stayed only three years before returning to the northeast as secretary of the Euroa Butter and Ice Factory. 'We can't replace Mr Maxfield,' one of his Cobden friends lamented as he departed. People should show more community spirit, James Edward replied. They should 'put their shoulder to the wheel and not sit at home by the fire'.

His lesson was not lost on his children. When England called in 1914, his eldest surviving son, Gordon, a 25-year-old bank accountant, did not hesitate to join up. He enlisted as a lieutenant in 1915, served at Gallipoli, and was promoted to captain in 1916. At the Somme and Fleurbaix he 'set an excellent example . . . by his coolness and self-control', winning a Military Cross. Like many of the Australians, however, he had begun to resent the apparently useless sacrifice of human life by the British high command. 'We have just come out of a place so terrible that . . . a raving lunatic would not imagine the horrors of the last 13 days,' he wrote to his parents after Pozières, warning them that the picture presented by the press was nothing like the reality. Weeks later, in April 1917, he was reported missing at the Battle of Bullecourt, one of the most disastrous Australian engagements of the war. He had led his men across the crater field to a position about five hundred yards (450 metres) beyond the Hindenburg line. There, while waiting for reinforcements, he was badly wounded by a German bomb. He handed over his command and attempted to return to the line, but never made it. When last seen, he was taking refuge in a shell hole from German sniper fire.

His parents endured several weeks of unbearable anxiety before the worst was confirmed: Gordon had apparently been blown to bits and his body could not be found. His mother, Jeannie, never really got over it, dying, quite literally, of a broken heart eighteen months later. Her husband began a polite but insistent correspondence with the military authorities, seeking more information about Gordon's death, his bodily remains, and the return of his possessions and decorations. Ever the community organiser, he sponsored a memorial for Gordon in St Peter's Anglican Church and presided over Euroa's first Anzac Day commemoration.

Gordon's second cousin Arthur Maxfield, son of Ted, a farmer like his father, had also joined up, as a private in the Second Pioneer Battalion. His was a less heroic war record than Gordon's, although also sacrificial in its way. Like Gordon, he served at the Battle of the Somme, mainly behind the lines, where the Pioneers built earthworks, roads and bridges. There he sustained an injury to his ankle which became ulcerated, and after some weeks in a field hospital was invalided out to a military hospital in Guildford, Surrey, only twenty kilometres from Hook, the village where his grandmother Susan had grown up. In an age before antibiotics, serious infections could be as fatal as a shell, but after almost two years Arthur was finally pronounced fit to travel, and he embarked for Australia in March 1919. He returned to the land, fathered two sons, and served as a director of the local butter factory. Two of his three grandchildren continued to live in Gippsland and maintained the Maxfield tradition of public service, one as a rural GP, another as a trade unionist and state Labor parliamentarian.

~

'All happy families are alike; each unhappy family is unhappy in its own way,' Tolstoy famously observed. In reality, few families are entirely happy or unhappy: like the Maxfields, most know seasons of joy and sadness, just as their members enjoy unequal measures of good fortune and bad. Yet Tolstoy was surely right in perceiving common characteristics that bind good families across generations. The Maxfields may not have been fortunate or happy in every way, but they were a good family who strengthened, and took strength, from the communities they helped to build.

Campbell's Creek, 1861. From Castlemaine the main road follows the creek valley, with the township spread out along its north-south axis. The shaded areas indicate the main alluvial deposits, with concentrations to the north, near Twenty Foot Hill and to the south near the Five Flags Hotel, each with a nearby Chinese Camp. Samuel Stephens's hay and corn store was located at the north end of the town opposite Campbell's Flat. (Map of Castlemaine, 1861 (detail), Victorian Mines Department)

CHAPTER SEVEN
Campbell's Creek

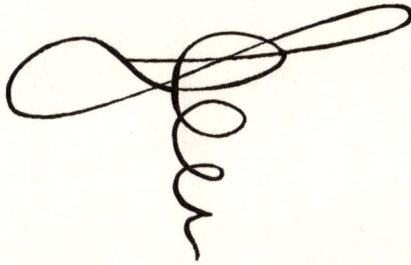

If you had asked me when I was a boy who we Hewetts and Davisons were, I would have had a ready answer. We were Methodists. My parents and most of my aunts, uncles and cousins were members of the church. We children all attended Methodist Sunday schools and youth groups. My grandfather Vic Hewett was a lay preacher and Bible class leader. My father was a trustee and sang in the choir, while my mother baked and sewed for the Ladies' Guild. The rituals of our faith, from the crowded Sunday school anniversary services and Cup Day picnics to the annual renditions of Handel's 'Messiah', were the high points of our year. We followed Methodism's austere moral code—no drinking, no gambling, no Sunday shopping or sport—almost to the letter.

Yet with this moral seriousness came the happiness and security of belonging to a large extended family. 'We all partake the joy of one/

163

THE STEPHENS OF CAMPBELL'S CREEK

Samuel Rowe Stephens
b. St Agnes Cornwall, 1819
d. Campbell's Creek 1872
m.
Martha Lloyd
b. Carmarthen, Wales, 1819
d. Campbell's Creek 1884

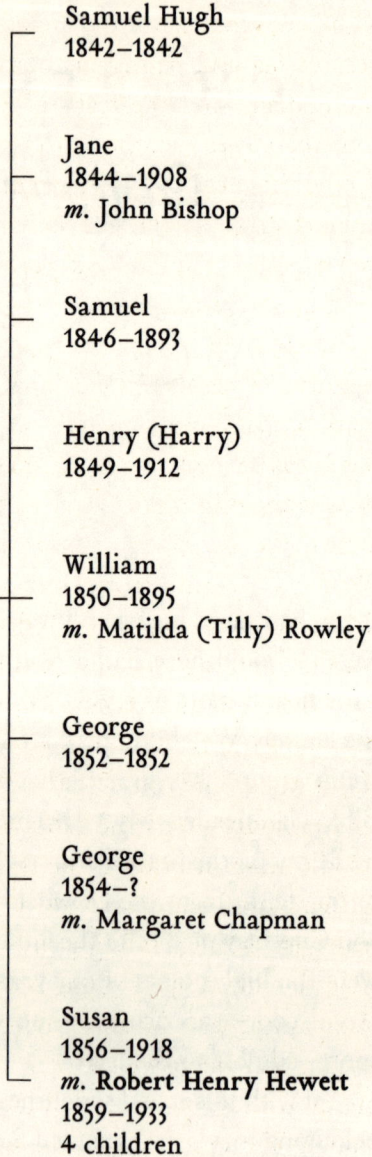

Samuel Hugh
1842–1842

Jane
1844–1908
m. John Bishop

Samuel
1846–1893

Henry (Harry)
1849–1912

William
1850–1895
m. Matilda (Tilly) Rowley

George
1852–1852

George
1854–?
m. Margaret Chapman

Susan
1856–1918
m. **Robert Henry Hewett**
1859–1933
4 children

The common peace we feel,' Methodism's co-founder, Charles Wesley, had written in one of the hymns we sang on festive occasions. My abiding childhood memory of Methodist gatherings is of conviviality rather than gloom. I remember the fervent hymn-singing in four-part harmony, the hum of excited conversation, the trestle tables laden with ham sandwiches and cream sponges, and the enormous enamel pots of tea and pannikins of raspberry cordial. The hallmark of Methodism, and the feature most despised by Wesley's educated contemporaries, was its 'enthusiasm'. Like the Romantics, the first Methodists challenged the emotional dryness of eighteenth-century rationalism. Over the succeeding two centuries, much would change in Methodist belief and practice, but this emotional warmth remained a feature of its communal life.

Methodism is now an almost extinct faith, but for almost two centuries it claimed about one-seventh of Australians and left its mark on large areas of national life, from the six o'clock closing of hotels to the moderate socialism of the Labor Party. In some regions, such as the mining fields of South Australia and Victoria, it became almost the dominant religion as judged by the number of active members. By the 1950s, Methodism was becoming more like other Protestant denominations, and was well down the path that ended with its merging into the Uniting Church of Australia in 1977. But even then, for those steeped in its history, doctrines and music (for Methodism was 'born in song'), it was much more than a creed, it was a way of life.

Methodism was the religion of the lower strata of the 'moral middle class'. It bridged the skilled working class (my father was a self-employed plumber) and the lower middle class (my grandfather managed a city printing firm). Post-war prosperity and university education lifted many young Methodists into the white-collar middle class, as teachers, nurses, accountants and engineers. The 1960s spirit of personal liberation dealt it a heavy blow, and only a minority of my own generation of Hewett descendants remained in the church. Yet something of the spirit of Methodism—its work ethic, its social conscience, its insecure middling position in the class hierarchy—marked us for life.

How did the Hewetts become Methodists? There was no trace of it, or of any religious enthusiasm, in the lives of the Hewetts and Fenwicks who arrived on the *Culloden*. The first hints of its influence came when Robert and Elizabeth moved to Forest Creek, where they lived near the first Methodist chapel on the goldfields, on what became known as Wesley Hill. Some of their neighbours, including the carpenter William Swalling, whose son John would marry their eldest daughter, Annie, were members of the Wesley Hill congregation. But both Robert and Elizabeth appear to have died, as they lived, nominal Independents.

In many families, religion was women's business. While the father's occupation determined the family's public standing, mothers often profoundly shaped its moral and spiritual outlook. Family historians following the male line may miss these spiritual lineages. A significant juncture in the history of the Hewett family came in 1880, the year after Elizabeth's death, when her eldest son, Robert Henry, married my great-grandmother Susan Stephens, youngest daughter of the staunchly Methodist Stephens family of Campbell's Creek. Susan's father, Samuel Rowe Stephens, had been born in Cornwall, where he was a miner, and migrated to South Australia, and later to Victoria where, after a brief venture into mining, he became a hay and corn merchant, volunteer soldier, shire councillor and a stalwart of the town. Cornwall was a bastion of Methodism, and Susan and her family helped transmit its influence into the goldfields of Victoria.

WHO WERE THE METHODISTS?

The first Methodist, John Wesley (born in 1703), the son of a rural clergyman, was educated at Oxford, where he embarked on a quest for personal holiness. His attempt to become a missionary in North

America failed, but on the return voyage he met a group of Moravians, members of a pietistic German sect, and shortly afterwards, in May 1738, at a meeting in Aldersgate Street, London, he at last found the assurance of personal salvation for which he had yearned. 'I felt my heart strangely warmed,' he recalled. This evangelical experience became the inspiration of a life-long crusade for the moral and religious salvation of England. Over the next forty years, Wesley travelled the length of the country on horseback, preaching to excited, sometimes hostile, crowds, usually in the open air.

Wesley's message struck a deep chord among the working people of Cornwall, South Wales, Yorkshire and the East Midlands, regions already feeling the first tremors of the Industrial Revolution. He visited Cornwall 32 times, including almost twenty visits to Samuel Stephens' birthplace, St Agnes, a tin-mining village on the northwest coast. 'I preached to a large multitude of quiet hearers, many of whom seem deeply affected; yet soon after I had done some began to divert themselves with throwing dirt and clods,' Wesley wrote in his journal after visiting the village in July 1746. His battle against a still vigorous local culture of wrestling, drinking, smuggling and magic continued for years. Forty years later, he was gratified to preach to 'the largest congregation I ever saw there'.

By the early nineteenth century, Cornwall had become a Methodist stronghold. 'The religion of the mass is become Wesleyan Methodism,' a local vicar observed. Almost one-third of Cornwall's population were members, and most of the rest were adherents. Methodism was partly filling the gaps left by the neglect of the Church of England and the older branches of religious nonconformity: 60 per cent of Wesley's converts came from the eleven English counties where organised Christianity was previously weakest. Within those regions, however, it appealed strongly to the young, including women, and to the skilled working class. In St Agnes, Methodism was as much a part of the atmosphere as the smoke billowing from the tall chimneys of the nearby tin mines.

THE MINING TRAIL

Tin had been mined in western Cornwall since the Middle Ages, but by the time of Samuel's birth in 1819, the youngest of nine children, St Agnes' mines had peaked. Steam engines, which enabled miners to go deeper with greater safety, had revolutionised mining, which remained, however, a hard and dangerous occupation, suitable only for fit young men. In the one photograph we have of him, taken in later life, Samuel seems to have inherited the stocky build of the typical Cornish miner. By 1841, aged 21, he was still living at home with his father Alexander, a blacksmith, his mother Mary and three siblings, and working as a tin miner in one of the local mines. Before the year was out, however, he had left St Agnes for Liskeard, 60 kilometres away in eastern Cornwall, where the discovery of rich deposits of copper had sparked a new mining boom. For the next five years he worked underground in the nearby South Caradon Mine, one of the largest and most advanced in Cornwall.

Soon after arriving, on 2 December 1841, he married Martha Lloyd, a native of Carmarthen in South Wales. A 22-year-old 'Martha Loyd' had been living, apparently in lodgings, in St Agnes earlier that year, and the couple may already have become engaged before they departed. Why she was living so far from her parental home is unclear, although the distance may have been less formidable than it now appears. Ships regularly crossed the Bristol Channel carrying copper and tin ore to the smelters of Carmarthen on the South Wales coalfields, and there was a constant flow of people between the two coasts. We do not know how they met, although the Wesleyan church, a home away from home for many young people, is the most likely setting. That they married in Liskeard Parish Church, rather than a Wesleyan chapel, may not signify much. Until the Marriage Act of 1836, only a priest of the Church of England could perform a legally valid wedding, and the custom of marrying in church was slow to die, even among Wesleyans.

Samuel and Martha's first child, Samuel Hugh, named after his father and maternal grandfather, died in infancy. A daughter, Jane, was born in 1844, and a second son, also named Samuel, in 1846. Both were baptised in the Wesleyan chapel when they were about eight weeks old. In reusing the father's name, Samuel, for their second son as well as their dead first child, the parents were following a tradition common until the early nineteenth century, although rarer by the mid-century. In an age when many children died in infancy, family honour and the sense of continuity symbolised by the inheritance of a name took precedence over the individuality that we now attribute to babies from birth. The birth of the second Samuel did not expunge the memory of the first, but it may have helped to compensate in some way for his loss. He was not to be the last replacement child.

In moving from St Agnes to Liskeard, Samuel Stephens was taking the first step on a journey that would end halfway across the world. Mining has always been a volatile industry, and miners, even in England, were used to moving jobs and houses as the map of opportunity changed. Two of Samuel's siblings had already migrated to Wisconsin in the United States. In the mid-1840s, as the Cornish copper mines entered harder times and industrial friction grew, reports appeared of new mineral discoveries in South Australia. Cornish miners had first arrived in the colony in the late 1830s, and by the mid-1840s a 'Little Cornwall' of tin- and copper-mining villages had grown up at Kadina, Moonta and Wallaroo on Yorke Peninsula.

In May 1846, an article in the *Cornwall Gazette* on 'The Mineral Regions of South Australia' announced an even more astounding discovery. At Burra, 160 kilometres north of Adelaide, miners had uncovered copper ores 'of extraordinary richness, and in such immense abundance, that very experienced miners from Cornwall, Wales and Germany, of whom there are now many in the province, have declared that they never heard of or saw anything to equal them'. The 'Monster Mine' of Burra Burra was soon hailed as one of the wonders of the world. Miners working on 'tribute', the traditional

Cornish system under which workers shared the proceeds of what they mined, were said to be earning as much as a pound a day.

Letters from Cornish miners in South Australia boasting of their success appeared in newspapers in South Wales, where the ore was smelted, as well as in Cornwall. 'Here is the place to live!' one emigrant exulted. 'The dogs here get more beef and mutton than we get in England.' An agent of the Colonial Land and Emigration Commissioners stationed at Plymouth, J.B. Wilcocks, toured Cornwall and Devon selecting the most suitable candidates for assisted emigration. In June 1846, the *South Australian News*, a promotional newspaper published in the west of England, predicted that five hundred Cornish miners with their wives and children would set sail for Adelaide over the following two months. More than one-third of assisted emigrants to South Australia between 1846 and 1850 came from Cornwall, a county with less than 3 per cent of the United Kingdom population.

Among them were Samuel Stephens, his wife Martha and their two children. Samuel had applied for a free passage early in August 1846. The decision seems to have been made in a hurry and perhaps under financial pressure. On 8 August, he swore an affidavit before a local magistrate attesting to his age, date of marriage and the ages of his children, explaining that 'the reason I cannot procure mine & my wife's registry of baptism is the great distance we are from our native homes and the expense it would incur in getting them is more than I could at present afford'. A week later, the Stephenses' certificates 'appearing to be correct and satisfactory', John Marshall and Company, London Agents of the South Australian government, issued an embarkation order admitting the family, upon payment of one pound for each adult passenger, to a free passage to South Australia on the ship *Abberton*. They were directed to present themselves just ten days later, on 25 August, at the Plymouth Emigration Depot.

At the last moment, Samuel secured a 'character', or reference, from his employer Thomas Kittow, 'Purser and large proprietor' of the South Caradon Mine.

The bearer Samuel Stephens has been employed in the above Mine for the last five years, during which period he has borne the character of a good miner, and I believe him to be a strictly honest man, and as such I can recommend him to the notice of any person, or Company who may require his services in the management of mining operations.

That word 'character' was a favourite of the mid-Victorians, for whom morality was the surest test of personal worth and an essential qualification for any job requiring trust and reliability. The signed piece of paper attesting a man's character was hard currency in a day when people travelled far and former employers could not be consulted easily. Kittow, a local yeoman before the discovery of the copper ores on his land, would become one of the largest mine proprietors in Cornwall, live to be 100 years old and leave a fortune of £75,000. Samuel would be relying on his employer's reputation to open up a responsible position, perhaps as a 'captain', or manager, in South Australia.

The *Abberton*, a 450-ton barque and a 'regular trader' on the Australian run, left London early in August under the command of Captain Thomas Pain before picking up the rest of its company, mainly miners from the west of England, at Plymouth. It set sail for South Australia on 1 September with eight cabin passengers and almost 190 assisted emigrants, males and females in almost equal numbers. About half, including the Stephenses, came as family groups. Most were agricultural labourers and miners, although there appear to have been a number of Irish female servants as well.

Inspired by reformer Edward Gibbon Wakefield's theories of 'systematic colonisation', the founders of South Australia wanted to build a respectable, prosperous society free of the convict taint of New South Wales and Van Diemen's Land. The new mineral discoveries boosted the colony's attractiveness to the skilled and respectable migrants it needed. When the *Princess Royal* left Plymouth in November with another two hundred emigrants, Mr Wilcocks the emigration agent was on hand to farewell them. 'The excellent character and satisfactory testimonials which you have produced assure me that your future conduct will be marked by frugal habits, persevering industry, and attention to your pursuits,' he declared. The farewell party adjourned to the captain's cabin for an excellent dinner 'with a bountiful supply of champagne and other wines'. Before the guests sat down, the emigrants assembled to hear their shipmate John Rowe, a miner from Lanhydrock in Cornwall, render his own composition, 'The Emigrants' Song':

> *Come on my brethren, let us sing,*
> *Unto that city bright;*
> *There need not one be left behind,*
> *For Christ does all invite.*
> *Chorus—And to glory we will sail, we'll sail,*
> *and to glory we will sail.*

At its conclusion, the singer was offered a glass of wine, but the devout Methodist and total abstainer politely declined. Altogether, the 'quiet and orderly conduct' of the emigrants presented a welcome contrast to 'the scenes of riot and debauchery' that had once accompanied the departure of migrant vessels.

AUSTRALIA'S LITTLE CORNWALL

After a three-month voyage, the *Abberton* arrived in Port Adelaide on 12 December 1846. One child was born and four children and one adult perished during the passage. Although it was described as a 'First Class Ship' with 'most regular accommodation', life on the *Abberton* was probably no more comfortable than on the *Culloden*, even if the passengers and crew were better behaved. Its arrival in Adelaide aroused interest because it brought news of the latest sales of copper ore from Burra to the Swansea smelters at prices markedly above those for mines in Devon and Cornwall.

Today Australians count ourselves lucky for our mineral wealth, but we are less reliant than South Australians were upon the country's first mineral boom. In less than five years, minerals grew from 10 per cent to over two-thirds of the colony's exports. 'You might safely say all South Australia was indirectly employed by the Burra mine,' Henry Ayers, secretary of the South Australian Mining Association, claimed with only a little exaggeration. Samuel and Martha had arrived at a critical moment, just as the most accessible ore bodies at Burra were being worked out. The company needed experienced Cornish miners and mine managers like Samuel to take charge of the next phase of its operations, as it sank shafts and drove tunnels into the deeper deposits of copper ore.

From Adelaide, the family made their way to Burra, perhaps hitching a ride on the return trip of one of the hundreds of bullock wagons carrying copper ore from the mining field to the coast. In the settlements surrounding the 'Monster Mine', they were in environmentally strange but socially familiar territory. Like its Cornish counterparts, Samuel's employer, the South Australian Mining Association, was a 'stern godfather to its employees', notes historian Geoffrey Blainey.

The people of Burra worshipped in chapels on land donated by the company, ate meat slaughtered in the company's abattoirs, drank water from the company's wells, brought their relatives from Cornwall at the company's expense, and were buried in the cemetery at whose gate the company's sexton presided.

Some lived in stone cottages erected by the company in villages scattered around the mine, while 1800 people lived in underground houses dug from the banks of a creek.

Although Samuel may have been better paid than at home, life on the mining frontier also brought hardship and sadness, especially for Martha. Three more boys were born during their residence in Burra, Henry (Harry) (1849), William (September 1850) and George

(September 1852), the last dying soon after birth. Far from home and without supportive kin, Martha must have felt this sorrow keenly, although she appears to have been slow to contact her family in the old country. She had left home in a hurry and may have been reluctant to re-establish contact. When at last she wrote, in 1849, her elder sister's reply must have come as a shock.

Mr Samuel Stephens, miner
Burra Burra Mine

Carmarthan
August 12 1849

My dear Brother & sister,
I have received your letter dated January 4th and was happy to hear from you, especially from such a remote part of the Globe. We were until the arrival of your letter quite at a loss to judge what had become of you whether dead or alive, or that you had entirely put us out of remembrance, but thank God I have now had the pleasure at last of receiving a most welcome and a long expected letter.

I am sorry of being under the painful task of informing you of the deaths of my Dear departed Father and my Sister Elizabeth. My poor Father Departed this life on the 13th day of November 1846 which is 3 years in November and it was on the 16th March 1847 that my sister Elizabeth died in childbirth on two little girls (twins). They lived a couple of months & died in their infancy leaving five small infant children to bewail their loss of an affectionate and tender mother, her husband is married to the second wife and lives in Pembroke. The children are all in the enjoyment of good healths.

I should have been extremely happy if the Lord had spared my poor father's life to have received a letter from you as his constant talk was about you and when he received the few words of your having sailed from England he said 'There is a nail in my coffin'. My youngest brother David is married in Merthyr and one child and doing remarkably well. Your brother George has removed from the Parade & keeps trade for himself as Boot & Shoemaker in King Street, Your sister Jane is doing well, she is in service with a gentleman. I am still single and at home keeping the house open as before. Your cousin Mary Lewis is married to Tom Llewellyn, the mason, of Lammas Street and does well. He has a little girl 8 months old her name is Martha. Wm Lewis's little boy Henry is dead these two years ago. Your Uncle and aunt Lewis are all well also the children who hand and heart join in love to you wishing to you the enjoyment of good healths and prosperity. Please to accept the united love of Jane and myself, your Brothers George and David also their families. And I beg to remain

My dear Brother & Sister
Your affectionate Sister
Mary Lloyd.

The fact that Martha kept this one letter is evidence enough of its impact. I wonder how often she reread her father's words 'There is a nail in my coffin' and blamed herself for leaving him without so much as a farewell visit. When she read her sister's barely disguised reproaches, did she try to heal the breach or decide it was irreparable? We do not know, but either way a shadow had fallen over the relationship. As with many other colonial families, emigration had exacted a heavy emotional cost.

A NEW RUSH

Australia's first mining boom was about to be eclipsed by its second, the rush to the goldfields of Victoria that began in September 1851. One of the lessons of the Burra boom was that luck favoured the first-comers. The easiest and most spectacular finds were made in the first phase of alluvial mining, when gold was literally picked out of the ground. And, of course, gold had an allure that simply outshone copper and tin. So when news of the finds at Ballarat and Forest Creek reached South Australia, it sparked an exodus by land and sea for the new fields. Mineral production in South Australia peaked in 1852 but plummeted the following year. The young and unattached were always the first to leave. Samuel and Martha, with their young family, were not among the first wave of departures but appear to have left sometime after the birth of George in September 1852. Their names do not appear in the lists of passengers sailing between Adelaide and Melbourne; like hundreds of others, they probably travelled overland by horse dray, bullock wagon or on foot.

A fellow Cornishman, Charles Rule, took just over five weeks to make the 750-kilometre journey in February and March of 1852. With five others he set out in a horse and dray. They crossed the lower Murray and skirted the Coorong before crossing the Ninety Mile Desert and heading into the Mallee scrub. They carefully picked a course between waterholes and soaks, purchasing flour, mutton and horse feed from sheep stations and pubs along the way. They encountered groups of Aboriginals, who warily observed them from a distance. Some other travellers fell by the wayside, their plans overturned by dead or lame horses, sparse feed, sickness and even the deaths of the travellers themselves. As he came within reach of his destination, the Mount Alexander diggings, Rule rejoiced in the hillier aspect of the country, a welcome relief from 'a continuous flat world' of the western plains. Seeing the Forest Creek diggings for the first time, he marvelled at the 'novel spectacle' of so many people living in tents. 'It puts one in mind of the ancient times spoken of by the writers of the Scriptures, when the patriarchs lived in tents and went from one country to another as the pastures gets scarce in one of them.'

When Samuel and Martha reached Castlemaine sometime in 1853, the first rush along Forest Creek was over, and miners were transferring their hopes to its southern tributary, Campbell's Creek, where the Cornish Methodists were already gathering. In 1852, James Bonwick camped there overnight. 'I was delighted with the sounds of psalmody proceeding from the opposite tent,' he recalled. When other, more profane campers struck up in opposition, they were cried down. 'The revellers yielded to the pressure from without, and again the sweet notes of praise to Jehovah resounded through the quiet glen.' The glen may have been Ranters' Gully, named for the Primitive Methodists, or Ranters as they were sometimes called, who congregated there. By the 1860s, about one-third of the town's adult males were Cornish.

In Samuel Calvert's 1864 view of Campbell's Creek, the Standard Brewery looms over a community of Methodist teetotallers, symbolised by its rival Wesleyan and Primitive Methodist churches. (State Library of Victoria)

By the time he arrived in Campbell's Creek, Samuel was in his mid-thirties and had been working underground for close to twenty years. Forty was commonly regarded as the practical retirement age for a working miner. He had four children, all below ten years of age. Two more children, George (born 1854 and replacing the George who died soon before their departure) and Susan (1856), would be born in Campbell's Creek.

Early in 1853, about three thousand people were at work along Campbell's Creek, most living in tents pitched along both sides of the stream. A year later, however, the population had levelled off, and by early in 1855 a visitor concluded that only 'a little gold is still left in these diggings'. Mining was 'chiefly confined to Chinese', yet by the end of the decade the population had swelled again and an estimated three thousand Chinese miners were living along the creek, most in two camps on the eastern slopes above the township and behind the Five Flags Hotel. Their population continued to fluctuate, but in 1871 they still comprised a third of Campbell's Creek's population.

European miners were meanwhile forming companies and small syndicates to extract gold from the deep leads and quartz bodies. Their camps were rapidly becoming permanent towns. 'One of the most pleasing features of this creek,' the *Mount Alexander Mail*'s local correspondent noted in 1858, 'is the number of neat and comfortable dwellings, many of them with small allotments of ground, trimly cultivated, attached . . . I am informed that most of these tenements belong to members of the Methodist connexion, a majority of whom are also teetotallers.' He likened these settlements to the villages on the edge of English industrial towns, especially in Cornwall, where miners had long enjoyed the opportunity to acquire their own bit of land and a cottage.

By 1858, Samuel had abandoned mining, at least as a full-time occupation, and set up as a hay and corn dealer. 'There is a spirit of enterprise abroad and building progress is going on which is worthy of all praise,' a visitor to the town observed, citing the recent appearance of Hobby and Huxted's ironmongery, Rowe's wheelwright's shop, Clifton's Drapery ('The People's Stores'), and 'Mr Stevens' [*sic*] hay and corn store and brick dwelling, a handsome erection'.

In the horse-and-buggy era, a hay and corn store was as important as a petrol service station is in the automobile era. Situated in the middle of the town, on the main road to Guildford and Daylesford (now the Midland Highway), halfway between the Wesleyan and Primitive Methodist churches, and just opposite the Rechabite Hall, Stephens' store and its adjoining dwelling, a sturdy four-room brick cottage with a pleasant veranda, was one of the social hubs of the district. As locals called in to buy feed for their horses, they exchanged news about local affairs, and Samuel himself became well known and trusted. Along with the house and store, he purchased nine other blocks of land in the town in his own name, and one each in the names of his four sons, Samuel, Henry, William and George. Like many old diggers, he also dabbled in mining shares, with small stakes in the local Cumberland, Phoenix and Nuggetty mines. He joined the First Castlemaine Volunteer Rifle Brigade as a bandsman (band music was another feature of Cornish culture), and in 1861 entered local politics as a member of the Campbell's Creek Roads Board, fighting for the abolition of the tollgate on the road between Castlemaine and Guildford. A corn merchant campaigning for free roads was rather like a service station owner fighting for freeways. When the Road District eventually merged with the Shire of Castlemaine, Samuel became a shire councillor; and when the government moved to establish a common (public) school in the district, he was an automatic appointee to the Board of Advice. 'Universally respected for his urbanity and strict integrity', Samuel had become a pillar of the community.

A motorist driving down the Midland Highway from Castlemaine today has only to blink and he would nearly miss Campbell's Creek, a once thriving town now reduced to little more than a hamlet. He would see little to remind him of the poppet heads, brewery, shops and houses that once lined the highway, and nothing at all of the large Chinese settlement that almost dominated, and often disturbed, its European residents. Some of the allotments Samuel purchased in the mid-1860s were on ground occupied only a few years earlier by the largest Chinese camp.

When I first began to reconstruct the lives of the Stephens family, I was following the religious thread—the Methodism that was their most distinctive legacy—but I soon began to wonder how their religion connected with other aspects of their lives. How did they cope with the realisation that the gold was running out and their town was gradually dying? How did they respond to the presence of so many Chinese in their midst? And why, when the town itself was declining, were the Methodists so prosperous?

HIGH-VOLTAGE RELIGION

In 1864, the Castlemaine circuit, or district, which included Bendigo and other nearby towns, claimed no fewer than 82 Wesleyan churches and chapels, 2339 members enrolled in class meetings, 5797 Sabbath school scholars, and 14,643 attending Sunday worship. Within the circuit, support for the church was stronger in the outlying villages than in Castlemaine itself. And the strongest of these, a contemporary noted, was Campbell's Creek, whose congregation 'as to strength of numbers and fervour of piety [stood] first in the Circuit'. In 1871, 42 per cent of Campbell's Creek's population were Methodists, more than three times their proportion throughout the colony.

'Methodism,' writes Alan Atkinson, 'was a religion of movement.' It was able to transplant itself into new communities like the Victorian goldfields with a minimum of ecclesiastical apparatus. (The term 'circuit' originated from the Methodist practice of ministers itinerating, or 'circulating', through a chain of chapels and preaching places.) With his Bible and hymnbook, the individual believer had almost all the spiritual aids he needed. Methodist local preachers—laymen with a rudimentary religious training—travelled in advance of its ordained clergy, establishing congregations and class meetings well before Conference, the central organisation, formalised their plantation.

There was a persistent tension within Wesleyan Methodism between centralised clerical control and local lay leadership. In 1810, these tensions had broken to the surface when a group of lay preachers in Staffordshire, led by the carpenter Hugh Bourne, began holding revivalist 'camp meetings' in the style of the Great Awakening, the religious movement that had recently swept through the eastern United States. Their actions precipitated a split between Wesleyan Methodism and the 'Primitive Methodists', as they became known. The Primitives spread rapidly from the industrial Midlands into East Anglia and Yorkshire, where their desire to recover 'the simplicity and uniformity of Primitive Methodism' won an enthusiastic response. In colonial Australia, especially in regions of rapid population change and social turmoil, like the copper belt of South Australia and the Victorian goldfields, the Primitives won a strong, if volatile, following.

'Shall we have a revival in Victoria?' the *Wesleyan Chronicle* asked in 1861. It had often lamented the spiritual state of the goldfields, where many Methodists had 'forgotten their religion' and 'the mass of the population [was] but a step from heathendom'. There had been small revivals in South Australia's Little Cornwall in the late 1840s and again in the late 1850s. Now the time seemed ripe for a fresh spiritual awakening. In 1863–64, an American evangelist, William 'California' Taylor, a six-footer with a stentorian delivery, preached to eager congregations in Melbourne and throughout the goldfields, including Castlemaine. Some Wesleyans were wary of the frank pragmatism and emotionalism of the American revivalists, but the evidence of spiritual growth was enough for most to put aside their reservations. 'Better a thousand times the wild hurricane than a calm miasma,' one argued. Between 1863 and 1865, Wesleyan membership in Victoria grew by 34 per cent.

During this period, Campbell's Creek Wesleyans experienced 'several mighty revivals . . . winter after winter, so that the membership was greatly augmented'. In 1863, there was a revival meeting every night for ten weeks, with prayer and preaching often extending into the small hours. The church's membership grew from 335 to 455 in the late 1850s, and by the mid-1860s it had reached 556. Meanwhile, their rivals, the Primitive Methodists, also witnessed 'a gracious revival', with camp meetings drawing new members to both the church and Sabbath school. Of the six hundred Primitive

Methodist members in the Castlemaine circuit, most were in the Campbell's Creek congregation.

Encouraged by their spiritual success, the Wesleyans and the Primitives vied to outdo each other with ambitious church-building programs, investing thousands of borrowed pounds on new Gothic churches and Sunday schools. As their town slowly declined, they buoyed their spirits with love feasts and anniversary tea meetings, teetotal extravaganzas so lavish that years later a former minister still recalled them with feelings of exhaustion. 'Again and again were the tables filled, while the fare itself was of that sumptuous description for which the place has become famous,' another remarked. Methodist festivity was shaped as a conscious 'counterpoise to the rollicking songs, banjos and tambourines, hurdy-gurdies and concertinas' of the competing pubs and gambling haunts.

Historians have often pondered the causes of these periodic eruptions of religious fervour. In a famous book, *The Making of the English Working Class* (1963), E.P. Thompson detected an oscillation between periods of high political excitement and the religious revivals that often followed them. Political disappointment, he argued, often drove its followers towards religious enthusiasm, 'the chiliasm of despair'. In Australia, where some contemporaries feared that the discovery of gold would plunge the colonies into violent disorder, Methodists were credited with a calming influence on the morals and politics of the populace. But if the revivals of the early 1860s had a social cause, it lay not in political disappointment—for, after all, the miners' protests had hastened political democracy—so much as in economic decline and uncertainty. In Cornwall, revivalist activity had often accompanied a slump in mining activity. 'Sudden release from old social pressures, and the personal disorientation to which this often led, exposed [mining communities] to religious excitement of a very high voltage,' one historian observed. As the excitement and optimism of the gold rush subsided, the Methodists turned back to the God of their Cornish and Welsh forebears.

To make apple cakes

Take 2 lbs of dough, roll it out thin, spread equally over it 5 oz each of coffee and sugar, a little allspice, and 2 oz of butter, then fold and roll it again 2 or 3 times; afterwards roll it out thin and spread over it 4 large apples, pared and chopped small, fold it up and roll till mixed, let it stand to rise after half a pound of butter may be added.

EXOTIC NEIGHBOURS

The revivalist preachers sought to reclaim the 'lost' souls of a gold-fields population they portrayed as mired in sin. John Wesley had stressed the free will of believers and the unbounded grace of God to sinners—even the 'harlots, publicans and thieves' addressed in one of his brother's most famous hymns. Closer, however, to the Methodists' homes than the harlots and publicans were the hundreds of 'heathen' Chinese miners living in camps on the outskirts of Campbell's Creek. During the 1850s, European miners had protested that it was a 'moral and physical impossibility' to continue living among the Chinese. Yet the Chinese stayed, and as the Stephens children grew up they must have been a familiar presence, walking between their mine workings and the camps. The smells from their large communal kitchens wafted across the town, and rumours of their exotic customs and beliefs circulated on the local grapevine. The young men of the town sometimes subjected 'John Chinaman' to tricks and taunts, as when they stole the food that mourners left beside Chinese graves in the cemetery. A reporter who visited the area in the late 1850s noted the regularity and quietness of the Chinese camps ('there is no boisterous carousing, no stentorian blaspheming, such as may be heard in more civilised neighbourhoods') but recoiled from the 'filthy sights and smells' of people who seemed to disregard English notions of hygiene. He admired their peaceful and orderly disposition but abhorred their addiction to opium smoking and gambling.

In fact, Europeans had their own addictions, to alcohol and gambling, which made the Chinese, in Methodist eyes, no worse than many of their other neighbours. In 1862, a Chinese missionary appointed by the Campbell's Creek Wesleyans attempted to persuade three Chinese opium smokers to give up the habit. 'They said it was no harm, Englishmen liked drink, Chinamen liked opium. I told them both practices were wicked, and hurt body and soul.' The missionary may also have struggled to justify the difference between the Chinese passion for mahjong and fantan and the addiction of many Methodist miners, including Samuel Stephens, to speculation in mining shares. While the Wesleyans sent their missionaries into the camps, the Chinese displayed little interest in joining communities that, for all their professed openness, were as redolent of their Cornish origins as the Chinese camps were of theirs. As closely as they lived to each other, the Cornish and Chinese residents of Campbell's Creek inhabited different worlds.

Some residents wished the races were even further apart. In 1874, shortly after the passage of the Victorian Education Act, they petitioned the colonial government to build a new, larger school on a site closer to the main concentration of the population. 'The present school no. 120,' they explained, 'is situated in close proximity to the Chinese Camp which is frequented by disreputable characters of both sexes (not Chinese) whose behaviour it is very undesirable that children should witness.' They may have been alluding to the white women who offered themselves as prostitutes to the predominantly male Chinese. Most of the signatories, including a 'Mrs Stephens'— probably Samuel's widow, Martha—came from Ranters' Gully, the Primitive Methodist stronghold on the northwestern side of the town. A rival petition, signed by residents in the vicinity of the Five Flags Hotel, including several Chinese, urged the government to extend the school on its present site. A ballot showed opinion among townsfolk to be almost equally divided, so the school remained where it was.

The prime targets of Methodist revivalism were not the heathen outside the church but the children within it. When the gold-rush generation settled down, married and began families of their own, they produced a baby boom, much like the one that hit Australia after the Second World War. By 1861, about half Campbell's Creek's population were children and young people under the age of 21. The Stephens family, whose children ranged from five-year-old Susan to seventeen-year-old Jane, was typical of many. For young Samuel, Henry, William and George, the creek and surrounding gold workings were like an enormous, but dangerous, adventure playground. Their parents, however, may have been more afraid of the moral quicksands of the gold towns than they were of the tunnels and mine shafts that surrounded them. 'We feel anxious to protect and benefit the rising generation, to save them from places that have an evil tendency, such as the ballroom, theatre, and the place most of all to be dreaded, the public house,' one of the town's Methodist ministers averred. It was imperative 'to bring them to the Saviour before they go out into the world to be cast on the sea of time, and exposed to all the glittering baits of sin'.

The Stephens family were Wesleyans and loyal members of the Campbell's Creek church. But how deeply were they affected by the revivalist enthusiasm of that era? One of the few items inherited through my grandfather and mother is a tiny leather-bound volume, just 95 by 50 millimetres, entitled:

A COLLECTION
OF
HYMNS
FOR THE USE OF THE PEOPLE CALLED
METHODISTS

BY THE REV. JOHN WESLEY A.M.
Sometime Fellow of Lincoln College, Oxford

Inside the front cover is the partially erased inscription:

Stephens
bell's Creek
February 1862

On the flyleaf are the numbers of the owner's favourite hymns: 343 ('Oh for a heart to praise my God,/A heart from sin set free'), 474 ('Captain of our salvation take/The souls we here present to thee') and 73 ('Away with our sorrow and fear,/We soon shall recover our home,/The city of saints shall appear,/The day of eternity come'). Salvation, commitment, assurance of eternal life—these were the perennial themes of the revivalist preacher. Inside the back cover, in a childish hand, Henry Stephens, the family's thirteen-year-old son, has written his name, with the date October 1863. The hymnbook passed in turn to his younger sister Susan, my great-grandmother, and eventually to my own mother.

THE EXODUS

Early in May 1872, Samuel joined the Castlemaine Volunteers on a weekend camp. It rained and he returned with a severe cold. The cold turned to bronchitis, and by Tuesday he was too ill to attend his usual Tuesday evening Mount Alexander Shire Council meeting. Twenty years working underground in dust-filled mines may have weakened his respiratory system. His bronchitis was further complicated by 'serous effusion of the brain', a kind of meningitis. Three days later the 53-year-old was dead. 'His sudden departure from our midst . . . will be severely felt,' the *Mount Alexander Mail* lamented.

Samuel had been a member of the Volunteers for eleven years, playing his tuba as a sergeant in the regimental band. Two days later, 71 comrades from the Castlemaine Rifles and Cavalry Troop assembled outside his house in Main Street to accompany him on his last journey. When his coffin was brought out, the procession presented and reversed arms before setting off, at a slow march, to the strains of 'The Dead March' from Handel's *Saul*. At the Campbell's Creek cemetery, Mr Williams the Wesleyan minister read the service, and a firing party discharged three volleys over the grave 'in a remarkably precise manner'. A large attendance of Samuel's friends attested 'the great respect' he had won throughout the locality.

On the tombstone Martha later erected over his grave, she acknowledged Samuel's birthplace ('late of St Agnes, Cornwall') and his public position ('For many years a Member of the Campbell's Creek Road Board and Shire Council'), and lauded his personal qualities: 'He passed his days in the practice of domestic virtue. May thy life, Reader, be as free from blame, and thy death be as deservedly lamented.' Here, in a public place, and in language evoking the Puritans', she made the death of her 'beloved husband' the occasion for a little homily in stone.

When Samuel died, his children were still living close to home. His eldest surviving child, 28-year-old Jane, had married another townsman, John Bishop, a native of Gwennap, near St Agnes. With their two children, Samuel and Martha, they also lived nearby in Campbell's Creek. The Stephenses' four surviving boys had not yet married, and continued to live and work in the district. Susan, the youngest child, was only fifteen when her father died. After so many boys, her parents seem to have doted on their baby girl, judging by the number of attractive studio portraits that survive. In the earliest, a self-possessed nine- or ten-year-old wears a hoop-skirted party dress and a necklace. Later photographs show a young woman of character, fashionably dressed, her hair tightly gathered, her cheek resting pensively on her hand, eyes fixed intently on the viewer. After Samuel's death, Susan stayed on at home, helping her mother, and she was 24, three years older than Robert Henry Hewett, when they married in 1880.

When and where they met we do not know. From Wesley Hill to Campbell's Creek was about seven kilometres by road, although Robert could have shortened the journey by cutting through the bush, down Poverty Gully and across Specimen Flat. Socially, the Stephenses had been a cut above the Hewetts, but Samuel's premature death had cost the family status. A more significant barrier may have been the religious one, but Robert, a handsome young man with a trade, was a good prospect and became a devout Methodist too. As a Methodist, he pledged himself to strict abstinence from alcoholic beverages and unceasing warfare against the drink traffic. After the wedding, Robert and Susan lived for a year or so with Martha in Campbell's Creek, where their first child, my grandfather Victor Stephens Hewett, was born in 1882.

Campbell's Creek was one of dozens of small communities created by the gold rush. Once the rush ended, they declined, often precipitously. Between 1871 and 1891, when Melbourne grew by almost 300,000, the goldfields lost about 50,000 people. Campbell's Creek declined even faster, more than halving its population, from 1875 in 1871 to 822 in 1891. The rosy expectations that had led Samuel to invest in local land and mining shares faded. The Methodist churches, erected with borrowed money in the wake of the revivals, struggled with shrinking congregations and crippling debts. 'The town and the district have . . . witnessed the departure, in droves, both of stalwart men, and of the rising and enterprising youth of the colony,' one of its former Methodist ministers lamented.

Gradually the Stephens family dispersed: Samuel junior, a butcher by trade, married a publican's daughter in Echuca; William became a contractor in Long Gully, near Bendigo; and George moved to Adelaide and later joined the 1890s gold rush to Western Australia. Only Harry, a bachelor, and Jane and her family remained in Campbell's Creek. Robert Henry and Susan lingered for two or three years, but after their mothers died there was less reason to stay. Elizabeth Hewett, as we have seen, died suddenly in 1879, and Martha Stephens in January 1884, just a few weeks after the birth of Reuben, Susan's second son. She was buried with Primitive Methodist rites beside her husband in the Campbell's Creek cemetery under an epitaph taken from the famous Evangelical hymn 'Rock of Ages': 'Nothing in my hand I bring/Simply to Thy cross I cling'.

THE SEA OF TIME

In 1880, the year of Robert and Susan's marriage, Robert Mitchell, a local councillor, founded the Castlemaine Pioneers' and Old Residents' Association. It was a gesture of respect for the town's founders, now beginning to pass from the scene. 'The work of pioneering in this colony is well-nigh over, but the spirit survives,' one of its members declared in 1888.

> *Better work will be done by the natives of this colony—the sons of the*
> *original pioneers—than can be expected from a spiritless class from*
> *the east end of London . . . The men who settled this country were*
> *of a very different stamp from the poor of London. They paid their*
> *own passage, and they cheerfully faced the dangers of the unknown.*

The Hewetts and Stephenses were among these pioneers, although only some had paid their own fares, and at least one, Elizabeth Fenwick, was recruited from the slums of London. Their virtues were a product not only of their homeland, but also of the distinctive culture of the goldfields. Their children, the natives in whom the pioneers reposed such confidence, would 'go out into the world to be cast on the sea of time'. Their survival, material as well as spiritual, would depend on how well they navigated the tides and currents, reefs and shoals of the world beyond the village and the chapel.

Goldfields Methodism was high-voltage religion. Its spiritual energy discharged slowly through successive generations like the current in a long-life battery. Later evangelists attempted to recharge it, but the fervour never quite returned to the levels of the early 1860s. By the time it reached North Essendon Methodist Church, which I attended in the 1950s, its morality and rituals seemed to have survived better than its Wesleyan inspiration. Among my old Sunday school companions I now recognise the Cornish and Welsh surnames—Jenkin, Skewes, Jones, Hughes, Rosewarne, Rule, Cadwallader—that also populated the congregations at Wesley Hill and Campbell's Creek.

'Protestants face God across infinite lonely space,' a historian of American revivalism writes. At the moment of their conversion this may have been so, and the hymns the converts sang so lustily ('Amazing love, how can it be/That thou my God shouldst die for *me*?') celebrate a vision of dramatic individual salvation. Yet Methodism was also a tribal religion, which reproduced itself generation after generation through its distinctive rituals of hymn singing, teetotalism and Sunday school picnicking. When they boarded the train for Melbourne, along with their Bibles and Wesleyan hymnals, Robert and Susan carried memories of the revivals and tea meetings and the rock-like faith of their elders. Methodist morality, with its industry, frugality and punctuality—characteristics Samuel and Martha Stephens acquired in the mining villages of Cornwall and Wales, and practised in the satellite towns of the Victorian goldfields—would prepare their descendants for life in an industrial suburb of the metropolis.

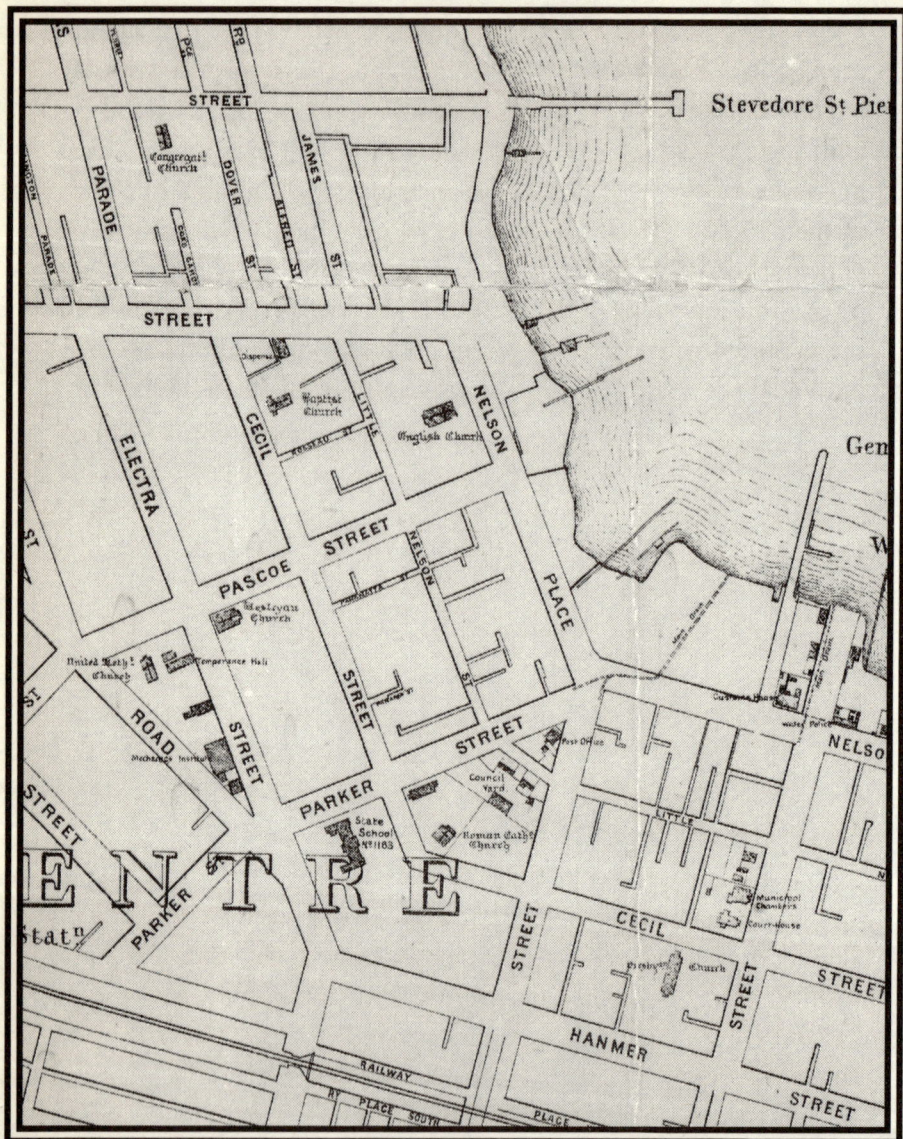

From their house in Parker Street, the Hewetts were within only a few minutes' walk of the Williamstown Beach Railway Station, the State School, the Mechanics Institute and the Electra Street Wesleyan Church. Nelson Place, facing the still-active waterfront, was only a step further away. (Plan of Williamstown, Department of Lands and Survey, 1894 (detail), State Library of Victoria)

CHAPTER EIGHT
Williamstown

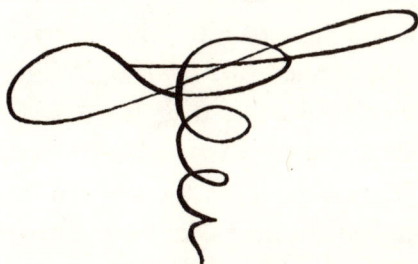

Long after the return of the *Culloden* to England, the Hewetts' fortunes continued to be shaped by the experience of migration. Robert Hewett and Elizabeth Fenwick had arrived in Melbourne on the eve of the gold rush, the biggest bonanza in Australia's colonial history. Thirty years later, four of my great-grandparents, Robert and Susan Hewett and William and Emma Seller, arrived in the city on the eve of another bonanza, the 1880s land boom. Over the following decade, 'Marvellous Melbourne' almost doubled its population and became the glamour city of Australia.

By 1885, they had all settled in Williamstown, a seaport suburb on the western shore of Port Phillip Bay. It was there that my grandfather Vic Hewett and my grandmother Emma Seller grew up, met and married, and where they are now buried. As a boy I travelled to Williamstown with my grandparents to attend the 110th anniversary of the Electra Street Methodist Church, where I heard them reminisce about the days of their youth. But I did not realise then that the Hewetts and Sellers had followed very different paths to Williamstown, or that Vic and Emma had defied their parents and conventional prejudice in order to marry.

ROBERT AND SUSAN'S STORY

Williamstown is as old as Melbourne. When Governor Richard Bourke visited the new settlement of Port Phillip in 1837, he ordered two towns to be surveyed, one on the river Yarra, the other on the bay. Williamstown was named after the King, William IV, a fact that locals cite in proof of their belief that their town, not Melbourne, was expected to be the capital. Even today Williamstown considers itself better than its neighbours in the western industrial suburbs. A peninsula surrounded on three sides by water, within sight of the city yet visibly separate, it feels more like a town than a suburb.

A decade after Robert and Susan arrived from Campbell's Creek, it was still a working seaport, drawing passenger and cargo ships from around the world. From the windows of Holy Trinity vicarage, the town's most famous resident, the novelist Ada Cambridge, wife of the local vicar, surveyed Hobson's Bay—'just a pond with a city round it'—and watched longingly as the ships passed from the mouth of the river towards 'the sea and the world'. Mrs George Cross, as she was known to locals, 'was not a popular personage in Williamstown'. After a crisis of faith in the mid-1880s, she had withdrawn from parish life. Yet she loved the seafront suburb. On Saturday afternoons she walked her fox terrier past the marine stores, cook-shops, sailors' pubs, railway yards and docks that lined Nelson Place. She sometimes stopped near the Alfred Graving Dock to chat to an old salt or explore the narrow passages between piers and shipyards, before arriving on the convict-built bluestone breakwater that terminated the peninsula. 'All around us here we feel the spirit of those old times, so stern and sad,' she reflected.

In fact, the Williamstown of old salts and sailing ships was fast disappearing. In 1886, the completion of the Coode Canal enabled ships to bypass Fisherman's Bend. Soon they were able to moor at the Victoria Dock, just a few hundred metres from Collins Street. Steam vessels now discharged their passengers at Port Melbourne rather than Williamstown. Slower, smaller sailing vessels continued to load wheat and coal at Williamstown's Railway and Breakwater piers, but their days were numbered.

As its port declined, however, the town got a boost from the most dynamic sector of Victoria's transport system. In 1884, the Minister for Railways, Castlemaine's James Patterson, introduced the biggest single instalment of railway construction in Australia's colonial history. 'The Octopus Act', as it was known because its iron tentacles reached the furthest corners of the colony, authorised the construction of over one thousand miles of new railway. Robert had come to the Williamstown Railway Workshops just as this boom got under way. In 1885, about four hundred railwaymen worked at Williamstown, but by 1890 the workforce had expanded to over 1500, almost all of them concentrated in a new 22-acre complex three kilometres away at Newport.

Newport, as an admiring observer noted in 1908, was 'the home, hospital and cemetery of every locomotive, carriage and truck in Victoria'. Today only the cemetery remains: the 1888 administration building with its impressive clock tower stands abandoned amidst a weed-infested graveyard of cavernous workshops, rusting boilers and bogies, windowless rail carriages and pensioned-off locomotives. Even the nearby Victorian Railways Museum, a retirement home for the state's most historic engines, has now closed. But a century ago, Newport was Victoria's industrial showplace. A state-owned enterprise, modern in outlook yet patriarchal in organisation, it was modelled on the great British railway workshops. Many of its managers were also British immigrants who had brought with them their high craftsmanship, austere moral standards and rigorous style of personal management. As a fitter, overseeing the construction, assembly and maintenance of locomotives, Robert belonged to the elite of a workforce steeped in these ideals. Long after other railway workshops had turned to professionally trained engineers, Newport promoted its managers from the shopfloor, and always from among the fitters, the trade with the most comprehensive view of the workshop's operations.

Robert was not the only Castlemaine boy at Newport. As we've seen, he probably entered the workshops as a 'supernumerary', or casual employee, through political patronage, but by 1899 he had risen to become a 'leading hand', on the third rung of a well-defined hierarchy of skill, etiquette and respect. At the top was the Newport manager, the conductor of an orchestra playing the tunes composed by the chief mechanical engineer, known as the CME, at the Railways head office in Spencer Street. Every month or so, the CME would visit Newport, where he was 'liturgically received—like a bishop making his solemn entry into his cathedral'. Next below the manager came the foremen and sub-foremen of the various departments. At Newport, the foremen's office was built high above the floor level 'like the warder's watch tower in a prison—so that the foreman could overlook the activity (or the lack of it) below him'.

In this industrial army, the leading hands were the 'NCOs of the Service', mediating between the 'officers' in the foremen's office and the 'other ranks' below. In the Erecting Shop, where locomotives were built and maintained, each leading hand directed work on three engines and oversaw the work of six fitters. The 'leading erectors', as they liked to be called, had a keen sense of their status, 'taking themselves very seriously', according to one veteran observer. They even had their own social club, separate from the managers and the trade union. As the face of the administration on the shopfloor, their personalities made a strong impression on their men. James Green was known as 'Dismal' because of his drooping moustache, while eagle-eyed Walter Grimshaw earned the name 'God' because

196

he seemed to be everywhere. Robert Hewett specialised in tank engines of the E, M and DDE class, the solid workhorses of the suburban railway system. 'A tall bearded man of immense dignity', he was nicknamed 'the Archdeacon'.

Robert Henry's secure, well-paid government job was probably the most significant upward step the Hewetts had taken since they migrated to Australia. By 1906, when Justice Higgins first defined the minimum wage as sufficient to meet 'the normal needs of an average employee, regarded as a human being living in a civilised community', and calculated it at seven shillings a day, Robert was earning twelve shillings and sixpence a day. No longer was his family dependent on the cycle of the seasons, the whim of a landlord, the luck of the prospector, or the uneven flow of building contracts in a declining town. This unprecedented economic security enabled Robert to pay off his mortgage, educate his family, contribute to a friendly society, and put money in the plate each Sunday. Just as important was the Eight Hour Day, a goal first attained by some Victorian working men in 1856, which enabled him to devote some of his leisure time to church and other activities.

~

Secure employment made for a more stable family life. Susan and Robert's first child, Victor, was born fourteen months after their wedding and their second, Reuben, a further fourteen months on. Had they continued at this rate, their family might have been as large as Robert's parents' (six live births) or grandparents' (nine). But after their second son, they paused for almost seven years before the births of two more sons, Frank (1890) and Robert John (John) (1894).

The Hewetts were following a trend: between the 1860s and the 1890s, the average completed Victorian family shrank from about six children to about four. Women in Susan's age cohort, in their late twenties and early thirties in the 1880s, were among the first Melbourne mothers to begin spacing their children. Families headed by skilled workers like Robert Henry had begun to reduce their offspring even before the 1890s depression further increased the incentive for family limitation. The causes of this change—one of the most important in our history—are still a topic of lively debate. Methods of artificial birth control, such as rubber condoms, pessaries and douches, were still unreliable and not widely known or available, at least until the 1890s. Avoiding an unwanted pregnancy probably required as much self-discipline as contraceptive technique. The Hewetts' Methodism—with its emphasis on abstinence and self-discipline—may have pervaded life in the bedroom as it did every other room of their home.

In 1885, Robert and Susan purchased 78 Parker Street, a five-room timber cottage in a pleasant tree-lined street halfway between Nelson Place and the Williamstown Beach railway station. When they first arrived, Robert walked to the nearby Williamstown Railway Workshops; even after his transfer to Newport, he could easily reach work, just two stops away, using his free railways pass. Susan had to walk only two hundred metres or so to the shops in Nelson Place. The picturesque belltower of the Williamstown State School (number 1183), a bluestone advertisement for the new dispensation of 'free, compulsory and secular' state education, was just across the street. A short walk around the corner into Electra Street, past the mechanics' institute and the Temperance Hall, brought them to the Electra Street Wesleyan (later Methodist) Church. Ten minutes in the other direction and they reached the Botanic Gardens and Williamstown Beach.

Towards the end of her life, my mother recalled her childhood impressions of the house in Parker Street. She found it hard to reconcile the sweet, loving nature of Susan, her grandmother, with the forbidding image of God portrayed in the framed samplers on its living room wall. 'Like a father pitieth his children, so the Lord pitieth them that fear him,' said one; 'Christ is the Head of this Home, the Unseen Guest at every meal, the Silent Listener to every conversation,' warned another. They were as much a part of conventional Protestant piety as the statues and holy pictures in

Catholic households, but the awe-inspiring, omnipresent God they portrayed was one that Robert and Susan's children, if not the parents themselves, would gradually come to question.

~

As the name implies, Methodism was a methodical, as well as a spontaneous, religion. In his *Rules of the Society of the People Called Methodist* (1738), Wesley directed that his followers should be gathered into groups, called classes, 'in order to pray together, to receive the word of exhortation and to watch over one another in love'. In his eyes, the class meeting was the most essential organisational feature of Methodism. 'Methodism and the class meeting must rise and fall together,' a Victorian Wesleyan minister warned in 1864. Robert and Susan Hewett were devoted members of their class meetings. They met separately in men's and women's groups led by elderly stalwarts of the faith.

The class meeting inculcated habits of self-discipline that permeated the rest of its members' lives. 'He had a great sense of self-discipline,' Ian Ward observed of his grandfather, Frank Hewett, Robert's younger brother, an inspector of works in the Victorian public service. 'He could see no need for the use of alcohol' and resolved to give up smoking the moment he realised that pausing to relight his pipe interrupted the flow of thought when reading. 'He was very methodical,' Ian added, citing Frank's habit as a cabinetmaker of always saving wood offcuts to use in later pieces, and of making compost for his vegetable garden.

By the 1880s, however, the Methodism of Wesley and his followers was gradually adapting to a more open, prosperous, urbanised society. Many Wesleyans no longer regularly attended class meetings. The congregation, rather than the class, was becoming the basic unit of a religion that was evolving from a 'sect' into a 'church'. 'We must either go back to the obscurity of a class religion, and the impotence of a moribund sect, or we must go forward into the blessed opportunities and far reaching beneficence of a national religion, which preaches the gospel to the poor,' warned Hugh Price Hughes, the prophet of contemporary British Methodism. Hughes' Australian disciples, like Reverend W.H. Fitchett and Williamstown's minister Francis Mason, sought to play a more public and national role, blending British patriotism and social reform with evangelical zeal.

'As Christians it was right that we should reside in Thanksgiving-street,' the chairman of the Electra Street church enthused in 1883. More prosperous times called for grand architecture, silver-tongued preachers, soul-stirring music and a program of activities for everyone. Williamstown's Methodists, mainly working-class men and women, first met in 1841 in a simple timber chapel in Ann Street, close to the waterfront, but in 1876 they moved to an imposing Gothic bluestone church on the corner of Electra and Pasco streets in the heart of the town. Designed by Methodist architect Thomas Crouch, it seated over four hundred in pews angled, like theatre seats, towards the main focus of worship, the pulpit. Ranged behind the preacher, a well-trained choir and thundering pipe organ filled the chancel. A vestry, two-storey parsonage, and Sabbath school accommodating more than three hundred pupils completed the complex.

One could just about live one's whole life in the bosom of the Electra Street church, and the Hewetts nearly did. As a skilled worker, Robert probably felt at home in a largely working-class congregation imbued with an ethos of respectability and social uplift. He became a Sunday school teacher, and ran a small mission school for the children of poor families in the nearby Temperance Hall. Susan, who also taught Sunday school, joined a circle of 'godly, self-sacrificing women' inspired by the Women's Christian Temperance Union to support 'cruelly deserted' unwed mothers and their babies. Together, they had embraced the ideals of domesticity and companionate marriage championed by contemporary feminists.

We may be inclined, from our position of relative affluence, to mock the code of working-class respectability, with its starched collars and strict morality. We too easily forget that in an era before state-provided welfare, when the economic weather could swiftly change and the perils of intemperance and improvidence were everywhere to be seen, it was one of the few defences against domestic disaster. Respectability, however, was a hard taskmaster. As they attained it, the Hewetts were more inclined to put their past, or at least the less respectable parts of it, behind them. Their black sheep, like the Fenwick sisters, the forger Richard Hewett and the maritally ill-fated John and Matilda Hewett, gradually dropped out of the family's memory.

A studio photograph taken around 1905 depicts the Hewetts as a model Methodist family. Robert, now in his mid-forties, his hair and beard whitening, his right hand clutching his lapel, smiles confidently at the camera, projecting the 'immense dignity' remembered by his workmates. Susan is greyer and plumper, and dresses more conservatively than the fashionable young woman captured in earlier photographs, yet radiates the same bright-eyed, winsome charm. Robert is flanked by his elder sons, Victor (usually known as Vic) and Reuben (later known as Robert or Bob), both above six feet: all three are dressed in dark Sunday suits with waistcoats, stiff wing collars and fob watches—badges of respectability in an era when sobriety and punctuality were its hallmarks. Frank, in his mid-teens, and Robert John, or John as he was usually known in the family, still in knickerbockers, stand closer to their mother, as though still preparing to join the adult men on the other side of the picture.

Vic, the eldest, had recently passed two milestones: the completion of his apprenticeship as a printer and his accreditation as a Methodist local preacher. In an age when higher education lay beyond all but a few, the printing press and the church were among the few gateways to knowledge for an ambitious working-class boy.

He seems to have always been a keen reader. At the age of thirteen he joined the Young People's Society for Christian Endeavour, preparing a paper on a devotional subject. He participated in distributing religious tracts to sailors on the wharf. By his late teens he was a Sunday school teacher, and proposed the formation of a reading circle for young women teachers. Years later, one of his contemporaries from 'the days in Williamstown when the pier bustled with sailing ships' recalled a 'young fresh-faced man lending out library books to scholars'. At fifteen he was apprenticed to Fyfe and Company, a local printer and publisher of a short-lived populist newspaper, *The People's Journal*, and later moved to the printing arm of the spiritualist and freethinker E.W. Cole, proprietor of the famous Coles's Book Arcade in Bourke Street, before completing his indentures with Clark and Company, publishers of the *Williamstown Advertiser*. During his seven-year apprenticeship he was expected to cover all facets of the trade, including bookbinding, paper ruling, lithography, engraving, etching and typesetting, as well as photography and electroplating, skills required for the new techniques of photogravure printing.

Alongside his apprenticeship, he was rising in the leadership of his local church. From the young men's Bible class and Mutual Improvement Society, he progressed to accreditation as a local preacher. For this he undertook a course of reading on the Bible and Methodist doctrine, under the supervision of his local minister, Thomas Copeland, a 'quiet, genial' man with 'an unquenchable thirst for knowledge'. In a different era, Vic's love for the spoken and printed word, thirst for knowledge, and moral seriousness may have found other outlets, but among the congregation of Electra Street Methodist Church, he was already viewed as a young man of promise.

WILLIAM AND EMMA'S STORY

As children, we knew almost nothing about our grandmother Emma's family. There is no genealogy of the Seller family in her husband Vic's notebook, and only one blurry photograph of her father, and none of her mother, in the albums I inherited from my mother. As a child I was not especially puzzled by this gap in the family's memory, for my grandmother appeared to have no family apart from the Hewetts. As a devoted Bible reader, she knew the Old Testament story of Ruth, whose famous vow of submission was often invoked as a model of wifely duty: 'Whither thou goest, I shall go, and where thou lodgest I will lodge: thy people shall be my people and thy God, my God.' It was a pledge that Emma seemed to have embraced without regret. Victor's people were her people and his God was hers.

Yet, of course, Emma did have a family of her own. Discovering their forgotten story has prompted me to see my grandparents' life together from a fresh perspective. Emma was seven years old when her parents arrived in Melbourne. I had not thought of her as an immigrant, but in retrospect I recall tones of voice and turns of phrase that were possibly a legacy of her North Country origins. Her parents, Brigham (or William as he usually called himself) and Emma Seller, were in their early forties when they boarded the *Norfolk* at Plymouth in October 1881. They had each already been on the move in their homeland before they arrived in Manchester, the city where they met and married. Mobility had 'loosened their moorings', in historian Eric Richards' apt phrase.

William was a native of Fridaythorpe, a tiny village in the Yorkshire Wolds. His grandfather and father, John and William Seller, were master wheelwrights, and William, the eldest son, was also apprenticed to the trade. His mother, Mary Ann, was the daughter of a local farmer, John Linton. Her brother, Thomas Linton, had migrated to Victoria during the 1850s gold rush; he would become a pathfinder and patron for later generations of the family, including William and Emma. The region had been a 'happy hunting ground' for Methodist preachers, so that by mid-century Wesleyans and Primitive Methodists outnumbered active Anglicans in the village by two to one.

In the 1860s, William crossed the Pennines to Manchester, where he became a joiner and general carpenter. Like many other rural craftsmen, he was adapting to the new imperatives of the steam and railway age. The wonder city of the Industrial Revolution was hit hard by the 'cotton famine' of the 1860s but revived in the 1870s. In 1870, William married 30-year-old Emma Parker and settled in Cheetham, once a village but now a densely populated industrial area. Emma was another industrial refugee. She had grown up in Coventry, where her family were cottage workers in the silk ribbon trade. At thirteen she was already filling shuttles with silk thread for her father, a master weaver; a decade later she was a silk weaver herself. Ribbon making as a cottage industry, however, was in terminal decline, and the Parkers soon moved to Manchester, probably in the hope of finding work in the cotton industry.

In 1874, the Sellers' first and only child, Emma, my grandmother, was born. Towards the end of the decade, the Manchester building boom collapsed. Encouraged by William's uncle Thomas Linton, now the proprietor of a successful bootmaking shop in Williamstown, the Sellers resolved to emigrate. They came with Emma's unmarried 38-year-old sister Catherine, a mantle-maker, who had been living with her married sister Elizabeth (Moore), Elizabeth's daughter, 26-year-old Eliza, and Eliza's new husband, William Metcalfe, a metal worker. Like the Hewetts' departure thirty years earlier, the Sellers' decision to emigrate was very much a family affair.

Steam had transformed the once long and dangerous passage to Australia. The *Norfolk*'s six-week voyage by way of the Cape of Good Hope took longer than the more usual route through the Suez Canal, but it was more comfortable, at least in Emma's estimation, and less than half as long as the Hewetts'. 'I did not come through the Canal,' she later explained to her brother William. 'That is the most trying way by far. We came through St Vinsons [Cape St Vincent] and Africa.' They arrived in Port Melbourne at the beginning of summer, and ran straight into a heat wave. 'I must tell you that yesterday and today is the hottest day we have had since we came,' William wrote to his family. 'It is 130 degs [54 degrees celsius!]. We shall soon be Black.' Yet, compared with the dank industrial city they had left, there was little to complain about. 'There is always plenty of fresh air, none of that choking stinking smoke and fog—thank God we have got clear away from that.' Already they were feeling the benefits of the move. 'My wife used often to be troubled with indigestion at home. She is a different woman now.'

William's job prospects were also looking up. 'I think I shall keep on working at my trade for some time yet as things seem to be very good at present.' They were at first discouraged by the high cost of housing in Melbourne. 'The rents are very high here as most people have there [*sic*] own house,' Emma explained. 'When we first came we could scarcely get a house to live in so uncle [Thomas Linton] sold us this. It has six rooms and very comfortable only the street is not very wide.' In his thirty years in the colony, Linton had acquired several properties, mostly modest timber cottages close to his own house in Stevedore Street, North Williamstown. The Sellers' house at 3 Braw Street, a short, narrow lane a block back from the Strand, was just around the corner from the Metcalfes, who rented another of Linton's houses, in Dover Road. All in all, the Sellers seemed to have made a happy landing.

~

Scarcely a year later, however, the family was suddenly overtaken by tragedy. A few months after their arrival, Emma's younger sister Catherine had married 66-year-old Samuel Cox, a farmer and stonemason, and departed to live on Cox's property at Wallaby Creek, near Whittlesea. She had previously purchased a four-room timber house in Albert Street, Footscray, withdrawing most of the £150 savings she had brought with her. On 23 December 1882, the Coxes returned to Melbourne to stay with the Metcalfes, and on Christmas Day they were joined by the Sellers for dinner.

Soon after one o'clock, the families were relaxing and preparing to go for a walk. Emma decided to clear up in the kitchen. Gas cooking was then still a novelty, and the Metcalfes, like most Melbourne families, cooked on a wood-fired stove. Emma scooped the ashes from the stove and spread them on the back lawn, believing the coals were now inert. She may have been following a common practice in England where potash was often used as garden fertiliser. Moments later, the grass ignited and quickly spread to the house. Soon the entire house was ablaze. The men rushed to find water but quickly realised it was futile, and turned to saving the couple's furniture.

Meanwhile, Catherine Cox had gone to retrieve some valuables from a box she had brought from Wallaby Creek. As the flames took hold, Eliza Metcalfe ran upstairs to save some jewellery. 'You must come down if you wish to escape,' she cried, but her aunt, who was hard of hearing, turned to get something from the box. Eliza ran down the stairs, which were now on fire, only to find the front door shut against her. She collapsed and fainted as she crossed the threshold; moments later, when she was hauled out and revived, she realised that she had burns on her head and legs. Catherine, however, was not so fortunate, and remained trapped in the upstairs bedroom. It took only fifteen minutes for the timber house to be consumed. The local volunteer fire brigade, who were on the train to Melbourne preparing to play a cricket match, were hastily recalled but arrived too late to save the adjoining property, also owned by Thomas Linton. Catherine's charred remains were later found in the ruins of the Metcalfes' house. The Coxes, it was reported, had brought with them their valuables (including the deeds of their properties), all of which were lost, although it later transpired that a fragment of Catherine's will, leaving all her possessions to Samuel, had survived the flames.

I am trying to visualise these events through the eyes of an eight-year-old girl, my grandmother 'little Emma' Seller. We know she was present on that fateful day, but how much of the inferno, the panic-stricken cries of her cousin and aunt, and the remorseful aftermath did she witness? How did she react to the sudden loss of her aunt, and to public knowledge of her own mother's unwitting part in her demise? I cannot draw on her own recollections, for, as far as any of her descendants know, she never spoke of this episode. Yet anyone who lived in Williamstown at the time must have known of the North Williamstown fire. It was reported in both the local and metropolitan press under the lurid headline 'Burned to Death', together with the painful statement that 'the fire is supposed to have been caused by Mrs Seller . . . throwing some ashes from the fireplace on the lawn'. At the inquest, everyone agreed that it was simply an unfortunate accident, and the coroner concluded that the house had caught fire 'by some unknown means'. The Sellers and Metcalfes remained firm friends into the next generation.

Yet memories of that black Christmas must have shadowed the family for a long time. My grandmother's silence may be more eloquent than words. She evidently decided, or her family tacitly agreed, not to mention it again. If I had stumbled on the story while she was still alive, I would probably have kept it to myself out of respect for her feelings. Even now, I wonder if telling it breaks some code of family loyalty. If I am to understand Emma and the place where she grew up it must surely be taken into account. Yet in telling it again, exposing a buried grief once more to public gaze, I wonder if I am placing my calling as a historian above some higher duty to my kin. History, writes the American historian Richard White, reflecting on a similar family dilemma, may sometimes seem like 'an unnatural act': 'By making the private public I risk hurting people, telling what they do not wish widely known, in the service of a dead thing—history.' My excuse is that the risks of hurt have now diminished, and the dividend of understanding has increased—but one can never be quite sure.

Only two fragmentary stories, told to her grandchildren, connect us with the world of Emma's childhood. One was her memory of sitting at a table, probably in the house in Cheetham, when a fireball suddenly appeared, whizzed through the house, touching every knife and fork, and disappeared again. Unlike that other fiery visitation, it left the household unharmed. She also liked to tell the story of Lady Godiva, which she had surely heard from her own mother, the Coventry ribbon weaver. According to the medieval legend, Godiva pleaded with her husband to relieve the poor people of Coventry of onerous taxes, and consented to ride naked through the town if he repealed them. In respect for her virtue, and to spare her shame, the people of the town closed their shutters and allowed the naked lady to ride through the streets unseen. We heard the tale of Lady Godiva with embarrassed giggles, but for Emma herself the predicament of a virtuous woman exposed to public gaze, and a sympathetic community who looked the other way, may have touched a more personal chord of sympathy.

In the early 1890s, the prosperity that had lured the Seller family to Melbourne suddenly vanished. For five years the local economy went into reverse. Building workers like William, now in his fifties, were worst affected by the depression. In 1899, as the depression lifted, Emma received a letter from her younger brother, 57-year-old William Parker, back in Manchester. Sometime in the 1880s, William's wife Rosetta had departed with her two daughters, leaving him to bring up their three sons, William, Lewis and Edgar, alone. After the tragic death of Catherine, Emma was his sole remaining sibling. Now he too was contemplating emigration.

'We should be glad to see you if you saw your way open,' Emma replied. 'You would find a comfortable home here.' She had made some enquiries on his behalf about job prospects. He was a small-goods manufacturer and his boys were also employed in the cotton industry. 'We are nine miles [14 kilometres] from the City it is ninepence return Foy and Gibson [the large clothing importer and manufacturer] is a tram ride the other side of the City.' As a Methodist, William was assured of a warm welcome among the Electra Street congregation, she noted, and her daughter relished the prospect of meeting her cousins. But emigrating at that stage of life was a risk that William should not underestimate. 'Commit thy way to the Lord and he shall direct thy path and if you are directed this way we will rejoice together,' she concluded.

On 26 July 1899, Emma wrote a second encouraging letter. In fact, William had already made his decision. On 5 August, accompanied by his two younger sons, twenty-year-old Lewis and nineteen-year-old Edgar, he boarded the *Orizaba* at Plymouth and set out for Australia. Just a few days earlier, however, on 31 July, Emma was suddenly seized with an acute attack of gastritis, and two days later she was dead at the age of 59. Did her husband cable the ship, warning William of the shock that awaited him? Or was it only on 13 September, when the *Orizaba* docked at Port Melbourne, that he learned that the long-anticipated reunion would not take place? Five years later, in July 1904, he too was dead. The Seller household in Braw Street had been reduced to just two people: 64-year-old William and his unmarried 30-year-old daughter, Emma.

'A VERY GOOD GIRL'

Like many young women of the time, Emma had left school early. She was never a great reader or scholar, unlike her husband, who would eventually build a library of several thousand books. I have kept one of the few she left, a copy of Mrs Henry Mackarness's *The Young Lady's Book* (1876). She won it, aged seventeen, as second prize in the Williamstown Wesleyan Sunday school. 'How common amongst our young ladies between school-days and [marriage] is the exclamation, "I have nothing to do",' it begins. The belief that young womanhood was a leisured interlude between school and marriage was far from being Emma's experience, but the model of useful, charitable activity the book describes was widely admired. In learning how to nurse the sick, visit and teach the poor, cook tasty and nutritious food, clean silver and mend upholstery, preserve fruit and arrange flowers, carry on a conversation and observe proper etiquette, the young woman was equipping herself to become a lady, an ideal to which many respectable working-class women also aspired.

A lady was a woman of superior character, not just high social standing. While her responsibilities centred on the home, they also extended into public life. In 1891, the year Emma won her Sunday school prize, her mother signed a 'monster' petition in support of female suffrage. 'Government of the People, by the People and for the People should mean *all* the People, and not one half,' it affirmed. The Williamstown branch of the Women's Christian Temperance

Union, which included many Methodists, led the local campaign for signatures. Winning the vote, the WCTU believed, would empower women to curb the brutal instincts of men and combat the evil influence of the drink trade. I like to think that my grandmother shared her mother's feminist ideals, although her daughters cannot recall her ever questioning her husband's opinion on anything.

By the late 1890s, when 'little' Emma Seller was in her mid-twenties, her life revolved around home, work and church. 'Emma is always busy with her dressmaking,' her mother observed. 'She gets 2.3 and 2.6 per day [about one-third of an adult male's minimum wage] . . . She is very industrious and a very good girl.' As proof of her goodness, her mother noted that at the end of a long day when she had travelled across the city to work, she still attended an evening service at Electra Street. Unlike the bored young women addressed in *The Young Lady's Book*, she could hardly say 'I have nothing to do', yet the little leisure she had was shaped by ladylike ideals.

From the mid-1890s her name appears frequently in the records of the Williamstown congregation's Young People's Society of Christian Endeavour. Founded in the United States in the early 1880s, the Society was an attempt on the part of the Protestant churches to meet the challenge of a burgeoning urban youth culture. It modelled the adult world of self-government through elected committees of young men and women. Emma was among the most active members of the Sunshine and Flower Committees, a band of young women who devoted themselves to visiting the sick and leaving posies of flowers as a memento of the visit. Yet, while reinforcing traditional gender roles, many of the Society's activities involved both sexes. And although attempting to provide a 'counter attraction to the hotels' and other 'doubtful forms of amusement', it also embraced some features of the contemporary youth culture. Judging by photographs of Vic and Emma among their church friends, they were quick to embrace new fashions in dress, and to take up novel pastimes like cycling.

VIC AND EMMA'S STORY

Both model Methodists, Vic and Emma might have been considered ideal marriage partners. But many people, including his parents, Robert and Susan, opposed the match. Vic was even locked out of the house after one angry exchange with his parents, according to my aunt Florence. The main objection was the almost eight-year age difference: in their eyes she was simply too old, and perhaps not good enough, for him. He was tall and quite good-looking; she was small and unprepossessing. He was an ambitious young tradesman in his mid-twenties; she was a seamstress well past thirty. He was bookish; she was practical. His family were labour aristocrats aspiring to join the middle class, and lived in one of Williamstown's better streets; hers were English working-class recent immigrants living in a backstreet in a poor part of town. The Hewetts were leaders of the Electra Street congregation, while the Sellers took a back pew. Coming from families that had struggled to get clear of poverty, did Robert and Susan fear that an alliance with the Sellers would take them back again? Family opposition, however, may only have driven the couple closer together. Emma later confided to Florence that they sometimes took refuge to kiss and cuddle under Gem Pier, in the dark, welcoming shadow of the promenade where, as young Christian Endeavourers, they distributed religious tracts to visiting sailors.

It was an era of long engagements, and some years passed before Vic's parents gave their reluctant consent to the marriage. Before then, in September 1906, Vic and his mate Will Roberts, a railway engineer, left Melbourne for New Zealand, where Vic worked as a printer at the Christchurch International Exhibition. In travelling to New Zealand, he was following in the path of his younger brother Reuben, another engineer, who was selling agricultural machinery and courting Nell Bayley, a Footscray girl who had migrated there with her family. At 24, Vic may have felt he needed to spread his wings before settling down. His parents may also have encouraged him to go in the hope that the year apart would end the relationship with Emma.

After the exhibition closed, Vic joined two of his workmates on a 'tramping' expedition across the South Island from Christchurch to Greymouth. In a memoir of the trip, the author ('tall, fair, but inclined to be dark . . . and known to his friends as Vic') rejoices in the comradeship of the track and the rigours of the alpine environment—the blistered feet, sore ankles and 'cold stiff clothes against our legs'. The three trampers climb tall peaks, wade through icy streams ('like a river of milk'), and camp on the properties of friendly farmers. After several invigorating days on the track, they reach Otira and catch the coach to Greymouth. There, Vic recounts, they sit on the breakwater and gaze across the Tasman, trying to see Victoria and Williamstown.

He returned to Melbourne in November 1907, spending a week in Sydney on the way. A few days later, at a church social, his friends at Electra Street 'heartily welcomed him home'. 'Notwithstanding the glories of Maoriland, Williamstown, with all its faults, was a desirable place to live,' he conceded. Had the glories of 'Maoriland' thrown the faults of his hometown into relief? Had he left something of himself, or another possible self, behind on the track? Whatever doubts he felt on his return, however, seem to have been quickly dispelled. Six months later, in a 'quiet little wedding' at 3 Braw Street, Vic and Emma were married. 'The pretty bride was daintily attired in white muslin, wearing a train and wreath and veil,' the *Williamstown Chronicle* reported. The family had made an effort to put the best face on what had probably been a difficult time.

For the newlyweds, Williamstown was apparently no longer 'a desirable place to live'. Soon after the ceremony, they moved with the bride's father to Taylor Street, Moonee Ponds. William was now in his late sixties, and Emma, who had kept house for almost a decade, could hardly leave him to cope alone. Less than two years later he was dead. The years in Australia had brought the Sellers much loss and heartache, but William had lived to see the birth of his first grandchild, my mother, Emma May, born in May 1909. The Hewetts were now all the family Emma had. Soon after William's death, Vic and Emma purchased their own home, 17 Edward Street, a new timber bungalow in a wide tree-lined street close to Essendon station. With their arrival in Essendon, in a house just a few blocks from my own childhood home, the gap between history and memory, between what I have heard or read and what I remember, has almost closed.

THE BROTHERS HEWETT

Williamstown was almost the last staging post in the Hewetts' colonial odyssey. From Hook Farm to Castlemaine, and from Castlemaine to Williamstown, each place and generation had brought big changes in the family's fortunes. There would be another stage in the Hewett story, beyond the scope of this book: the arrival of my father, George Davison, the infant son of John and Ada, who emigrated from Birmingham in 1911, and his marriage to my mother May, the eldest of Robert's grandchildren, in 1940.

The death of 62-year-old Susan Hewett, Vic's mother, in 1918 effectively closed the Williamstown chapter. 'Fair as the morning, bright as the day', she had been the spiritual centre of the household in Parker Street, and with her going the ties that had bound them all to Williamstown were loosened. Her widower Robert stayed on until 1922, when he married Sarah ('Say') Bayley, the elder sister of his daughter-in-law Nell. They lived at first with her mother and sister in Essendon, but Robert's 'smelly pipe' and Say's bossy mother made it an uneasy arrangement, so they moved to Wesley Hill, where Robert purchased an old two-storey house—'The Ranch'—just a few doors from the house his father had built in the 1850s. There he cultivated his vegetable garden, smoked his pipe, entertained his grandchildren, chatted to his sisters—still living in the parental home—and attended the pioneer church that gave Wesley Hill its name until his death in 1933.

While Robert retreated to his hometown, his four sons had already embarked on another journey, from working-class Williamstown to middle-class suburbia. The respectable, frugal household in Parker Street was the launching pad for lives that would diverge from the pattern of their parents'. Vic, Reuben, Frank and John would each take something of their Williamstown Methodist legacy with them, but what they each took and what they made of it was very much their own.

~

Coming to adulthood amidst the optimism of Federation Australia, the brothers cannot have anticipated the testing time that lay ahead. When we think about the great events of history, such as war, revolution and depression, we acknowledge the divisions of class and gender, but often miss the equally profound differences between the experiences of generations separated, sometimes, by only a few years. Young Australian men born in the mid-1890s, for example, were more than three times as likely to enlist in the Great War as those born a decade earlier. In turn, they were more likely to be hard hit by the Great Depression and to father sons who served in the Second World War. The unequal sacrifices, and differing perspectives, of Australia's 'war' and 'peace' generations still reverberate in Australian history. The emergence of Anzac as our primary national myth, coupled with the boom in family history, has given new salience to the question posed in a famous contemporary recruitment poster: 'Daddy, what did you do in the Great War?'

At the outbreak of war in 1914, several younger members of the Maxfield family, like Gordon (born 1890) and Arthur (1889), were single and of military age, but only six of Robert and Elizabeth's sixteen grandchildren were males, and only two were of military age. My grandfather, Vic Hewett, was 32, already married with three daughters, when war was declared. He was among the approximately three-quarters of Australian men in their early thirties who did not enlist. He would have had his reasons, family responsibilities probably first among them, but as far as I know he did not divulge them. However, he cannot have escaped the moral dilemmas that the war presented to young men of his generation. When he and Emma moved to Edward Street, they joined the North Essendon Methodist Church. Lower-middle class and mainly Protestant, Essendon was a fertile recruiting ground for the 58th Infantry or Essendon Rifles, the volunteer company raised by the charismatic Lieutenant-Colonel Harold 'Pompey' Elliott, who chose the red and black of the Essendon Football Club as his unit's colours.

Many Methodists abhorred the prospect of war. 'We know that when the war-drum throbs, the passions of men boil over, and reason and Christian principle, for the time being, are set aside,' the Methodist newspaper, the *Spectator*, warned in August 1914. But many others, including Prime Minister Joseph Cook, a former Primitive Methodist local preacher, were convinced that the war was a godly crusade. Once the AIF departed, the voices of the pacifists died away. And when news of the first casualties arrived, sympathy for their families stifled debate about the cause for which they had died.

Pompey Elliott's men were among the first Australians ashore at Gallipoli. D Company of the Seventh Battalion, mostly Essendon lads, were assigned the task of covering the left flank of the invasion force. Because the landing craft did not make the rendezvous, they were forced to row themselves and wade ashore weighed down with waterlogged equipment. Instead of arriving on a sandy beach they faced the steep ridges and ravines of Ari Burnu and the withering fire of the Turkish defenders. The Seventh suffered heavier casualties than any other AIF battalion, and D Company the heaviest of all. Elliott was wounded and evacuated. 'Only about half of the Essendon boys left,' he wrote sorrowfully in his diary a few days later, 'and only a little over a hundred of the men I took from Broadmeadows [the recruitment camp].'

In the following weeks, Essendon learned of the catastrophe as local clergymen broke the news to grieving families. 'While they sorrowed at the death of their boys, they could not help feeling proud of the magnificent response their district had made to the Empire's appeal,' the mayor declared. 'Though the Essendon casualties were heavy, every one was a sparkling gem in the crown of honour.' Among the first to fall was 21-year-old First Lieutenant Earl Chapman, a member of the Young People's Guild at the North Essendon Methodist Church. Wounded on the first day of the Gallipoli landing, he was evacuated but died and was buried at sea before the ship could return to Alexandria.

A few months later a party of fresh Methodist recruits from the nearby Broadmeadows camp led by Reverend Thomas Woodfull joined the church's Sunday school anniversary celebrations. Woodfull called upon the soldiers to stand among the children and to sing a verse of 'Onward, Christian soldiers', a spectacle which 'roused the audience to the highest pitch of enthusiasm'. He unveiled a new honour roll, headed by Earl Chapman, the hero of Gallipoli, and paid tribute to the 'sacrifice, not only of the men, but of the mothers, sisters and sweethearts, who were called upon to give their best and bear the heaviest load of sorrow'.

The Great War cast a long shadow over the congregation at North Essendon. Even in the early 1950s when I was a Sunday school pupil there, it seemed darker even than that of the Second World War. Sixty-two other members of the church had joined Lieutenant Chapman on the honour roll, eleven of whom made the supreme sacrifice. I sat with my family in a pew towards the back of the church, just behind my Sunday school teacher Arthur Jones and under the memorial window for his older brothers Ray and Llew Jones killed at Bullecourt and St Quentin. The photograph of Llew in the church's book of honour is uncannily like my school friend Evan Jones, the nephew he never knew. Many of the participants in that patriotic tableau of 1915, including choirmaster Mr Dibb, organist Ethel Quayle and local preacher Bill Northey, were still at their posts almost forty years later.

Where was my grandfather, Vic Hewett, during this testing time? Was he a patriot, eager to do his bit but held back by family responsibility? Was he a shirker, fearful of the fight? Or was he a man of peace, compelled by 'reason and Christian principle' to resist the headlong rush to war? I do not know the answer to these questions, and perhaps even he did not know his motives exactly. Such quandaries were the unsettling legacy of staying rather than going.

The war was a seismic eruption in Australian society, dividing friends and families, and overturning cherished beliefs. 'In the beginning', writes Brian Lewis in his perceptive memoir *Our War*, 'we believed everything that we were told; at the end we believed nothing.' Whatever Vic Hewett believed at the outset of the war, by its end he was convinced, as were many others, of its insanity. 'He hated war,' my aunt Florence succinctly remarked. So, it seems, did his younger brother Reuben who told his own son Harry that he had not enlisted because he considered the war a European brawl and not Australia's business. He had married Nell Bayley, the Footscray girl he had followed to New Zealand, in Christchurch and Harry was born just a month after the outbreak of war. Their younger brother Frank, then 24, did not enlist either, perhaps because his job, as a marine engineer employed by the Melbourne Harbour Trust, was considered important to the war effort. He married May Webster, another member of the Electra Street church, in 1915, and their first child, Olive, was born in April 1916. Only the youngest brother, John, who turned 20 in 1914, joined up two years later as an ambulance man in the Australian Navy.

As a boy, John won first prize for attendance at the Electra Street Sunday school, and he later followed his eldest brother into the printing trade, completing his apprenticeship at the *Williamstown Chronicle*. But in his late teens he came under the influence of the charismatic vicar of Holy Trinity, Frank Lynch, and began the journey that eventually led him into the Anglican priesthood. In 1915, Lynch drew national attention when he stepped down from the platform of a local recruitment rally to knock out a heckler who had dared insult Australia's 'tinpot Navy'. In March 1917, John joined the Australian Navy as a medical orderly and sailed for England aboard the troopship *Canowra*. In signing up, albeit in a non-combatant role, perhaps he sought to accommodate the cross-pressured loyalties of family and religion.

AFTER THE WAR

By the end of the war, all four brothers had begun to distance themselves from their origins. Frank was the only one to stay on in Williamstown, eventually inhabiting a fine house on the Esplanade overlooking the sea, and fathering two attractive daughters who married sons of Williamstown's small-business elite. A happy-go-lucky character, he quickly shed the moral austerity of 78 Parker Street. He became a popular figure in Williamstown's waterfront community and a favourite uncle to his nieces and nephews. 'He was a wag,' his cousin Millie recalled. When he died, aged only 56, he was described as a 'prominent member of the Electra Street Methodist Church' although, as far as anyone can recall, he seldom darkened its doors.

Meanwhile, Reuben had entered the motor trade, first as a manager of the Canada Cycle and Motor Company, and later as proprietor of his own business, Hewett Motors, an agency for Dodge cars, located next to Wesley Church in Latrobe Street, Melbourne. It was at this point that he changed his first name to Robert, for fear that the Jewish associations of 'Reuben' might be bad for trade. With the coming of the depression, he closed the business, and lived for the rest of his life on investments supplemented by odd jobs. His marriage to Nell had run into difficulties, and in 1933, when he took a long voyage to Europe, he travelled with a business associate. He visited the Pyramids and London's National Gallery and played golf at St Andrews in Scotland. By middle age, his religious interests had become more private and less orthodox. While seldom attending church—although the Hawthorn Presbyterian Church was next door to the family home in Grove Road, Hawthorn—he continued to read the Bible, and sometimes the Koran, and to dabble in theology, philosophy, psychology, spiritualism and Egyptology. An active freemason, he retained something of the spiritual intensity and strict morality of Methodism, but forsook its doctrines and disciplines.

John, the youngest, travelled furthest geographically and denominationally but remained truest to his parents' evangelical beliefs. One afternoon early in the war, while strolling in the Williamstown Botanic Gardens, he met an attractive young woman, Winifred ('Win') Dakin from Roseville in Sydney, an Anglican who was staying with her Melbourne cousins. They continued to correspond, and by January 1916 they were engaged. At the end of the war, John moved to Sydney to be with Win and study at Moore Theological College. Only after he became a curate in 1922, six years after their engagement, did they at last marry. In an evangelical diocese, he was a voice of moderation. 'I'm not a high churchman or a low churchman,' he would say, 'I'm an all round churchman.' As a long-time state and national secretary of the Church Missionary Society, he travelled widely in Africa and Asia. 'The day of the white sahib is gone, and we are being forced to learn this in the most unpleasant way,' he observed during the 1950s Mau Mau rising in Kenya. In between, he served as vicar of several parishes, mostly on Sydney's North Shore. Eventually the son of a railway engineer nicknamed 'the Archdeacon' became an archdeacon himself. When he visited Melbourne, he reminded his relations that John Wesley, the founder of Methodism, had remained a member of the Church of England to his dying day. In becoming Anglican, John Hewett insisted, he had simply come home.

Of the four brothers, Vic was, at least outwardly, most faithful to his Methodist origins. He was an active member of the North Essendon church. As a local preacher, he walked for miles rather than break the Sabbath by taking a tram to preach at outlying churches. (He never drove a car.) Within a marriage of singular sweetness and mutual devotion, he and Emma inhabited separate spheres; while she attended the Ladies' Guild and the Women's Association for

Overseas Missions, he was increasingly drawn beyond the local and domestic scene. Their daughters cannot recall them ever quarrelling. At night, as the girls lay in bed, their parents' voices could be heard through the wall, chuckling as they reviewed the days' events. Strict though fond parents to the eldest of their five daughters, they became relaxed, even indulgent, by the youngest.

In writing about Vic and Emma, my grandparents, I have crossed the threshold between history and memory. Much about their youth and courtship was unknown to me until I dug into the slender paper record, but in writing about their adult lives I inevitably draw on memory, that of my parents and sister as well as my own. As the eldest of their grandchildren, and the first boy to arrive after a generation of girls, I was close to my grandfather, but I realise how little of their lives was visible to me as a child and adolescent. Memories of my grandparents—their physical presence, voices, gestures, posture—are fused with memories of the sounds, smell, tastes and sights of their home.

In the late 1930s, Vic and Emma moved to 18 Salmon Avenue in North Essendon. The handiwork of English-born builder Fred Todd, a fellow Methodist, it was solidly built, in red clinker bricks, with the small windows, white walls and dark-stained architraves fashionable in that era. I can picture every room, from the folk-weave fabric of the sleep-out curtains to the Lionel Lindsay etchings on the wall. Every Sunday afternoon—or so it seemed—we dropped in for afternoon tea. (I cannot recall my grandparents ever visiting us, even though we lived only a mile away.) Two of the pictures on their dining room walls are etched in my memory. *The Foundation of Australia* depicts the scene at Sydney Cove in 1788 as Governor Arthur Phillip raises the British flag. It is a reproduction of the painting executed in 1937, in anticipation of the sesquicentenary celebrations, by the English painter Algernon Talmage. On the opposite wall is another coastal scene, a darkly lit study in browns and purples. A steep winding street descends between rows of English cottages towards a rocky harbour. The work of another English painter, George Ayling, it depicts a place Vic had never visited, except in imagination, the Cornish birthplace of his grandfather Samuel Stephens.

As I recall that room, I hear the rattle of china cups and saucers as my grandmother emerges from the kitchen pushing a wooden tea trolley. The sound evokes the taste of seedcake, gingernuts, lemon cordial and damson jam, the scent of old ladies' perfume, and the musty smell of old books. My grandparents themselves seem, by comparison, shadowy presences. Emma is a petite figure dressed in a mauve floral dress, her hair tightly wound in a bun. Vic, tall, stout and jovial, rubs his hands with glee as he shows off another acquisition for his library. I feel their affection and approval but struggle to recall their voices and words; their conversations are part of an adult world I have yet to enter. Only years afterwards, talking with my parents, and reading the books I inherited from my grandfather's library, do I reconstruct his mental world.

In the notebook where he drew the Hewett family tree, Vic also recorded the landmarks of his own life: the dates of his apprenticeship and local preacher's certificate, the places of his employment, and the birthdays of his children and grandchildren. After his marriage, he worked for a number of city publishing firms, some with Methodist connections, but soon sought wider opportunities. He began as a compositor: a photograph of the interior of the printing shop where he worked in Christchurch shows him standing in a white apron composing a line of type in the traditional way. But he was an eager innovator, eventually becoming the factory manager and a director of one of Melbourne's leading fine colour printers, the Specialty Press. When I was eight or nine years old and he was still in charge, he showed me around the Little Collins Street premises. From his office, a windowed cubicle in the middle of the plant, he could keep the entire operation of the place in view. He patiently explained the techniques of colour separation and showed me the large rotary presses used for colour gravure printing. He loved books as works of art and taught his children and grandchildren to handle them reverently. He had an expert knowledge of typography and a keen

Portable lemonade

Take of tartaric acid ½ oz, loaf sugar 3 oz,
essence of lemon ½ drachm. Powder the
acid and the sugar very fine in a marble
mortar, not use a metal one. Mix them
together and pour the essence of lemon
on them by a few drops at a time, stirring
the mixture after each addition, till the
whole is added, then mix them well and
divide it into 12 equal parts, wrapping each
up separately in a peice of white paper.
When wanted for use it is only necessary to
dissolve it in a tumbler of cold water, and
fine lemonade will be obtained, containing
the flavour of the juice and peel of the
lemon and ready sweetened.

eye for book design, often advising authors, such as the landscape designer Edna Walling.

Printing was his entrée to the wider world of books and ideas. V.S., as he was known in these circles, became a discerning collector, haunting second-hand bookshops in search of first editions, purchasing airmail covers of Charles Kingsford Smith's historic flights, and commissioning designs from local artists for his own bookplates. At dinners of the Bread and Cheese Club, a fellowship of middle-aged litterateurs and businessmen dedicated to 'mateship, art and letters', he filled his tankard with lemonade instead of beer. He was a 'keen admirer' of the writings of Henry Lawson, eager 'to keep his memory fresh and the things he stood for alive'. Lawson's portrait, along with Lionel Lindsay's etchings of bush life, hung from the walls of his library. The things Lawson stood for—not to mention the vices he fell to—may seem a far cry from my grandfather's life as a respectable, teetotal suburban Methodist; but perhaps it was the very settled, domestic lives of the Bread and Cheesers that stirred their imaginative identification with 'the romance of the swag'.

By middle age, Vic had forsaken the evangelical certainties of his youth. He embraced the fruits of critical biblical scholarship and the teachings of the social gospel. The writings of Gandhi, the English journalist and politician Norman Angell and the Japanese Christian pacifist Toyohiko Kagawa, and the influence of his neighbour, Labor politician Maurice Blackburn, informed his anxiety about the threat of international war. He became active in Toc-H, the organisation founded by army parson 'Tubby' Clayton to provide friendship and support to men broken by the Great War. 'We are not yet certain that the present civilisation has survived the last war. It is very doubtful if it could survive another war,' he wrote in the late 1930s. He was addressing the young men's Bible class at his local church. The vigorous debates among this circle of young men—it included two of his future sons-in-law—stimulated Vic's reading and reflection on politics, history, literature and theology. Their idealism was roused by the problems of poverty and social inequality exposed by the Great

Depression. Vic assisted his friend the Methodist accountant and social activist Oswald Barnett to harness the young men's energies in support of the Methodist Babies' Home ('to save the neglected Babies—White and Brown') and slum abolition. When war came again, some of his protégés volunteered, some served in non-combatant roles, some were in reserved occupations, and some were conscripted. Vic supported them all. Characteristically, he took refuge in the power of the written and printed word, editing and despatching over three thousand copies of a newsletter to keep servicemen in touch with their home community.

I was sixteen when my grandfather died. He was then just a few years older than I am now. Like so many of his Hewett forebears he succumbed to stroke ('apoplexy'), and for several months he lay semi-comatose, halfway between life and death, no longer able to speak but still, it sometimes seemed, aware of our presence. To support my grandmother, my father often spent the night at Salmon Avenue. I sometimes kept him company, sitting by my grandfather's bed, praying he would get well again but knowing in my heart that I was saying a long, fond goodbye.

I knew, even then, that he had shaped my life. I would inherit his Methodism, his love of the spoken and printed word, his passion for literature and history, his moderate leftist politics, and his sense of humour. In time, I would shed some of his beliefs—his teetotalism was one of the first to go, his pacifism rather later—and his personal influence would be modified by the influence of others. But often, it seemed to me, I was following paths that he would have followed himself, if the world had been as kind to children of his class and generation as it was to mine.

Of all family relationships, none—save for the relationship between husbands and wives—is as mysterious as that between the generations. What parents most aspire to pass on may not be what children most want to take. How children see their parents seldom corresponds with how parents see themselves. Robert and Susan, Vic's father and mother, were dedicated parents at a time when, according to family historians, improving economic conditions permitted parents to invest more, both financially and psychologically, in their children. They had high hopes for their four sons, and all four could be said to have advanced beyond their parents. Yet the directions they took, and the uses they each made of their heritage, were very different. Native temperament and talent, birth order, parental preference, sibling rivalry, not to mention the effects of schooling and religious socialisation, all doubtless played a part. So too, of course, did the times and places in which they lived. Between the world that Robert and Susan entered, in a small declining town at the close of Victoria's golden age, and the one their sons inherited, in a burgeoning metropolis in the early twentieth century, there was a gulf at least as wide as the famed 'generation gap' of the 1960s. The high-voltage religion of the parents was a powerful shaping influence on the sons' childhood, but as adults they adapted, renovated and sometimes rejected it.

While remaining in touch, and retaining things in common—not least their boisterous sense of humour—the brothers' lives increasingly diverged. A photograph of the four taken aboard ship as John departed overseas sometime in the late 1930s captures something of their personalities while celebrating the fraternal bond. Robert (Reuben) stands stiffly, his eyes avoiding the camera; John, hatless and wearing his dog collar, solemnly faces it; Frank, his fedora hat set at a jaunty angle, radiates charm; while Vic, leaning easily against the ship's rail, looks presidential. Late-middle-aged middle-class men in business suits, they have outgrown the awkwardness of the four working-class boys who posed with their parents thirty years earlier. They have risen in the world and absorbed some of its knocks. All four now have families of their own, fourteen children in all: eleven girls but just three boys to carry on the Hewett name. Soon there will be grandchildren. When they die, Vic, Robert and Frank, together with their wives, will be reunited in the same plot, under a shady tree, at the entrance to the Methodist section of the Williamstown cemetery.

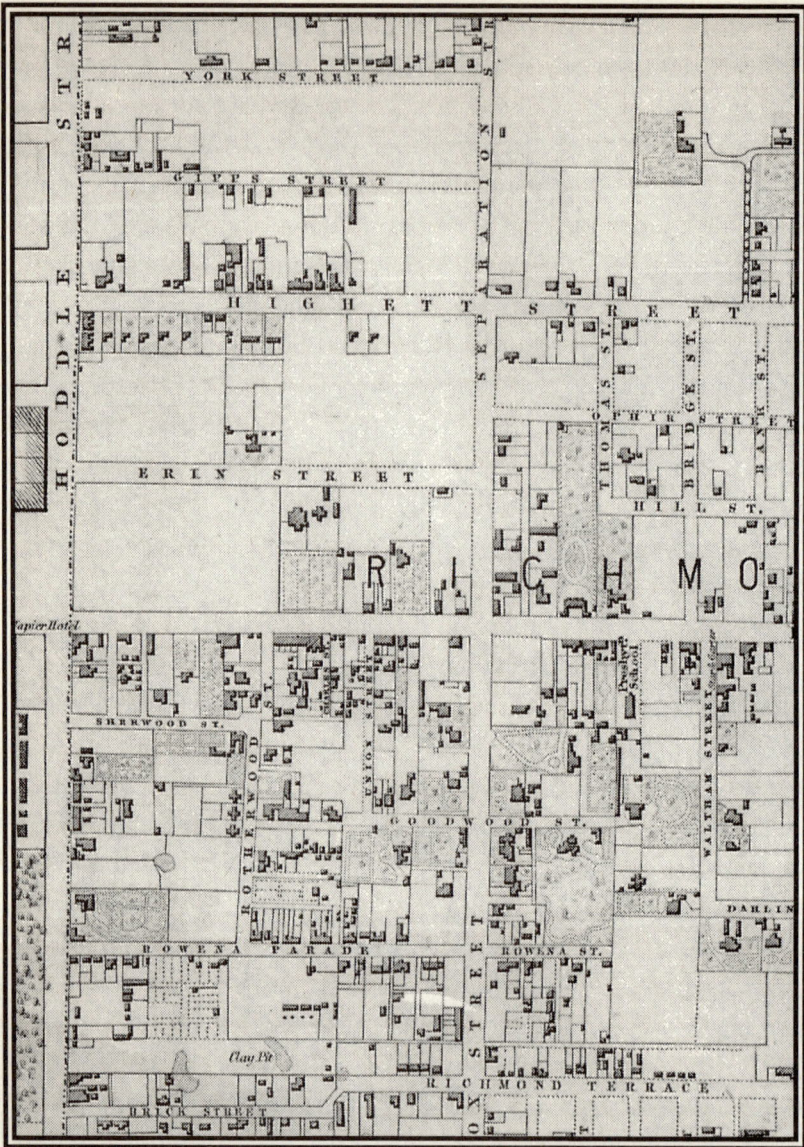

In the 1850s, Richmond was one of an inner ring of suburban townships, formed by the overflow of population from the gold-rush city. Separated from the city by parklands, it attracted some of the city's elite, whose villas and spacious gardens clustered on the top of the hill. Jane Hewett and her daughter were among the poorer cottage-dwellers who settled on the slopes to the north. (James Kearney, Melbourne and Its Suburbs, *1855 (detail), State Library of Victoria)*

CHAPTER NINE
Richmond Hill

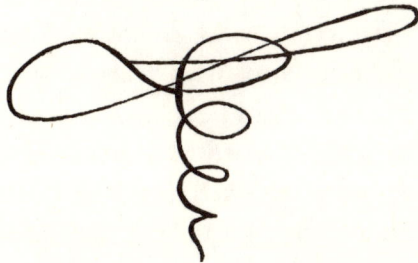

'Men do not emigrate in despair, but in hope,' the historian W.K. Hancock famously remarked. We can only guess what hopes Jane Hewett and her family carried to Port Phillip in 1850. The fact that they emigrated as a family is surely significant. It testifies to the bonds of mutual dependence nurtured by life on a family farm and consolidated by the premature death of their husband and father. But if Jane had expected her family to continue farming and living together in the new land, she must have been disappointed. By the mid-1850s, with her eldest son dead, and all but two of her other children married and scattered across the colony, Jane and two of her daughters, Mary Ann and Jane, alone remained single. Mary Ann, as we related in Chapter 6, became a monthly nurse and farmer in Gippsland, but what happened to the two Janes?

Theirs was not an unusual predicament. At the peak of the rush, many women were left to wait in Melbourne as their menfolk pursued their dreams of gold. 'While in no country is wife desertion so common as this, in no country is it harder for the poor woman to live, and maintain herself and her children in an honest way,' the Melbourne *Argus* observed in 1860. Widows and single women, like Jane and her daughter, may have been little better off. They gravitated to the cheapest housing they could find, within walking distance of the low-paid, insecure employment, as domestic servants, charwomen (cleaners), laundry women, hawkers, needlewomen and street-sellers, that was all that stood between them and poverty, or prostitution.

Women without partners or children leave only the faintest footprint in the official record, so we do not know with any certainty where the widow Jane lived, or with whom, for the next decade. Perhaps she accompanied one of her children to country Victoria— Lucy, the eldest daughter, married to a well-to-do businessman, is the most probable. But more likely she was already living where we next find her, in a cottage on the outskirts of Melbourne. Jane Hewett was 68 years old when her name appeared for the first time in the 1859 *Victorian Directory*, in Lennox Street, Richmond. Five years later she was listed in the local rate book at the same address, as owner and occupier of a four-room timber cottage rated at £26 a year. Located just under the brow of the hill, their home was only a few blocks from the house of Edward Bell, the governor's secretary, who had employed Elizabeth Fenwick as a servant when she arrived in Melbourne in 1850. Two hundred metres or so to the north, however, Lennox Street threads through a pocket of crowded, low-lying timber houses later condemned as a slum. (In the mid-twentieth century it was cleared to make way for Housing Commission high-rise flats.) Halfway between the hill and the flat, respectability and poverty, Jane and her daughter had become members of that ill-used class, the genteel poor.

Although cramped by our standards, Jane's cottage was typical of the houses of the time: more than two-thirds of Richmond houses were built of wood, and three-quarters had four rooms or less. A cottage like hers would have cost around a hundred pounds, or about two-thirds of a workman's yearly wages, in 1861. How she acquired it is unknown. Perhaps, after selling up the family's possessions at Hook Farm, she had saved enough for a modest home in Australia. Perhaps her relatives—brother-in-law James, or one of her children—helped out. Or perhaps her carpenter son Robert contributed in kind. However she managed it, the Richmond cottage became the rock of her salvation.

I have often walked down Lennox Street, usually with a group of students or other historical tourists in tow. Richmond was the subject of my honours dissertation, my first extended effort at writing history. I spent many weeks combing through council rate books, mapping houses and tracing individuals, yet somehow never encountered, or recognised, the name of my great-great-great-grandmother. It did not occur to me that one of my forebears could have passed that way. I had come from lower-middle-class Essendon in search of the Victorian working class, not realising that I was descended from one of them. I walked the backstreets of Richmond photographing humble cottages much like Jane's without knowing that an ancestor's home could be in my viewfinder. Years later, when I designed a walking tour of the area, I plotted a route along Bridge Road, down Judd Street, where the boot manufacturer and staunch Methodist Daniel Bedggood established his factory, and back to Lennox Street, turning the corner just where Jane's house used to stand. Now, alas, it has gone, demolished to make way for an annex of the nearby Epworth Hospital.

As I thought about the lives of the two Janes, mother and daughter, my sympathies were aroused for the many other women who found themselves alone in a new colony, without a male breadwinner or protector, and far from the homeland networks of kin and neighbours. In Richmond, young women between fifteen and 30 years of age outnumbered men by 60 to 40, yet the opportunities for their employment were severely limited. In 1859, one of the Hewetts' neighbours, Harriet Clisby, a homeopath and feminist, living with her husband in Highett Street, wrote to the *Argus* newspaper to raise the problem of female employment. 'The paths that are generally open to women are full to overflowing,' she observed. 'And then what a miserable pittance is received for the 10, 12, and 14 houred day compared to what men receive for their eight hours. All women don't want to be needlewomen, governesses or servants.' Nor, she pointed out, did they necessarily want to be wives.

> *All women do not wish to marry, whilst others lose their husbands; and what would be done with these? They may have means and they may not. In either case, they need work, whereby they may come out of that state of uncertainty and incompleteness which at present is the state of their minds—the state of their home life.*

Local charities were keenly aware of the predicament of Richmond's female unemployed. 'The cases relieved during the past year have been of the ordinary kind—widows, deserted wives, and fatherless children; and not a few cases arising from sickness, and want of employment,' the Richmond Ladies' Benevolent Society reported in 1870. Their assistance, in many cases, came in the form of a sewing machine, the entry ticket into the standard form of paid employment for women.

Jane Hewett, 'widow', continued to be listed as owner and occupier of the house at 46 Lennox Street until 1874. When she died, in October 1875, aged 84, after a five-month illness, she was living at Longwood with her eldest daughter, Lucy. A 'gentlewoman', according to her death certificate, she was buried in the Longwood cemetery, close to the old Hume Highway and within view of the rugged foothills of the Strathbogie Ranges. Thirty-six years had passed since she and her children had gathered in another graveyard, half a world away amidst the soft green fields of Hampshire, to bury their husband and father, John Hewett. As her own life neared its close, did Jane relive her fateful decision to emigrate, and ponder the chain of consequences that flowed from the voyage of the *Culloden*? Had it all been worthwhile?

In 1876, Mrs Jane Hewett, widow, was succeeded by Miss Jane Hewett, dressmaker, as owner-occupier of the Lennox Street cottage. 'Dressmaker' was a small step up from 'needlewoman', implying more skill and a semi-professional relationship with a clientele of respectable well-to-do women whose clothes were 'bespoke', made to measure, rather than manufactured for sale off the peg ('slops'). But if the title carried more respect, it did not necessarily offer much more pay. She was edging uncomfortably close to the situation her sister-in-law Elizabeth Fenwick had emigrated to escape and that her nieces Clara and Elizabeth in Wesley Hill still endured. Her brother John took a kindly interest in her welfare, leaving her a small bequest of £50 in his will. Her residence at 29 Lennox Street—the number changed when the street was renumbered in the early 1880s—was undisturbed for the next decade, but after 1888 she suddenly disappears from both the Richmond rate book and the directory. In 1889, the 'Misses Hewett dressmakers' appear in Gore Street, Fitzroy, but a year later their names have disappeared. A 'Mrs Jane Hewitt' (*sic*) arrives in Rule Street, Richmond, in 1891, disappears, and is succeeded by a 'Miss Hewett' at 97 Church Street in 1894.

What had happened to disturb the apparently settled existence of the middle-aged spinster? The late 1880s was an optimistic time when house prices rose dramatically and there was a good deal of speculative development on Richmond Hill. Could Jane have decided to sell the house and invest in a dressmaking business in Fitzroy (with her sister Mary Ann or her niece Clara perhaps?) only to succumb to the financial crash of the early 1890s? Or was it simply that, with advancing age, she was unable to earn a living and sold her house for income? Whatever the reason, by the end of the 1890s, she had lost the Richmond cottage and become a bird of passage, moving from one rented house to another. When she next appears, on the 1908 electoral roll, it is as co-tenant with a widow, Anna Thomas, in a house owned by John Lennox at 19 Bowen Street, Richmond, just around the corner from her old abode.

Jane was now over seventy years of age, one of the thousands of gold-rush settlers whose fortunes had been blighted by the 1890s depression. In the midst of the crisis, Melbourne's charitable institutions, the only source of relief for indigent old people, almost collapsed under the pressure of demand. In 1899, the Victorian government had recognised their plight by introducing one of the world's first old-age pension schemes. In order to qualify, applicants had to show not just that they were indigent but also that they no longer had family able to care for them. Jane's sister Mary Ann had died in 1892 and her only surviving sibling, Lucy, was now a widow herself. If Jane did not qualify soon after the scheme was introduced, she would certainly have done so after Lucy's death in 1912. After two decades of anxiety and insecurity, she was about to enter perhaps the most serene stage of her long life.

In 1915, John Traill, manager of Huddart Parker, a shipping company, and a leading member of the Charity Organisation Society, nominated Miss Jane Hewett for admission to the Old Colonists' Homes in Fitzroy. Its council 'unanimously' agreed to accept her. The Homes had been established by the Old Colonists' Association in 1872 'to assist the poor and distressed pioneers of this colony whose position and services entitle them to a more congenial home than the Benevolent Asylum'. The words 'pioneer' and 'old colonist' had a definite meaning: they applied especially to the first-comers, those who had arrived before Separation in 1851, although eligibility was later extended to those who arrived before 1855. Admission to the homes, like the old age pension, was meant as a reward for those who had suffered the privations of the 'early days'. So we can appreciate why, when Vic and Emma visited Jane in the Old Colonists' Homes in the 1920s, she reminded them that she had arrived 'before the gold rush'. Preference was also given to 'those who had been in superior positions in life previously', that is, to the genteel poor. That Jane was 'unanimously' accepted suggests that she was seen as deserving not only because of her poverty but also because of her respectability.

A little village of old people, housed in Gothic cottages clustered in a garden setting, the Old Colonists' Homes were a colonial adaptation of a traditional English ideal. Jane may have felt as though she was returning to one of the sixteenth-century almshouses in the yard of All Saints Church in her mother's old town, Odiham. While residents each had their own cottage, guests were not permitted, or only as a special favour. 'I have pleasure in informing you that the Council has granted you permission to have your friend Miss McDonald to stay with you during the Christmas and New Year holidays,' the secretary wrote to Jane in December 1916. Once a year, the cottagers were taken on a picnic excursion to Sorrento, and occasionally Jane travelled to the country herself to stay with friends.

In 1925, a *Herald* reporter visited the Homes to spend 'An Hour with the Old Colonists'. Their cottages, he noted, were a picture of 'comfort and cleanliness'. Though subject to regular inspection, 'each house is really its occupant's castle', 'neat as doll's houses, furnished to the taste of the resident', each with its own neatly stacked pile of firewood. More than half the residents were women. Two of them, 'in their cradles when Victoria was crowned', contested the honour of being the oldest. Three years earlier, Jane had held the title, but now a new resident, Mrs Susan Soward, 94, beat her by three months. The reporter returned a year later to find Jane—'the most wonderful old lady I have ever met'—writing Christmas cards, without even the aid of spectacles. 'Glasses make my eyes tired when I'm writing,' she explained, handing over half a dozen addressed envelopes for inspection. The writing was firm and straight. 'My sight is good, I hear as well as ever I did. I haven't an artificial tooth in my head, and so can chew my food like a youngster, my health is perfect, and I'm 96 years old.' (She was actually 94, but the ambition to best Mrs Soward may have been irresistible.)

'I'm from Hampshire. Hook Farm, Hampshire, where my father and his father were born,' she continued. 'All my sisters married here, but I was the odd one out. I remained single. I'm a real old maid.' Had she forgotten her spinster sister Mary Ann, or did the reporter mishear her? She pointed to a row of photographs on the mantelpiece. 'There's portraits of some of the young men in my family.' A previous press article depicting her as the oldest inhabitant of the Old Colonists' Homes may have prompted her great-nephews Vic and Bob to visit and record her story. Bob, a keen photographer, posed the old lady with representatives of the succeeding generations. Alongside the photographs of her 'young men' was one of the Prince of Wales (later Edward VIII), who had recently visited Australia. 'And you have a distinguished young man's picture there, I see,' the reporter observed. 'Oh, the Prince of Wales. Yes indeed. A fine young man too, Prince Charming. I'm as loyal as they make 'em.'

Two years later, on 9 October 1928, Jane Hewett, 'lady's companion', suffered a fatal heart attack. At 96 she was still the second-oldest inhabitant of the Old Colonists' Homes: her rival Mrs Soward outlived her by a year. The next day, a two-line advertisement appeared in the *Argus* announcing her death. She was buried the same afternoon, with as little fuss as she had caused in life, in the Boroondara cemetery. On a recent visit, I stopped by the gatehouse and collected a map showing the location of her grave, and followed a path along the western wall to a shady spot under a row of pines. There, between the solid granite tombstones of two worthy Presbyterians, the last of the family to embark on the *Culloden* lies in an unmarked grave.

CONCLUSION
Legacies and life chances

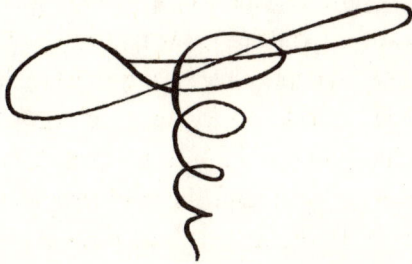

Family history may be the oldest kind of history. Since Old Testament times families have collected genealogies and handed down stories of their tribe. 'Let us now praise famous men, and our fathers who begat us,' begins the psalmist. Most family histories are acts of homage offered by descendants to their forebears. They magnify their ancestors' virtues and achievements and gloss over, forget or at least forgive their faults. By the time the youngest of Robert and Elizabeth's children, Frank Deacon Hewett, died in 1954, his parents' story had been shaped to provide a suitable pedigree for a respectable public servant. Robert was now described as a 'contractor', not just a carpenter, while Elizabeth was said to have come from aristocratic 'Berkly Square' rather than humble Old Kent Road. She emigrated 'with her family' rather than as a 'distressed needlewoman'. Other

Hewett descendants imagined a glorious ancestral past. Robert and Elizabeth's daughter Clara regaled her niece Millie with tales of the lost 'Fenwick millions', while their grandson John Hewett vowed, as he left on a trip to England, to visit the Hewetts' 'ancestral castle'.

Like other Australian families, the Hewetts shaped their story as a colonial Book of Genesis. By the early twentieth century, they had begun to cultivate a sense of their history, photographing the last of the pioneers, recording their stories and revisiting the sites of their first settlement. They looked back to the voyage of the *Culloden* with gratitude and respect, as the gateway to their own fortunate lives. There was real heroism, mixed with desperation, in the decision of Jane and her children to set sail for Port Phillip. In 'pitching his tent' on the Castlemaine goldfields, Robert Hewett became our Abraham, the first-comer to our Promised Land. Their children followed in the path they had set, adding further members to the tribe. The first tellers of this story, like Jane Hewett, the maiden aunt with whose memory this book began, tactfully passed over the misfortunes of the diseased and unfruitful branches: the black sheep, hard cases, solitaries and drifters. They forgot or suppressed the memories of bereavement, dispossession, penury, imprisonment, bankruptcy, scandal, and premature and sudden death that shadowed, and often shaped, their lives.

In a post-Freudian age, we may deplore or pity their reluctance to confront the demons in their past. Only if the secret sins and pains of the past are laid bare can we hope to be healed from them—or so it is often said. Yet many of the sad events I recount here were too long forgotten to affect more recent generations, and even when they were not, I wonder whether stoic silence was always more hurtful than disclosure. I did not begin this book looking for skeletons in my family's cupboard, but once the cupboard was opened, they simply fell out. As a historian, I had no choice but to include them in my story, but the point of revealing them is not healing so much as an enlarged understanding.

Interest in family history usually grows stronger towards the end of life, as our past grows longer and our future shrinks. Genealogy and family history have flourished as baby boomers review their roller-coaster ride from the austere 1940s and 1950s, through the liberated 1960s and 1970s, to their chastening years of maturity. In a famous essay, 'The Eight Ages of Man', the psychoanalyst Erik Erikson defined the goal of old age as 'the acceptance of one's one and only life cycle as something that had to be and that, by necessity, permitted of no substitutions'. 'An individual life,' he continues, 'is the accidental coincidence of but one life cycle with but one segment of history.' Investigating family history, placing oneself in the intersection between one's own unique life cycle and the history of our times, may be a step towards the integrity Erikson sees as the ultimate goal of life.

Family history grounds our identity in a past deeper than our own memory. Asked when they feel most connected with the past, many people talk about looking at old family photographs, visiting museums and touching heirlooms or other objects associated with their family's history. A tangible past—a history one can see, touch and feel—often seems more evocative than one based on words alone. In touching heirlooms, we may feel closer to the person who made or used them than we do in simply hearing or reading about them. Anthropologist Diane Bell suggests that heirlooms have a special significance for women in maintaining links between generations otherwise obscured by marriage. Apart from their old home at Wesley Hill and the photographs in my mother's album, only a handful of commonplace objects survives to connect us with the lives of Robert and Elizabeth Hewett. My kinsman John Boothroyd treasures a spokeshave rescued from Robert's workshop by another descendant, Roy Mussett, and a small silver button, part of a riding jacket said to have been brought by Elizabeth aboard the *Culloden*. (What possible use did a London needlewoman have for such a getup?) Beth Pidsley, a distant cousin now resident in Queensland, inherited Robert's painted sea chest, the Bible and Prayerbook presented to Elizabeth

237

by the Female Emigration Society, and a brooch supposed to have been made from a gemstone given by Robert to Elizabeth. In a short story, 'The Heirloom', Beth imagines Robert picking up a milky white stone from the beach as they landed in Australia. "'Robert, we shan't have a betrothal ring," Elizabeth declares. "This, our very first possession in our new land, can do instead.'" Heirlooms lend themselves to such flights of fancy; they are relics, designed to stir sentimental attachment, not reliable testimony.

Beyond sentimental attachment or ancestral homage, family history, especially in our times, has become a search for self-understanding. It offers an answer to the question 'Who do you think you are?' In tracing where we came from, we hope to understand who we are now. Perhaps, we think, we are not products of our genes and upbringing alone, but of a longer chain of ancestry in which talents, values and foibles, as well as physical characteristics, pass mysteriously from generation to generation. 'Who does she take after?' parents and grandparents anxiously enquire about a new addition to the family. They are looking for traits of personality as well as physical resemblance. The answers we give are often wishful, always conjectural, yet we would be unwise to dismiss them entirely.

Personal identity is formed first of all in the family setting. Our most significant role models are usually family members. I was aware as I grew up of my parents' admiration for my grandfather, the printer, bibliophile and Methodist preacher Vic Hewett. More than anyone else, he modelled and encouraged my interest in history and literature. Even after he died, his influence continued through the books I inherited from his library. Albert Schweitzer's *The Quest of the Historical Jesus*, *The Poems of Wilfred Owen* and Francis Adams' *The Australians*—to select just three books among many—mapped my intellectual journey as they had his before me. Vic Hewett, in turn, was formed by the interests, skills and religion of his parents and grandparents, influences I understand better now than I did before I began to write this book. Yet in writing it I have resisted the temptation to create my forebears in my own image, or my generation's. The Hampshire farmer John Hewett and his wife Jane lived a world away, in time and space, from our Australia. I am now more aware of the ruptures, as well as the continuities, in the lineage that connects those worlds. And more aware, too, of what I have taken from it, and rejected.

Yet continuities there were. The family was English and Protestant, loyalties maintained through four generations by intermarriage with other mainly English, Protestant families. The regional origins of their partners, from Cornwall to Yorkshire and from rural Hampshire to central London, were diverse, but only one family of Scottish and none of Irish descent appeared in its family tree before the fourth generation. In this respect, the Hewetts were probably not unusual: religious sectarianism, or tribalism, was a powerful binding and dividing force in Australia, at least until the Second World War.

As yeomen farmers, the Hewetts were people of 'the middling sort', a rank in society that their emigrant descendants largely maintained. In wishing his sons to learn a trade, yeoman John Hewett established a pattern of skilled handwork continued by his son Robert, a carpenter; his grandsons, the engineer Robert Henry and the building inspector Frank; and his great-grandsons, the printers Victor and John, the mechanical engineer Robert (Reuben) and the marine engineer Frank. Not all of the Hewetts' Australian descendants were able to maintain a respectable position in society, and some fell into poverty. During the gold era, meanwhile, Jane's eldest girl Lucy and her husband James Maxfield rose a step higher, although by the 1870s, when their business failed, they, like their sister and brother Susan and Robert Maxfield, settled for 'middling' occupations, much like those they had left in England. As in many immigrant families, the second and third generations prospered more than the first.

For almost a century, Hewett men tended, unconventionally, to marry women older than themselves. John Hewett, the farmer with whom this story began, was 25 years old, five years younger than Jane Parsons; Robert Hewett three and a half years younger than

Elizabeth Fenwick, Robert Henry three years younger than Susan Stephens, Victor seven years younger than my grandmother Emma, and my own father, George Davison, two years younger than my mother, May. In the 1880s, Victorian grooms marrying for the first time were on average about four years older than their brides, so the marriage pattern of the Hewetts flouted contemporary norms. An older man who marries a younger woman potentially increases the size of the couple's family, although at the risk of a shorter working life over which to rear them. An older woman who marries a younger man, by contrast, may produce a smaller family but may be able to rely on her husband's longer working life to see them educated and launched into adulthood. Whether by accident or design, the Hewetts' marriages seem to have reinforced the 'self-discipline' and prudential restraint that marked their working, family and religious lives.

Yet as the voyage of the *Culloden* and the fortunes of its passengers remind us, migration was not a sure recipe for success. Jane Hewett brought her eight children to Australia hoping to improve their prospects and keep her family together, but it was not long before the family scattered, and of her eight children only five appear to have left descendants. 'Settler colonies,' Janet McCalman reminds us, 'were not only sites of dispossession and destruction, they were also severe testing grounds for those who took possession and transplanted their culture and social forms.' Some single men and women led fulfilling lives, either alone or within the family circle, but others ended their lives as 'solitaries, drifters and failures'. Their deaths, unlamented and sometimes conveniently forgotten, were simply written out of family history.

Jane's eldest son, Henry, who died alone in the bush at the age of 32, and her fourth son, Richard, who served time in Maitland Gaol for forgery, were among the casualties of colonisation. Her second son, John, married in haste but appears to have repented at leisure, while two of her daughters, Mary Ann and Jane, remained single, each relying, however, on family support to stay afloat. My own forebears, Robert and Elizabeth, were perhaps the most fruitful, if not the most fortunate in every way. Of their five adult children, four married, giving them, in turn, sixteen grandchildren, 45 great-grandchildren and over a hundred great-great-grandchildren, although—such was the predominance of girls among the second and third generations—few still bear the Hewett surname. Robert, the bush carpenter, is our Abraham, and Elizabeth, the distressed needlewoman from London, is our Sarah. I bless them both, as I also salute Robert's widowed mother, and their childless brothers and sisters.

Family history, according to one view, should instil pride, a warm glow of satisfaction with the achievements of one's forebears and an incentive to later generations to conserve their heritage. We visualise our ancestors marching bravely into the future, confident of where they were going, plotting a steady course towards a glorious destination—us. I have no quarrel with those who view it in that light. But family history, understood more broadly, should also foster a measure of family humility. It should embrace the black sheep as well as the white, the wanderers and stumblers as well as the confident marchers. In reclaiming our lost relations, we may learn compassion for those who were caught in the riptides of history, and for those who struggle against them still.

Acknowledgements

In February 2013, I accompanied my sister, Helen Hobbs, then visiting us from England for a birthday celebration, back to the Hewett family's old homes in Castlemaine and Campbell's Creek. Some of our cousins and children accompanied us. As the self-appointed guide, I had previously made a few enquiries into the family's history. The story of Elizabeth Fenwick, previously unknown to us, caught my interest and I decided to write a short account for family members. Over the following months, however, the thread grew longer and the story expanded; this book is the result. I wish to thank Helen for the stimulus of her visit and her continuing support for the project. I also thank my cousin Philip Jackson, who accompanied me on an expedition to Flynn's Creek, and my aunts Marjorie Jackson and Florence Lear for their recollections. Richard Jackson and the folk at the Orient Expresso provided excellent coffee and cheerfully endured my progress reports.

Only when the research was well under way did I make contact with John Boothroyd, who had already compiled a genealogical table of the descendants of Robert and Elizabeth Hewett and interviewed a number of surviving Hewett descendants in the early 1980s. He generously allowed me to make use of his collection and read some draft chapters of this book. I also thank him for introducing me to other Hewett descendants, Colin and Iris Maxfield, Maree Kininburgh, Beth Pidsley and Roy Mussett, who have eagerly supported the project, also making documents and photographs in their possession available. Joy Crawford, daughter of my great-uncle John Hewett, provided valuable details on his life. Geoffrey Fairbairn pointed me towards the panoramic photograph of Campbell's Creek and helped identify the probable site of the Stephens house. In England, I thank Nick, Mimi and Anne Hart of Llangarron, Penny and Paul Shewry of Malvern, Barry Stapleton of Portsmouth, and archivists at the Hampshire and Wiltshire record offices. In Australia I acknowledge help from librarians and archivists at the Public Record Office of Victoria, the State Library of Victoria, the Uniting Church Archives, Castlemaine Historical Society, the Williamstown branch of the City of Port Phillip Library, Carringbush Library, and Euroa Historical Society. Tony Dingle and Charles Fahey placed their knowledge of mining houses at my disposal, and Tony accompanied me on a visit to Wesley Hill where, thanks to the kindness of Dugald McLellan and Adrian Saunders, we were able to inspect the two Hewett houses. Janet McCalman kindly enabled me to draw on data gathered for her long-term study of maternal health and child mortality.

I wish to thank Janet and my colleagues John Hirst and Marian Quartly for their helpful comments on the manuscript, Tom Griffiths and Andrew May for leads into the literature on family history, and publisher, Elizabeth Weiss, copyeditor Clara Finlay, and editorial manager Angela Handley of Allen & Unwin for their encouragement, incisive criticism and support. Barbara Davison has been a more than tolerant supporter of my late conversion to family history: sharing the journey with her has been one of its special rewards. Our children Jim, Lucy and Mim have also taken an interest: this book is for them and their children too.

GD
May 2014

Picture acknowledgements

The photographs in this volume come mainly from private family sources. As the eldest daughter, and a photographer herself, my mother took a keen interest in old family photographs; her family albums are the principal source. My niece Elizabeth Tranter helpfully digitised and organised some of these images. I am grateful to John Boothroyd, Beth Pidsley and Colin and Iris Maxfield for images in their own collections. Images from public collections are acknowledged in the captions.

Notes

I have made extensive use of the standard genealogical sources, such as parish registers, official registrations of births, marriages and deaths, probate records, city directories and British census records, often accessing them through Ancestry.com, Find My Past and other online sources. These are too extensive to cite except in cases where critical judgement was required.

ABBREVIATIONS

EA	*Euroa Advertiser*
HA	*Hampshire Advertiser*
KFP	*Kilmore Free Press*
MC	*Morning Chronicle*
MAM	*Mount Alexander Mail*
TR	*Traralgon Record*
WC	*Williamstown Chronicle*

INTRODUCTION

Charles Taylor on identity in his 'The politics of recognition' (1992), in David Theo Goldberg (ed.), *Multiculturalism: A critical reader*, Blackwell, Oxford, 1994, 79; family reunions, Paul Ashton and Paula Hamilton, *History at the Crossroads*,

Halstead Press, Sydney, 2007, 32; family history boom in my *The Use and Abuse of Australian History*, Allen & Unwin, Sydney, 2000, 80–109; family history as a gateway to the national past in Roy Rosenzweig and David Thelen, *The Presence of the Past*, Columbia University Press, New York, 1998, 15–22; Paul Ashton and Paula Hamilton, 'At home with the past: background and initial findings from the national survey', in Paula Hamilton and Paul Ashton (eds), *Australians and the Past*, special issue of *Australian Cultural History*, vol. 22, 2003, 5–30; critical remarks on digital family history in my 'Speed-relating: family history in a digital age', *History Australia*, vol. 6, no. 2, 2009, 43.1–43.10.

CHAPTER ONE: HOOK FARM

On Newnham see Nigel Bell, *Newnham: A short history of the parish and its church*, The Church, n.d. and William Page (ed.), *A History of the County of Hampshire, Volume 4*, Victoria County History, 1911, 156–8; wills of James and Lucy Hewett, 1808 and 1809, Hampshire Record Office Ad 21/2 and Letters of Administration 1827, AD 36; on spinsters, Michael Anderson, 'The social position of spinsters in mid-Victorian Britain', *Journal of Family History*, vol. 9, no. 4, 1984, 377–93; on 'yeoman' see William Cobbett, *Rural Rides*, Nelson and Sons, [1822–26], Project Gutenberg, 2010, 16, and G.E. Mingay, *Rural Life in Victorian England*, Futura Publications, London, 1977, 63; Vancouver's description in his *General View of the Agriculture of Hampshire*, Richard Philips, London, 1810, 8 and 14, and compare Bob Edwards, *Historic Farmsteads and Historic Character in Hampshire, Report for English Heritage*, English Heritage, Blandford Forum, UK, 2005; configuration of Hook Farm in Newnham Tithe Apportionment, 1839–40, Newnham Tithe Map, Hampshire Record Office, 21M65/F7/168/1 and 21M65/F7/168/2, Tithe Award for the Parish of Nately Scures, WRO 21M65/F7/165/1; Vancouver's description of farmers in his *General View*, 75–7; ages of yeomen marriages in J.H. Porter, 'The development of rural society', in G.E. Mingay (ed.), *The Agrarian History of England and Wales, Volume VI: 1750–1850*, Cambridge University Press, Cambridge, 1989, 866–77; Jane Austen's opinion of the yeomanry in her *Emma* [1816], Everyman Edition, London, 1906, 23; women and children in rural workforce in Mingay, *Agrarian History*, 683–8; size of farming families in Michael Anderson, 'Social aspects of demographic change', in F.M.L. Thompson, *Cambridge Social History of Britain 1750–1950, Volume 1*, Cambridge University Press, Cambridge, 2005, 38–9 and 52; on income sources of farmers, Leigh Shaw-Taylor, 'Family farms and capitalist farms in mid nineteenth century England', *British Agricultural History Review*, vol. 53, no. 2, 2005, 158–91; Robert Stares in Select Committee on Agriculture, House of Commons Sessional Papers, 465, 1836; local responses to

Swing riots, *HA*, 27 November 1830, and compare E.J. Hobsbawm and George Rudé, *Captain Swing*, Penguin University Books, London, 1973, 261–2; John Hewett's Will A 1939 52, Hampshire Record Office; George Eliot, 'Mr Gilfil's Love Story', in her *Scenes of Clerical Life* [1856], Everyman Edition, London, 1910; Barry Stapleton's study of Odiham wills in his 'Family strategies: patterns of inheritance in Odiham, Hampshire, 1525–1850', *Continuity and Change*, vol. 14, no. 3, December 1999, 385–402; coming of railway in *HA*, 9 October 1830, and R.A. Williams, *The London & South Western Railway, Volume 1: The formative years*, David and Charles, Newton Abbot, 1968, *passim*; rival verdicts on conduct of navvies in Terry Coleman, *The Railway Navvies*, Hutchinson, London, 1965, 72–101 and David Brooke, 'The railway navvy: a reassessment', in Mike Chrimes (ed.), *The Civil Engineering of Canals and Railways before 1850*, Ashgate, Aldershot, 1997, 309–19; arrival of railway, *MC*, 19 September 1838; Fernand Braudel on Voltaire in Braudel's *Capitalism and Material Life*, Harper and Row, New York, 1967, 7; R.G. Collingwood on rethinking the past in his *The Idea of History*, Oxford University Press, New York, 1957, 218; Dickens on arrival of railway in his *Dombey and Son*, [1848], Penguin edition, London, 1970, 354; 'ease and smoothness', *The Standard*, 11 June 1839; 'delightful prospects' in *Bradshaw's Descriptive Guide to the London & South Western Railway*, E.L. Blanchard, London, 1845, 32–5; on 'apoplexy', see Pandora Pound, Michael Bury and Shah Ebrahim, 'From apoplexy to stroke', *Age and Ageing*, vol. 27, 1997, 331–7; mobility of agricultural labourers in Mingay (ed.), *Agrarian History*, 661–4 and 683–8; diet, Vancouver, *General View*, 383–7 and Cobbett, *Rural Rides*, 245; Tyssen's illness and family crisis, Florence Horatio Suckling, *A Forgotten Past: Being notes on the families of Tyssen, Baker, Hougham, and Milles, of five centuries*, G. Bell and Sons, London, 1898, 91 and 116; his sons in Australia, *Geelong Advertiser*, 7 March 1842 and *Australian Chronicle*, 15 March 1842; transactions on his Hampshire estates, 'Hooke' and 'Nightingales' (Parishes of Odiham, Nately Scures) 1835–67, Harris of Rotherwick, Hampshire Record Office 287 M87/8; sale of farm, Odiham, Sale Particulars of 'Hook and Nightingale' Farm, 1846, Hampshire Record Office, 10 M 57/SP 527; insecurity of tenant farmers, Mingay (ed.), *Agrarian History*, 611–17, *HA*, 16 January 1847 and David R. Stead, 'The mobility of English tenant farmers, c.1700–1850', *Agricultural History Review*, vol. 51, 2003, 186–8; outcome of sale, William Charles King and others to Charles Tyssen, 1 October 1853, Hampshire Record Office, 10 M 57/SP 527; sympathisers to *The Times*, 21 February 1845, Gloucester farmer's plea in *ibid*. 21 January 1845; protest about advice to small farmers in *ibid*. 18 October 1845; *Morning Post*, 7 August 1849, 'I have tried in vain', *Morning Post*, 18 September 1849; Surrey petition, *Daily News*, 9 March 1849; on Hook Independent Chapel see William Page (ed.), *A History of the County of*

Hampshire, vol. 4, Victoria County History, London 1911, 156–8; and for details of local landowners and church livings, *History, Gazetteer and Directory of Hampshire and the Isle of Wight*, William White (ed.), Sheffield and London, 1859, 490; Cromwell's troops at White Hart in Hook Timeline, www.hookinhampshire.co.uk/historic_hook.php, accessed 11 November 2014; Hampshire religious composition from *Census of Great Britain, Religious Worship England and Wales*, 1851, HMSO London, 1853, ccxii, 23, and for social character of Independents A.D. Gilbert, *Religion and Society in Industrial England: Church, chapel and social change, 1740–1914*, Longman, London 1976, 97–121; marriage certificates of John, Robert and Lucy Hewett; attitudes to emigration, James Belich, *Replenishing the Earth: The settler revolution and the rise of the Anglo world*, Oxford University Press, Oxford, 2009, 145–76; Eric Richards, *Britannia's Children: Emigration from England, Scotland, Wales and Ireland since 1600*, Hambledon and London, London, 2004, 145–59, also compare Nancy L. Green, 'The politics of exit: reversing the immigration paradigm', *Journal of Modern History*, vol. 77, no. 2, June 2005, 263–89; wages of Berkshire labourer, *MC*, 27 October 1849; labour in Port Phillip, *Hampshire Telegraph and Sussex Chronicle*, 29 December 1849; Australian emigration counties, see James Jupp (ed.), *The Australian People*, Angus and Robertson, Sydney, 1988, 388–406; Jupp, *The English in Australia*, Cambridge University Press, Melbourne, 2004, 52–68; Chisholm on emigration, *MC*, 4, 11, 16, 28, 30 January, 9 February, 29 March 1849; *The ABC of Colonization in a Series of Letters by Mrs Chisholm*, John Ollivier, London, 1850, 7–8; on the scheme, Margaret Kiddle, *Caroline Chisholm*, Melbourne University Press, Carlton, 1950, reprinted 1990, 97–121; advantages of family groups, *MC*, 17 July 1850; on Dickens' interest see Margaret Mendelawitz (ed.), *Charles Dickens' Australia: Selected essays from household words 1850–1859, Book Two: Immigration*, Sydney University Press, Sydney, 2011, 79–82; Poor Law guardians in Odiham, see Barry Stapleton, 'Inherited poverty and life-cycle poverty: Odiham, Hampshire 1650–1850', *Social History*, vol. 18, no. 3, October 1993, 353; on reasons for emigration, compare Belich, *Replenishing the Earth*, 128–32 and Richards, *Britannia's Children*, 145–9.

CHAPTER TWO: LONDON

W.K. Hancock in his *Australia*, Benn, London, 1930, 58; Elizabeth's birth on 28 November 1824 in Parish Register of Newington St Mary, London Metropolitan Archives; on the London 'season' see Leonore Davidoff, *The Best Circles: Society, etiquette and the Season*, Cresset Library, London, 1973; industrial character of London in P.G. Hall, *The Industries of London*, Hutchinson, London, 1962, *passim*; on the carriage trade, George Dodd, *Days at the Factories*, Charles Knight

& Co, London, 1843, 435, 441 and 453–4; effects of seasonality on employment, Gareth Stedman Jones, *Outcast London: A study of the relationship between classes in Victorian London*, Clarendon Press, Oxford, 1971, 33–51, 376 and 382; study of St George's, C.R. Weld, 'On the condition of the working classes in the inner ward of St George's Parish, Hanover Square', *Journal of the Statistical Society of London*, vol. 6, no. 1, April 1843, 18; on overcrowding, Weld, 'On the condition', 18, Stedman Jones, *Outcast London*, 159–78, Anthony Wohl, *The Eternal Slum: Housing and social policy in Victorian London*, Edward Arnold, London, 1977, 5–20; effects of 'improvement', Select Committee on Metropolis Improvements, House of Commons Sessional Papers, no. 517, 1836, 8, also see *ibid.*, no. 661, 1837–38, 60–6 and 279; displacement, Jerry White, *London in the Nineteenth Century*, Vintage Books, London, 2008, 34; Dickens' sweeper in Judith Flanders, *The Victorian City: Everyday life in Dickens' London*, Atlantic Books, London, 2013, 189; on Quadrant see Hermione Hobhouse, *A History of Regent Street*, Macdonald and James, London, 1975, 60ff; Roy Porter, *London: A social history*, Penguin, London, 1994, 154–6; Regent Street as 'ulcer', Albert Smith as quoted in William Acton, *Prostitution*, [1857], Mackibbon and Kee, London, 1968, 218, and Acton's own observation in Flanders, *Victorian City*, 398–401, see also White, *London in the Nineteenth Century*, 300; notoriety of lodgings in Quadrant, see Quadrant (Regent Street), Copy of a circular letter addressed by the Commissioners of Her Majesty's Woods, Forests and Land Revenues to the Lessees of Houses in the Quadrant, House of Commons Sessional Papers, no. 519, 1847–48; on numbers of domestic servants see Sally Alexander, *Women's Work in Nineteenth Century London*, Journeyman Press, London, 1976, 20; 'maid of all work', Francis Sheppard, *London 1808–1870: The infernal wen*, Secker and Warburg, London, 1971, 368–75; Kennington Common meeting, R.G. Gammage, *History of the Chartist Movement, 1837–1854*, [1894], Merlin Press, London, 1969, 296–7; Jerrold in Charles and Mary Cowden Clarke, *Recollections of Writers*, 1878, as quoted in E.P. Thompson, 'Mayhew and the *Morning Chronicle*', in E.P. Thompson and Eileen Yeo, *The Unknown Mayhew: Selections for the Morning Chronicle 1849–50*, Penguin, Harmondsworth, 1971, 9; shift in Mayhew's writing, see Anne Humpherys, *Travels into the Poor Man's Country: The work of Henry Mayhew*, Caliban Books, Firle, Sussex, 1977, 1–30, Thompson and Yeo, *The Unknown Mayhew*, *passim*; on seamstress as figure of pity, Christina Walkley, *The Ghost in the Looking Glass: The Victorian seamstress*, Peter Owen, London, 1981; as exploited in west, see Alexander, *Women's Work*, 59; Mayhew on needlewomen, in Thompson and Yeo, *Unknown Mayhew*, 177–81 and *MC*, 13 November 1849; my 'friendship' with Mayhew, Graeme Davison, David Dunstan and Chris McConville (eds), *Outcast Melbourne: Essays in social history*, Allen & Unwin, Sydney, 1985, 29–58; 'The Unsociable Sociologist—W.S.

Jevons and his survey of Sydney, 1856–8', *Australian Cultural History*, no. 16, 1998, 127–50 and compare Seth Koven, *Slumming: Sexual and social politics in Victorian London*, Princeton University Press, Princeton, 2004; Herbert's response, *MC*, 5 December 1849; *Sidney Herbert, Lord Herbert of Lea: A memoir by Lord Stanmore*, John Murray, London, 1906, 111–12; Jo Chimes, '"Wanted: 1000 Spirited Young Milliners": The Fund for Promoting Female Emigration', in Beth Harris (ed.), *Famine and Fashion: Needlewomen in the nineteenth century*, Ashgate, London, 2005, 228–41; 'safety valve', *MC*, 31 December 1849; Herbert to Gladstone in *Sidney Herbert*, 114; questionnaire, *Daily News*, 21 March 1850; *Fund for Promoting Female Emigration, First Report of the Committee*, March 1851, 2–4 (Mitchell Library); critics in *Morning Post*, 14 February, 28 January 1850; *Economist*, vol. 7, 1849, 1437–41; information on applicants, *MC*, 27 November 1850, *Fund for Female Emigration, First Report*, 4; origins of servants and applicants, compare Chimes, '"Wanted"', 234 and Stedman Jones, *Outcast London*, 136–8; handbill for *Culloden* in Heather Curnow, *The Life and Art of William Strutt, 1825–1915*, Alister Taylor, Martindale, New Zealand, 1980, 12; on conditions for assisted emigrants, Robin F. Haines, *Emigration and the Labouring Poor: Australian recruitment in Britain and Ireland, 1831–60*, St Martin's Press, New York, 1997, 275.

CHAPTER THREE: THE VOYAGE OF THE *CULLODEN*

Emigration Society Home, *Fund for Female Emigration, First Report*, 28; report of departure, *MC*, 26 February 1850; on Dickens' possible attendance see letter to Daniel Maclise in Madeline House, Graham Story and Kathleen Tillotson (eds), *The Letters of Charles Dickens*, Clarendon Press, Oxford, 1988, 25 and Peter Ackroyd, *Dickens*, Sinclair-Stevenson, London, 1990, 586–7; Thackeray's account, 'Waiting at the Station', *Punch*, 9 March 1850, attributed to Thackeray in *Times Literary Supplement*, 1 January 1949, 4; on the snob as a social type, see Thackeray, *The Book of Snobs*, London, 1848 and my 'R.E.N. Twopeny and town life in Australia', *Historical Studies*, vol. 16, no. 63, October 1974, 292–305; passengers aboard the *Culloden*, Ian A. Hughes, *Passengers to Port Phillip from Southern England & Ireland 1849–51*, the author, Northcote 1981, compiles a list of 154 individuals on board the *Culloden*, including an unspecified number of people who are listed simply as 'families' (he appears to have simply added names from several sources, principally newspaper lists, such as the *Argus*, 6 July 1850, *Port Phillip Gazette*, 6 July 1850, and *Melbourne Morning Herald*, 6 July 1850, together with those listed as assisted immigrants in the Government Passenger lists, PROV. Lists of unassisted immigrants to Port Phillip survive only from 1852. The newspaper lists were evidently transcribed from handwritten lists supplied by the agent J.B.

Were, and Hughes' compilation includes a number of transcription errors. Many of the names appearing on the list are simply variants of the same name); marriages of cabin passengers, *Argus*, 17 July 1850, *Launceston Examiner*, 20 January, 5 February 1851, Australian Marriage Index 1853; Paul de Serville describes the Bawtrees as 'gentleman merchants' in his *Pounds and Pedigrees: The upper class in Victoria 1850–80*, Oxford University Press, Melbourne, 1991, 16 and 274; on 'respectability', see G.M. Young, *Portrait of an Age*, Cambridge University Press, Cambridge, 1936, 5, also compare Geoffrey Crossick, *An Artisan Elite in Victorian Society*, Croom Helm, London, 1978, 135ff and Janet McCalman, *Struggletown: Public and private life in Richmond 1900–1965*, Melbourne University Press, Carlton, 1984, 20–9; Strutt's view of fellow passengers, Strutt to his mother, 9 July 1850, as quoted in Curnow, *The Life and Art of William Strutt*, 13; quotations from Strutt's journal in George Mackaness (ed.), *The Australian Journal of William Strutt ARA*, Australian Historical Monographs, Halstead Press, Sydney, 1958; scene on board, *MC*, 26 February 1850; Dickens' view in *David Copperfield*, 1850, chapter 57, and compare Janet C. Myers, *Antipodal England: Emigration and portable domesticity in the Victorian imagination*, SUNY Press, New York, 2009, and Coral Lansbury, *Arcady in Australia: The evocation of Australia in nineteenth century English fiction*, Melbourne University Press, Carlton, 1970, 92–107; Herbert on the voyage, *MC*, 14 January 1852, compare La Trobe to Herbert, 6 December 1850; Lucy Edwards, L_M_E to her father, 13 July 1850, in *Fund for Female Emigration, First Report*, 53: Lucy Edwards' letter is one of several published by the Emigration Society and sometimes republished in newspapers. The writers are identified only by their initials but it is often possible to identify them by reference to the names listed in the archival and Port Phillip immigration records; Strutt's account of pirate incident in *The Australian Journal of William Strutt*, 4; incidents of crew insubordination, *Argus*, 17 July 1850 and compare 'An Old Shellback', *ibid.*, 22 July 1850; Ferguson and Tisdall, see John Patterson and John Sullivan, Immigration Office, to Superintendent La Trobe, 13 July 1850, Papers relative to Emigration, House of Commons, Sessional Papers, 1851 (347); Statement of Margaret Burney in Proceedings of an inquiry into certain circumstances relating to the conduct of the Master and Surgeon of the Ship 'Culloden' and some of the Female passengers by that ship, 5 August 1850, CO 201/431, Australian Joint Copying Project, Reel 622; accounts of arrival, Strutt, *Australian Journal*, 6 and Lucy Edwards in *Fund for Female Emigration, First Report*, 53; La Trobe and Perry hail arrival of ship, C.J. La Trobe to Rt Hon. Sidney Herbert, 19 July 1850, in Papers relative to Emigration to the Australian Colonies, House of Commons Sessional Papers 1851 (347), 59–60, *Argus*, 4, 11 July 1850; La Trobe's recantation, C.J. La Trobe to Rt Hon. Sidney Herbert, 6 August 1850, La Trobe Correspondence, PROV; investigation reported in Proceedings of an inquiry into certain circumstances relating to the conduct of the Master and Surgeon of the Ship 'Culloden' and some of the Female passengers by that ship, 5 August 1850, CO 201/431, Australian Joint Copying Project, Reel 622; Herbert's response, Draft Letter from Sidney Herbert [to La Trobe] regarding the *Culloden*, 3 January 1850 [1851?], Sidney Herbert Papers, 2057/F8/VIII/47a, Wiltshire County Record Office (it is unclear whether this draft letter was actually sent); letter of complaint about *Duke of Portland*, 2 September 1850, 2057/F8/viii/, 48b, Wiltshire County Record Office; Ellen Clacy's opinion in her *A Lady's Visit to the Gold Diggings of Australia in 1852–3*, Hurst and Blackett, London, 1854, [University of Sydney Library edition], chapter xvi; departure of *Culloden* from Sydney, *Sydney Morning Herald*, 10 August, 2 November 1850; its fate in Crimea, *Morning Post*, 22 December 1854.

CHAPTER FOUR: FIVE WEDDINGS AND A FUNERAL

On instant cities, Gunther Barth, *Instant Cities: Urbanization and the rise of San Francisco and Denver*, Oxford University Press, New York, 1975 and my 'Goldrush Melbourne', in Iain McCalman, Alexander Cook and Andrew Reeves (eds), *Gold: Forgotten histories and lost objects of Australia*, Cambridge University Press, Melbourne, 2001, 52–66; quick employment of needlewomen, *Fund for Female Emigration, First Report*, 51; La Trobe's private misgivings in letter to Herbert, 6 August 1850; employment situations in *Fund for Female Emigration, First Report*, 41–2; Mathilda Read in *Occasional Paper* extracts in *MC*, 8 January 1852; Elizabeth Madgely?, *Sydney Morning Herald*, 19 June 1852; Fanny Hickmott quoted in Henry Morley, 'A rainy day on the "Euphrates"', *Household Words*, vol. 4, no. 96, 409–15; Jane Hewett's address, *Port Phillip Directory*, 1851 and also see advertisement by Archibald Williamson in *Argus*, 21 September 1852; marriage register of John Hewett and Matilda Walker, 19 November 1850, no. 3933, 1850; butcher's shop, Shire of Warrnambool Ratebook, 1874, Hewitt Butcher's Shop, rented from Mark Conway; Richard Osborne, *The History of Warrnambool*, H. Worland, Warrnambool, 1900, reprinted Chronicle Printing, 1980, 102–16; the first indubitable evidence of Matilda in Melbourne appears in the 1880 *Sands and McDougall Melbourne Directory*, which lists 'Mrs Matilda Hewett, dressmaker' at Selina Terrace, Harmsworth Street, Collingwood, but a 'Mrs Hewett' is previously listed at 63 Francis Street, Collingwood, in 1877, and in Bendigo Street, Prahran, as early as 1871; mothers with large numbers of infant deaths, Janet McCalman, 'The past that haunts us: the historical basis of well-being in Australian children', in Sue Richardson and Margaret Prior (eds), *No Time to Lose: The well-being of Australia's children*, Melbourne University Press, Carlton, 2005, 38–9; epidemics of measles etc., Barnard Barrett, *The Inner Suburbs: The evolution of an industrial area*, Melbourne University Press, Carlton, 1971, 55–8 and F.B. Smith, *Illness in Colonial Australia*, Australian Scholarly Publishing, Melbourne, 2011, 93–5; effects of summer heat, McCalman, '"All just melted with heat": mothers, babies and "hot winds" in colonial Melbourne', in Tim Sherratt, Tom Griffiths and Libby Robin (eds), *A Change in the Weather: Climate and culture in Australia*, National Museum of Australia, Canberra, 2008, 104–15; geography of infant deaths, Shurlee Swain, 'Towards a social geography of baby farming', *The History of the Family*, vol. 10, no. 2, 2005, 155; reciprocity between household characteristics and reproduction, Janet McCalman and Ruth Morley, 'Inequalities of gender and health 1857–1985: a long-run perspective from the Melbourne Lying-In Hospital birth cohort', *Australian Journal of Social Issues*, vol. 43, no. 1, Autumn 2008, 28–44; Jerrome funeral, *Argus*, 3 December 1874; will of John Hewett, 1887, Probate 1888, PROV no. 36/927; Alice Litchfield, Death Certificate, 28 January 1895, no. 1373; Matilda Jenetta Hewett, Death Certificate, 8 August 1899, no. 16625; Robert Hewett's 'Blackguard Conduct', *Argus*, 12 March 1851; Robert Hewett Prisoner, Central Register of Male Prisoners, VPRS 515, PROV; Fanny Hickmott's advertisement, *Argus*, 19 January 1853; John Veevers in 1856 Electoral Roll; Richard Hewett's marriage and death of child, Birth Register of Richard Edward Hewett, 1860, Wollombi, NSW, died 22 October 1862; headstone: *Campbell's Hill Cemetery, Church of England Section Headstone Inscriptions*, Maitland Family History Circle, 2001, 162; Richard Hewett's conviction and imprisonment, *New South Wales Police Gazette*, 3 May 1865, 18 December 1867, *Maitland Mercury*, 8 June 1865, Gaol Entrance Book, East Maitland Gaol, 1865, NSW Archives; Richard as witness, *Maitland Mercury*, 25 October 1879; Richard Hewett's death, NSW Inquests, *Maitland Mercury*, 15 October 1881; James Maxfield isn't shown in Port Phillip immigration records but his death certificate shows date of arrival in colony as 1850; on Hereford forebears, 1841, 1851 and 1861 censuses, *Kelly's Directory of Herefordshire*, Hereford, 1856 and tombstone of Edward and Mary Maxfield, St Dienst Church, Llangarron (for further sources see chapter 6); inquest on Henry Hewett, NSW Archives, Burial Certificate 1556 vol. 43A; on Henry Elliott, *Border Post*, 17 April 1858; on Williams station at Little Billabong see J.H. Winston-Gregson, 'People in the landscape: a biography of two villages', *Australian Historical Archaeology*, vol. 2, 1984, 27–37, and for shearers' migration patterns and 'rogues and runaways' see my 'People moving', in Graeme Davison, J.W. McCarty and Ailsa McLeary (eds), *Australians 1888*, Fairfax, Syme and Weldon, Sydney, 1987, 250–1; I have been unable to find a record of Henry's burial in cemetery records—he is not recorded in Albury, for example; archaeologist's report on Little Billabong cemetery, *Little Billabong: Hume Highway Duplication, Environmental*

Assessment, vol. 3, Appendix F, March 2007, 164–5 and Winston-Gregson, 'People in the landscape', 28–9; giving convicts a respectable pedigree, John Hirst, 'An oddity from the start: convicts and national character', *The Monthly*, July 2008, 36–42; Claus on family and identity, *OpenLearn*, 10 May 2005, www.open.edu/openlearn/history-the-arts/history/heritage/family-and-identity, accessed 2013; 'havens in a heartless world' from the title of Christopher Lasch, *Haven in a Heartless World: The family besieged*, Norton, New York 1995.

CHAPTER FIVE: WESLEY HILL

On pummelled landscape see Geoffrey Blainey, 'History of a pummelled landscape', in M.R. Banks and J.B. Kirkpatrick (eds), *Landscape and Man*, Royal Society of Tasmania, Hobart, 1977, 305–12; like a burial ground, James Robertson in *Records of the Castlemaine Pioneers*, Rigby Limited, Adelaide, 1972, 47; 'pitched his tent', phrase used by Gladys Boothroyd (née Hewett) quoting her father, Robert (Reuben) Hewett, when he pointed to the spot where his grandfather had first settled; 'unspeakable squalor', James Robertson in *Records*, 47; Bonwick as quoted in Robyn Annear, *Nothing but Gold: The diggers of 1852*, Text Publishing, Melbourne, 1999, 123; 'wee bit o' garden', *MAM*, 26 August 1854; 'few of the tents', *ibid.*, 3 August 1855; causes of child deaths, A.R. McMillen, *The Pennyweight Kids*, the author, Harcourt, 1988, 87ff; relations with Whitings noted in V.S. Hewett notebook; details of the family's history in England come from English censuses and vital registrations, birth of Robert Whiting at Forest Creek recorded in Victorian birth registers; Joseph's mixed fortunes, *Ballarat Star*, 21 February 1866; Robert Whiting's success, *Argus*, 28 June, 17 October 1929; Wesley Hill as Methodist shrine, *Wesleyan Chronicle*, 1864, 147 and Methodist *Spectator*, 23 November 1906; anticipation of 'suburban' land sales, *Argus*, 25 June 1856; Robert's purchase, Certificate of Title, 7 May 1857, Copy in Castlemaine Historical Society Collection, VCMHS 2007/16; home ownership in Castlemaine, Tony Dingle, 'Miners' cottages', *Australian Economic History Review*, vol. 50, no. 2, July 2010, 162–77 (I am indebted to Tony Dingle for permitting me to read a longer, unpublished version of this paper with fuller data on home ownership in Castlemaine); Robert's partnership with Borland, *MAM*, 31 December 1942 and *Castlemaine Directory*, 1862–63; Robert's bankruptcy, *Argus*, 10 October 1861; 'excellent tradesman', *MAM*, 14 May 1894; building by stages, Dingle, 'Miners' cottages', 170–2; Robin Boyd on 'colonial cottage', *Australia's Home*, Melbourne University Press, Carlton, 1952, 8–10; 'born under canvas', obituary of Robert Henry Hewett, *WC*, 19 August 1933; average family sizes in Castlemaine, see Patricia Grimshaw and Charles Fahey, 'Family and community in nineteenth century Castlemaine', in Patricia Grimshaw, Chris McConville and Ellen McEwen (eds), *Families in Colonial Australia*, Allen & Unwin, Sydney, 1985, 97–8; living flexibly, see also Joseph Elliott, *Our Home in Australia: A description of cottage life in 1860*, Flannel Flower Press, Sydney, 1984; arrival of railway, *Argus*, 16 October 1862; 'a good time coming', *Bendigo Advertiser*, 2 March 1859; numbers of railway workers, see local returns of employment in 1861 Victorian census; the Dickens short story entitled 'Railway Dreaming' is in *Household Words*, 10 May 1856, 386–8, an idea developed by Alan Atkinson, *The Europeans in Australia, Volume 2: Democracy*, Oxford University Press, Melbourne, 2004, 274, and compare Wolfgang Schivelbusch, *The Railway Journey: Trains and travel in the nineteenth century*, Blackwell, Oxford, 1980, 41–76; 'Collection of Valuable Recipes', photocopy in possession of John Boothroyd; death of Elizabeth, *MAM*, 25, 26 June 1879; John Swalling, *MAM*, 25 March 1941 and Richard J. Rowe, *St Alphage to Sandhurst: The lives of William and Harriet Swalling*, privately printed, 1994, 25–7; Robert Hewett as help to younger tradesmen, *MAM*, 14 May 1894; Frank as apprentice, *Horsham Times*, 20 November 1953, 5 April 1954; Orbelar on educational neglect, First Report of the Commissioners of National Education, 1852, 6 and *Votes and Proceedings of Legislative Council*, 1852; 'nomadic barbarism', *MAM*, 15 April 1856 as quoted in *State School 119 Castlemaine Centenary 1855–1955*, The School 1956, [14]; pleas for railway workshops, *Argus*, 20 October 1885, *Bendigo Advertiser*, 12 May 1883; rumours of jobs, *Argus*, 23 March 1880; Patterson's renunciation of patronage, *ibid.*, 10 February 1883; on survival of 'supernumeraries', *ibid.*, 11 July 1885, 11 February 1892; death of Robert Hewett, 14 May 1894, memorial card (copy in possession of author); Clara's occupation, Electoral Rolls 1924 and 1931, and interview of John Boothroyd with Millie Burke (née Morecroft), 7 April, 5 May 1985, and author with Roy Mussett, 25 February 2014; on feminisation of goldfields population, see Grimshaw et al., *Families in Colonial Australia*, 86; Alf Mussett's return, *Castlemaine Mail*, 21 May 1918, also see Service Record of Alfred Mussett, no. 16285; van Heurick obituary, *Argus*, 6 February 1941.

CHAPTER SIX: THE MILLERS' TALE

William Howitt's opinion in 'A few words from Australia', *Illustrated Magazine of Art*, vol. 3, no. 14, 1854, 82; on diggers' diet, Robyn Annear, *Nothing but Gold: The diggers of 1852*, Text Publishing, Melbourne, 1992, 102–16; fear of famine, *Argus*, 1 May 1854, see also *South Australian Register*, 13 May 1852; Allan's Kilmore mill, Lewis and Peggy Jones, *The Flour Mills of Victoria 1840–1990: An historical record*, The Flour Millers' Council of Victoria, Melbourne, 1990, 104–6 and Rowland Ward, 'Robert Allan & his bequest', *The Presbyterian Banner*, March

2006; wheat-growing districts, E. and L. Dunsdorfs, *Historical Statistics of the Australian Wheatgrowing Industry: Acreage and average yield in countries and divisions New South Wales, Victoria, South Australia, Western Australia, 1792–1950*, University of Melbourne, 1956; Edgars Dunsdorfs, *The Australian Wheat-Growing Industry 1788–1948*, Melbourne University Press, Carlton, 1956, 114–86; Irish in Kilmore, Oliver Macdonagh, 'The Irish in Victoria in the nineteenth century', in James Jupp (ed.), *The Australian People*, Angus and Robertson, Sydney, 1988, 578–83; old-timer's recollections, 'From bullocks to motors', *KFP*, 6 June 1935; buildings on Sydney Street, Lorraine Huddle and Associates, Mitchell Shire Stage Two Heritage Study, vol. 4, Kilmore Town Centre Precinct, 278; Kilmore on fire, *Argus*, 11 February 1851; cheapest market, *Portland Guardian*, 20 February 1856, *Argus*, 20 January 1853; Maxfield takes over mill, *Argus*, 11, 13 January 1853; opening of new mill, Jones and Jones, *The Flour Mills of Victoria*, 105; Maxfield political manifesto, *Argus*, 23 August 1859; O'Shanassy and sectarian politics, Geoffrey Serle, *The Golden Age: A history of the colony of Victoria 1851–1861*, Melbourne University Press, Carlton, 1863, 15–16 and Margaret Pawsey, *The Popish Plot: Culture clashes in Victoria 1860–1863*, Studies in the Christian Movement, Manly, 1963, 74–6; election, *Argus*, 30 August, 2, 5 September 1859, *Ballarat Star*, 31 August, 13 September 1859, *Portland Guardian*, 2 September 1859; mill became valueless, *KFP*, 25 August 1887; northeastern railway, *Argus*, 16 April, 4 December 1858, 30 September 1859, 19 October 1863, 27 October 1864; Broadford mill, *KFP*, February 1862, as quoted in 'Old Kilmore', *KFP*, 20 July 1935, and B.J. Fletcher, *Broadford: A regional history*, Lowden Publishing, Kilmore, 1975, 13 and 79; drought, Jenny Keating, *The Drought Walked Through: A history of water shortage in Victoria*, Department of Water Resources, Melbourne, 1992, 33–48; Maxfield's public role, Fletcher, *Broadford*, 14; Seymour mill, *KFP*, 22 August, 21 November 1867; insufficient grain, *Kilmore Advertiser*, 20 August 1887; sale of Broadford mill, *Argus*, 11 October, 5 December 1870, *Australasian*, 24 October 1874, *Argus*, 11 November 1875; Longwood history, *EA*, 1 October 1920; Reedy Creek, *KFP*, 12 April 1883; J.E. Maxfield's family and community life, *EA*, 19 October, 19 December 1884, *Argus*, 12 February, 9, 22 November 1886; death of James Maxfield, *EA*, 26 August 1887; will and Probate of James Maxfield, 11 January 1888; effects of drought, *EA*, 26 November 1897; J.E. Maxfield's departure, *EA*, 30 March, 30 August 1900; mills in Sale, Reminiscences of W.D. Leslie, *Gippsland Times*, 19 November 1928, 21 March, 30 May, 6 June 1862, *Argus,* 8 April 1862, 10 April 1863, 8 July 1864, 21 May 1865; supporter of Grant Land Act, *Bendigo Advertiser*, 19 June 1869; settlement of Latrobe Valley, Patrick Morgan, *The Settling of Gippsland: A regional history*, Gippsland Municipalities Association, Leongatha, 1997, 107–15; Kathleen M. Huffer, *A History of Loy Yang 1844–1978,*

Traralgon District Historical Society, 1979, 14 and 29; Maxfield family selections, Robert Maxfield, Application for License under Land Act of 1869, 1871, VPRS 625, 5956; Mary Ann Hewett, Application for License under Land Act of 1869, 1871, VPRS 625, 5953, PROV; acquisition of neighbouring properties, application of Robert Maxfield for transfer of lease of James Dolan, March 1877, VPRS 625, 9529/19.20; application for transfer of lease of Patrick Howard, October 1879, VPRS 626, 419/19.20; description of Flynn's Creek property, *TR*, 1 October 1901; introduction of separator, *TR*, 6 April 1886 and compare G.S. Brinsmead, '1888—turning point in the Victorian dairy industry', *Australia 1888*, no. 5, September 1980, 67–79; railway league, *TR*, 26 April 1889, 27 June, 15 July 1890; verdicts on free selection, compare Stephen Roberts, *A History of Australian Land Settlement 1788–1920*, Macmillan, Melbourne, 1929, 247–58 and 300–6, and Alison Bashford and Stuart Macintyre (eds), *The Cambridge History of Australia*, Cambridge University Press, Melbourne and Cambridge, 2014, 198–200 and 282 with Charles Fahey, 'The wealth of farmers: a Victorian regional study, 1879–1901, *Historical Studies*, vol. 21, no. 82, April 1984, 29–51; Ted's purchases and sale, *TR*, 21 July 1908, 8 July, 22 October, 7 December 1909; Robert Maxfield obituary, *Gippsland Times*, 26 February 1912, and widow, *Gippsland Farmer's Journal*, 6 November 1917; J.E. Maxfield in Cobden, *Camperdown Chronicle*, 23, 30 May, 10 September 1903; death of Gordon Maxfield and military record, Service Record of Gordon Loris Maxfield, Officer no. Z1883, Australian Archives, C.E.W. Bean, *Official History of Australia in the War of 1914–18, Volume III: The Australian Imperial Force in France: 1916*, 817 and 872, *Volume 4: 1917*, 467–9; mother's death, *EA*, 21, 28 February 1919; James's memorial activity, *EA*, 7 November 1919, 30 April 1920; Arthur Maxfield, Service Record of Arthur Maxfield, no. 3144, Australian Archives, and personal communication, Colin Maxfield.

CHAPTER SEVEN: CAMPBELL'S CREEK

'Born in song', introduction to *Methodist Hymn Book*, 1933, 1; on the moral middle class, Judith Brett, *Australian Liberals and the Moral Middle Class*, Cambridge University Press, Melbourne, 2003; expansion of Methodism in England, Robert Currie, 'A micro-theory of Methodist growth', *Proceedings of the Wesley Historical Society*, vol. 36, October 1967, 65–73; in mining communities, John Graham Rule, 'The labouring miner in Cornwall c. 1740–1870: a study in social history', PhD thesis, University of Warwick, 1971, 214; Wesley's visits, *The Journal of Rev John Wesley*, Everyman Edition, J.M. Dent, Glasgow, 1906, vol. 2, 25 (4 July 1746), 391 (4 September 1758), vol. 4, 329 (28 August 1785); 'religion of the mass', Rule, 'Labouring miner', 262–3; grows where Church was weakest,

Robert Currie, *Methodism Divided: A study in the sociology of ecumenicalism*, Faber, London, 1968, 21; women and skilled working class, Clive D. Field, 'The social composition of English Methodism to 1830: a membership analysis', *Bulletin of the John Rylands Library*, vol. 76, no. 1, 1994, 153–69; growth of Liskeard, Rule, 'Labouring miner', 7–9; links with Wales, Peter H. Stanier, 'The copper ore trade of south west England in the nineteenth century', *Journal of Transport History*, vol. 5, 1979, 18–35; sibling names, Lawrence Stone, *The Family, Sex and Marriage in England, 1500–1800*, Penguin, Harmondsworth, 1979, 408–12 and D.S. Smith, 'Continuity and discontinuity in puritan naming', *William and Mary Quarterly*, vol. 51, no. 1, January 1994, 67–91; article on mineral regions, *Cornwall Gazette, Falmouth Packet and Plymouth Journal*, 1 May 1846; letters from South Australia, quoted in Ian Auhl, *The Story of the 'Monster Mine': The Burra Burra mine and its townships 1845–1877*, Investigator Press, Adelaide, 1986, 76–88; *South Australian News*, as quoted in Auhl, *The Story*, 84; for Wilcocks' activities, *South Australian News*, December 1846, 89, and Robin F. Haines, *Emigration and the Labouring Poor*, 106–8; proportions of Cornish, *ibid.*, 44; Samuel Stephens' embarkation order and testimonial, copies in author's possession; ship's company of *Abberton*, Barry Leadbeater, *South Australian Passenger Lists*, Family History SA, and *South Australian Register*, 16 December 1846; departure scene, *The South Australian News*, December 1846, 89–90; growth of mineral production, Auhl, *The Story*, 67; Ayers' boast, Geoffrey Blainey, *The Rush That Never Ended: A history of Australian mining*, Melbourne University Press, Carlton, 1963, 112; and 'the people of Burra', *ibid.*, 111; Martha's death certificate (1884) records the following children: Samuel dead, Jane 39, Samuel 37, Henry 35, William 32, George dead, George 29, Susan 27; the first George's death is recorded in Jennifer Carter (ed.), *Burra 1845–1851, A Directory of Early Folk*, Shalimar Press, Latrobe University, 1996, 116; Mary Lloyd letter, copy in author's possession; overland journey, Charles Sandry Rule, Log Book, 1852, State Library of South Australia D7486; Bonwick's impressions in his *Notes of a Gold Digger and Gold Diggers' Guide*, [1852], Hawthorn Press, Melbourne, 1942, 29; estimate of Cornish adult male population of Campbell's Creek is Charles Fahey's, personal communication, see also his '"A poor man does not improve his position much by emigrating to this country": the Cornish on the Victorian Goldfields, 1861–1901', in Charles Fahey and Alan Mayne (eds), *Gold Tailings: Forgotten histories of family and community on the Central Victorian Goldfields*, Australian Scholarly Publishing, North Melbourne, 2010, 152–78; 'one of the most pleasing', *MAM*, 10 July 1858; Cornish tradition of home ownership, Damaris Rose, 'Home ownership, subsistence and historical change: the mining district of West Cornwall in the nineteenth century', in Nigel Thrift and Peter Williams (eds), *Class and Space: The making of urban society*, Routledge, London,

1987, 113–24; 'spirit of enterprise', Campbell's Creek, *MAM*, 3 May 1858, see also R.A. Bradfield, *Campbell's Creek . . . Some Early History,* Castlemaine Mail, Castlemaine, n.d., 7; Samuel Stephens Land Holdings, VPRS 11862, 1862; 'urbanity and integrity', obituary in *MAM*, 13 May 1872; Castlemaine circuit, *Wesleyan Chronicle,* July 1864, 147 and W.L. Blamires and John B. Smith, *The Early Story of the Wesleyan Methodist Church in Victoria*, Wesleyan Book Depot, Melbourne, 1886, 177; 'a religion of movement', Alan Atkinson, *Camden: Farm and village life in early New South Wales*, Oxford University Press, Melbourne, 1988, 170; on the Primitives, H.B. Kendall, 'The Primitive Methodist Church and the Independent Methodist Churches', in W.J. Townsend, H.B. Workman and George Eayrs (eds), *A New History of Methodism*, Hodder and Stoughton, London, 1909, 562; Bible Christians, W.R. Ward, *Religion and Society in England 1790–1850*, Batsford, London, 1972, 83; 'Shall we have a revival', *Wesleyan Chronicle*, 31 January 1861, 37; 'short step from heathendom', *Victorian Miscellany and Wesleyan Chronicle*, no. 1, July 1857, 10, Charles Grandison Finney, *Revivals of Religion*, [1835], Morgan and Scott, London, 1860, 5; 'better hurricane', *Wesleyan Chronicle*, 1863, 126, revivals in Campbell's Creek, H.R. Jackson, *Churches and People in Australia and New Zealand 1860–1930*, Allen & Unwin, Sydney, 1987, 51–2; Blamires and Smith, *The Early Story*, 184; R. Thomas Chenoweth, 'Campbell's Creek Methodism in the 60's and 70's', *Spectator*, 1 February 1907, 189–94, *Primitive Methodist Miscellany*, 1867–67, 12–13 and 182, Primitive Methodist Church, Castlemaine Circuit, Box 5, Schedules and Reports, 1866, 1877; Box 9, Trustees Meetings, 0334, Uniting Church Archives, Elsternwick, Victoria; tea meetings, *Wesleyan Chronicle*, 1862, 142; Thompson and Halevy's theses, E.P. Thompson, *The Making of the English Working Class*, Penguin, London, 1968, 411–40 and A.D. Gilbert, *Religion and Society in Industrial England: Church, chapel and social change 1740–1914*, Longman, London, 1976, 187–98; Methodists and goldfields' population, Blainey, *The Rush That Never Ended*, 41–2 and Serle, *The Golden Age*, 336–43; Renate Howe, 'The dynamic and progressive influence of Victorian Goldfields Methodism', draft chapter for a history of Methodism in Australia; 'high voltage', Ward, *Religion and Society in England*, 79; Chinese, Bradfield, *Campbell's Creek*, 11–14, Miners' Petition 1857 as quoted in Kathryn Cronin, *Colonial Casualties: Chinese in early Victoria*, Melbourne University Press, Carlton, 1982, 69, *MAM*, 3 May 1858, *Wesleyan Chronicle*, 1862, 142 and compare Keir Reeves, 'Echoes on a cultural landscape: glimpses of Chinese community life in Castlemaine', in Fahey and Mayne (eds), *Gold Tailings*, 178–95; Stephens' shareholdings listed in M. McAdie, *An Index to Shareholders in Mining Companies, 1857–1886*, State Library of Victoria; dispute over location of school, Campbell's Creek Petitions, 31 July 1874, 7 July 1875, 19 September 1876, VPRS 795, Unit 58, PROV; 'anxious to protect',

Primitive Methodist Miscellany, 1866–67, 13 and 215; death of Samuel, *MAM*, 13, 15 May 1872; loss of goldfields population, A.R. Hall, *The Stock Exchange of Melbourne and the Victorian Economy*, ANU Press, Canberra, 1968, 53, and Angus B. Wilson, *Vanishing Burgesses—Emerging Citizens*, privately printed, 2010, 65; exodus, Blamires and Smith, *The Early Story*, 185–6, Primitive Methodist Church, Castlemaine Circuit, Quarterly Meetings, 20 December 1870, 29 March 1876, UCA Archives 0334; Old Pioneers, *Journal of the Pioneers and Old Residents' Association*, Castlemaine District, no. 3, January 1889, 52; 'Protestants face God', Paul E. Johnson, *A Shopkeeper's Millennium, Society and Revivals in Rochester, New York, 1815–1837*, Hill and Wang, New York, 1978, 96.

CHAPTER EIGHT: WILLIAMSTOWN

The author's history of land-boom Melbourne, Graeme Davison, *The Rise and Fall of Marvellous Melbourne*, Melbourne University Press, Carlton, 1978 and 2004, 8 and 102; Ada Cambridge in Williamstown, 'A Williamstown novelist', *WC*, 1 June 1945, and Ada Cambridge, *Thirty Years in Australia*, [1903], London, reprinted by Sydney University Press, Sydney, 2006, 190–4; railway expansion, Robert Lee, *The Railways of Victoria 1854–2004*, Melbourne University Publishing, Carlton, 2007, 80–5; Newport workshops, 'Railway Workshops at Williamstown', *Illustrated Australian News*, 13 June 1883, Employees in Railway Workshops, *Victorian Parliamentary Papers*, vol. 1, C11, 1886, *WC*, 14 July 1888, *Victorian Municipal Directory*, 1889, 'The Newport Railway Workshops', *Bacchus Marsh Express*, 6 April 1889, and G. Doenau, 'The Newport story', *Australian Railways Historical Society Bulletin*, no. 506, December 1979, 249–88; 'home, hospital', *Argus*, 13 June 1908; Robert Henry's employment, *Government Gazette*, vol. 1, 1899, 433, vol. 3, 1904, 4719; Workshop Employees Service and Conduct Register, Rolling Stock Branch, 1885–1912, VPRS 12736, PROV; 'Archdeacon', Doenau, 'Newport story', 281–3; comfort of employees, William Elsum, *The History of Williamstown*, Williamstown Council, Craftsman Press, 1934, 52–3; 'Justice Higgins', Stuart Macintyre, *The Oxford History of Australia*, vol. 4, 1902–1942, Oxford University Press, Melbourne, 1986, 102–4; family spacing, Ann Larson, *Growing Up in Melbourne: Family life in the late nineteenth century*, Demography Program, Australian National University, Canberra, 1994, 27–60; Parker Street house, Williamstown Ratebooks, Central Ward 1885, Port Phillip Library; class meeting, *Rules of the Society of the People Called Methodist*, 1842, 1–2, *Wesleyan Chronicle*, 1864, 3; Robert and Susan as members, Williamstown Circuit Members Roll, 1897, Box 1/1; Leaders' Meeting Minutes, 18 May 1904, 22 December 1909, Box 5/2, Uniting Church Archives 1280; on Frank Hewett, Ian Ward to John

Boothroyd, 30 June 1983 (copy in author's possession); decline of class meeting, Renate Howe, 'The Wesleyan Church in Victoria 1856–1901: its ministry and membership', MA thesis, University of Melbourne, 1964, 33–40; sect to church, H.R. Jackson, *Churches and People in Australia and New Zealand 1860–1930*, Allen & Unwin, Wellington, 1987, 77–9, and see the church–sect distinction in Ernst Troeltsch, *The Social Teaching of the Christian Churches*, [1917], English translation, Allen & Unwin, London, 1931; 'Forward Movement', *Methodist Times*, 19 March 1885 as quoted in K.S. Inglis, *Churches and the Working Classes in Victorian England*, Routledge and Kegan Paul, London, 1963, 70, and compare Robert Currie, *Methodism Divided*, 178ff; 'Thanksgiving Street', *WC*, 15 December 1883; social composition of congregation, Renate Howe, 'Social composition of the Wesleyan Church in Victoria during the nineteenth century', *Journal of Religious History*, vol. 4, no. 3, June 1967, 209, and compare her 'The Wesleyan Church in Victoria', Appendix 8; Robert and Susan's church activities, *WC*, 9 December 1911, 3 May 1913, 24 May 1930, 19 August 1933, and recollections of May Davison to author; temperance and companionate marriage, Marilyn Lake, 'The politics of respectability: identifying the masculinist context', *Historical Studies*, vol. 22, no. 86, April 1986, 116–31; respectability and punctuality in my *The Unforgiving Minute: How Australia learned to tell the time*, Oxford University Press, Melbourne, 1994, ch. 3; 'fresh-faced man', *Essendon Gazette*, 29 August 1957; Victor's jobs listed in his notebook, author's possession; training of printer, R.T. Fitzgerald, *The Printers of Melbourne: The history of a union*, Isaac Pitman and Sons, Melbourne, 1967, 103–7; on Copeland, Irving Benson, *A Century of Victorian Methodism*, Spectator Publishing Company, Melbourne, 1935, 297; 'loosened their moorings', Margretta Kleinig and Eric Richards (eds), *On the Wing: Mobility before and after emigration to Australia*, Anchor Books, Melbourne, 2013, 7; Fridaythorpe, *Baines' History, Directory and Gazetteer of the County of York*, Edward Baines, Leeds, 1823; Methodism in East Riding, Census of Great Britain, 1851, *Religious Worship in England and Wales*, 1854, and Ward, *Religion and Society in England*, 76; ribbon trade in Coventry, John Prest, *The Industrial Revolution in Coventry*, Oxford University Press, Oxford, 1960, 96–113; collapse of Manchester building boom, Brinley Thomas, *Migration and Urban Development*, Methuen and Company, London, 1972, 30–1; letters of William and Emma Seller, Emma Seller to William Parker, [1897], William Seller to [his family], c. 1882, letters in possession of the author (these letters were found among my mother's possessions; how they came to be in Australia is a mystery, but those from Emma were probably brought back with her brother William); Thomas Linton, *WC*, 6 February 1904; Will of Thomas Linton, VPRS 89/810, 1904; Will of Catherine Cox, VPRS 24/840, 1882; fire and inquest, *WC*, 26, 30 December 1882, *Argus*, 27 December 1882; historian

Richard White's reflections in his *Remembering Ahanagran: A history of stories*, University of Washington Press, Seattle, 1998, 95; William's history from English censuses, Rosetta lived in England till her death in 1923; William's voyage and Emma's death, Emma Seller to William Parker, 8 February and 26 July 1899, Outward Passenger lists for *Orizaba*, 1899, Death Certificate for Emma Seller, 2 August 1899; Mrs Henry Mackarness (ed.), *The Young Lady's Book: A manual of amusements, exercises, studies, and pursuits*, Routledge, London, 1888, 1; Emma Seller signs petition, Women's Suffrage Petition, 1891, PROV, also see Diane Gardiner, 'Women's suffrage in Victoria', *Agora*, vol. 45, no. 4, 2010, 54–8; WCTU campaign in Williamstown, *WC*, 27 July, 24 October 1891; 'a very good girl', Emma Seller to William Parker, 8 February 1899; youth culture, Simon Sleight, *Young People and the Shaping of Public Space in Melbourne, 1870–1914*, Ashgate, London, 2013; Christian Endeavour, Electra Street Methodist Church Leaders Meeting, 12 May 1909, UCA Archives, 1280, Box 5/2, and compare F.E. Clark, *The Work of the Committees of the Young People's Society of Christian Endeavour*, The Society, Boston, 1887; Vic's New Zealand tour, handwritten memoir dated 1908, in the author's possession; homecoming, *WC*, 30 November 1907, and marriage, *WC*, 23 May 1908; death and in memoriam of Susan, *WC*, 26 October 1918, *Argus*, 22 October 1919; estimates of generational participation in war based on figures in L.L. Robson, 'The origin and character of the First AIF, 1914–18: Some statistical evidence', *Historical Studies*, vol. 15. no. 61, October 1973, 743; *Census of the Commonwealth of Australia*, 1933, Part XVII, War Service; strength and character of pre-war peace movement, Margaret Macmillan, *The War that Ended Peace*, Profile Books, London, 2013, 266–94; 'war-drum throbs', *Spectator*, 7 August 1914 and for Methodist pacifism see Don Wright and Eric Clancy, *The Methodists: A history of Methodism in New South Wales*, Allen & Unwin, Sydney 1993, 129–34; Joseph Cook's view in his diaries cited in Douglas Newton, *Hell-Bent: Australia's leap into the Great War*, Scribe, Melbourne, 142–3; Elliott and Essendon Rifles, in Ross McMullin, *Pompey Elliott*, Scribe Publications, Melbourne, 2002, 64, 79, 115–17, 125, 132, 134 and Arthur Dean and Eric W. Gutteridge, *The Seventh Battalion*, Melbourne, 1933; on Chapman, McMullin, 128 Service Dossier E.H.S Chapman, NAA B2455; Essendon response to deaths, *Age*, 11 May 1915, *Spectator*, 21 May 1915; Woodfull's remarks, *Essendon Gazette*, 28 October 1915; 'we believed everything', Brian Lewis, *Our War: Australia during World War I*, Melbourne University Press, 1980, 3; Robert (John) war service, *WC*, 10 July 1915; 'tinpot Navy', *Argus*, 13 July 1915; obituary of Lynch, *WC*, 12 October 1929; Robert John Hewett, Enlistment Papers and Service Record, Australian Archives, CP 979/2/5411; Frank, obituary, *WC*, 29 March 1946 and Millie's recollection in interview with John Boothroyd, 1983; Reuben (Robert), research compiled by John; later career of Robert (John), Susan Hewett to Winnie Dakin, 14 January 1916, copy in possession of the author; Kenya, *Hobart Mercury*, 1 June 1954; author's recollections, conversations with Joy Crawford (daughter of John Hewett); death of Vic, recollections of May Davison and Florence Lear, daughters, miscellaneous writings in possession of the author, Vic Hewett obituary, *Essendon Gazette*, 21 August 1957; Speciality Press, Don Hauser, *Printers of the Streets and Lanes of Melbourne*, Nondescript Press, Melbourne, 2006, 130–1; Bread and Cheese Club, H.W. Malloch, *Fellows All: The chronicles of the Bread and Cheese Club, Melbourne*, The Club, Melbourne, 1943; Lawson Society, *Grenfell Record*, 18 May 1939.

CHAPTER NINE: RICHMOND HILL

'Men do not emigrate', W.K. Hancock, *Australia*, Ernest Benn, London, [1930], Jacaranda Press, 1961, 39; 'wife desertion', *Argus*, 20 June 1860, as quoted in Christina Twomey, *Deserted and Destitute: Motherhood, desertion and colonial welfare*, Australian Scholarly Publishing, Melbourne, 2002, 27; my walking, Graeme Davison (ed.), *Melbourne on Foot*, Rigby, Adelaide, 1980, 84–97; Harriet Clisby, H.C.W., 'The claims of women', *Argus*, 28 June 1859, also see her 'Female employment', *ibid*., 13 September 1859 and 6 August 1860; for a reply, see H.M., 'Prostitution', *ibid*., 24 June 1859; compare Kathleen Thomson, 'Clisby, Harriet Jemima Winifred', *Australian Dictionary of Biography, Volume 3, 1851–1890*, Melbourne University Press, Carlton, 1969, 430–1; Richmond Benevolent Society, Richmond and East Melbourne Ladies' Benevolent Society, *Annual Report 1870*, Melbourne, 1870, 8; ageing of the gold-rush generation, Graeme Davison, '"Our youth is spent and our backs are bent": the origins of Australian ageism', *Australian Cultural History*, no. 14, 1995, 4–62; Old Colonists' Homes, Frances O'Neill, *A Place of their Own: The Old Colonists' Homes in Victoria*, Australian Scholarly Publishing, North Melbourne, 2005, 38; Jane's entry, secretary to John Traill, 29 May, and to Miss Jane Hewett, 1 July 1915, Old Colonists' Association Letterbooks, Ms 12726, Box 6, 1912–15, State Library of Victoria; visits and excursions, secretary to Jane Hewett, 19 December 1916, 26 June 1918, Old Colonists' Association Letterbook; newspaper articles on Jane, *Herald*, 3 December 1925, *Argus*, 22 March 1922, *Herald*, 27 December 1926.

CONCLUSION: LEGACIES AND LIFE CHANCES

Frank Hewett, *Horsham Times*, 5 April 1954, Ian Ward to John Boothroyd, 30 June 1983 (copy in author's possession), and John Boothroyd interviews; Book of Genesis, Graeme Davison, *Narrating the Nation in Australia*, Menzies Lecture,

Menzies Centre for Australian Studies, London, 2009, and Davison, 'Victorian genesis: founding histories', *Victorian Historical Journal*, vol. 80, no. 2, November 2009, 191–210; Erikson, see his *Childhood and Society*, Penguin, Harmondsworth, 1967, 260; on heirlooms, Paula Hamilton and Paul Ashton, 'At home with the past: initial findings from the survey', *Australian Cultural History*, no. 22, 2003, 14–15, Diane Bell and Ponch Hawkes, *Generations: Grandmothers, mothers and daughters*, McPhee Gribble/Penguin, Melbourne, 1987, 244, and Beth Pidsley, 'The Heirloom', *Prime Time*, September 1985, 8–9; recipes, photocopy in possession of John Boothroyd; Hewett marriages, compare Peter F. McDonald, *Marriage in Australia: Age at first marriage and proportions marrying 1860–1971*, Australian Family Formation Project, Monograph No. 2, Australian National University, Canberra, 1975, 105; McCalman on drifters, Janet McCalman, 'To die without friends: solitaries, drifters and failures in a New World society', in Graeme Davison, Pat Jalland and Wilfrid Prest (eds), *Body and Mind: Historical essays in honour of F.B. Smith*, Melbourne University Publishing, Carlton, 2009, 172–94.

Index

Page numbers in *italics* refer to illustrations